Luxury for All

Luxury for All

Milestones in European Stepped Terrace Housing

Gerhard Steixner
Maria Welzig
(Eds.)

Birkhäuser
Basel

Inner-City Hybrids

Introduction

Gerhard Steixner, Maria Welzig

The growth spurt in European cities has been a catalyst for the question of eco-solar housing concepts and, with global migration, is taking on new political urgency. The overheating of cities and current tendency to reduce the housing question to one of mere accommodation suggests that attention should once again turn to a prototype that was developed internationally in the late 1960s, conceived as the ideal solution to the question of housing for great numbers of people, namely stepped terrace housing.

Housing for the broad mass of the population—a relatively new challenge in the history of humankind—is not defined as mere accommodation here, but aims to achieve the highest possible quality of housing and living while at the same time conserving land resources. A modified urban approach for the changed society of the twentieth and twenty-first centuries.

A prototype, moreover, which represents one of the most effective ways of creating ecological cities. The starting point for this is consistent planning considerations for vehicular traffic. The greening of residential terraces combined with generous communal greenspaces contributes significantly to the improvement of the urban climate. Stepped terrace housing as an urban model of densification that contributes to a green(er) city. The regained contact with nature this provides is also essential for individual wellbeing: smells, sounds, colors, insects, birds, and the changing seasons—the fundamental experience that we humans are a part of nature.

Just as important as the improvement of individual living situations are the ample spatial and functional opportunities that these terraced projects create for the community and for a dense urban use. The ambition of creating "the greatest possible happiness for the greatest possible number of people" with these new stepped terrace housing and urban concepts also received the political support it needed during and around the pivotal year of 1968. In the years to follow, London, Paris, Berlin, Munich, Vienna, Graz, Ljubljana, and many other cities showed that the "realization of utopia" is possible. Vienna holds a special position for its use of the stepped terrace model in social housing. In no other city has stepped terrace housing of such immense quality been realized to such a vast degree.

This book brings together 12 selected stepped terrace housing estates built in Europe during the 1960s and 1970s and offers a current evaluation after about forty years. Today, after several decades of service, the examples presented can undoubtedly be qualified as sustainable. Resident satisfaction is extraordinarily high compared to conventional housing estates. The acceptance by the residents is also reflected in the way the housing estates have been preserved and in the care and appropriation of the private and communal open spaces.

We have gathered together international experts to examine housing estates in London, Munich, Ljubljana, Berlin, Ivrea, Graz, and Vienna, studying their history, significance to architecture, urban planning, and society, how they were received and appropriated, and relevance for residential and urban development today. Karen Beckmann (Hanover), Paolo Enrico Dalpiaz and Giulia Maria Infortuna (Turin), Silke Fischer (Vienna), San-Hwan Lu (Vienna), Natalie Heger (Berlin), Nataša Koselj (Ljubljana), Clare Melhuish (London), Gerhard Steixner (Vienna), Mark Swenarton (Liverpool), and Maria Welzig (Vienna) have all contributed their specialized knowledge to this book.

The schemes show alternatives to the urban and housing concepts from pre-democratic times, which are still, or becoming once again, common (reconstructions of the highly economical grid cities of the nineteenth century). These alternatives are aligned with the social and technological conditions of the twentieth and twenty-first centuries. The selected housing estates reveal the diversity of typological variants and the numerous ways to implement them under different conditions.

While most stepped terrace housing complexes remained one-off projects, in Vienna, the architect Harry Glück together with GESIBA, the city's non-profit housing and construction corporation, succeeded in building numerous stepped terrace housing estates with park-like communal greenspaces, high-quality shared facilities, and urban density. This provided concrete proof of the economic feasibility, social viability, and ecological success of such concepts. Over the decades, Glück documented his research and findings on the issue of urban housing question in numerous (little known) essays, publishing them in a work titled The Potential of the Green City. An annotated and illustrated excerpt from Glück's essay in this book introduces the foundations of a Green City. Comprehensible and concise, Glück puts the questions of residential construction into a broad historical context and links them to the essential needs of life. The manner in which Glück writes reflects his approach to housing; he is writing for the great number.

In the chapter "The *Invention* of Stepped Terrace Housing," the editors examine the development of this new typology during the twentieth century, taking a particular look at the sociopolitical context of 1968, which provided the opportunity to realize the stepped terrace model. An outlook essay analyzes the conditions necessary for this eco-solar housing model and presents current modified approaches to the resumption of such compact terrace schemes.

This book is aimed at readers interested in housing, housing construction, and the (green) city.

The Potential of the Green City

Harry Glück

How it all began

In the decades before and after 1800, a period historians regard as the beginning of the Industrial Age, scientific and technological developments began in Europe that led to the growth and emergence of great cities. According to a report by the United Nations Population Fund, by 2050, 70 percent of the world's population will live in cities.

In 1765, the engineer James Watt invented the steam engine, in 1798 doctor Edward Jenner invented the smallpox vaccination, and in 1840, the chemist Justus Liebig invented artificial fertilizer, which multiplied agricultural yields and thereby refuted the theories of economist Thomas R. Malthus, who had predicted in 1798 that food production would not be able to keep up with increases in the world population. From Louis Pasteur to Robert Koch and Paul Ehrlich, it was a heroic age of discovery and invention. In 1847, Ignaz Semmelweis discovered the cause of childbed fever, and Werner Siemens built the first electric motor in 1866.

The ideals of the Enlightenment, seemingly submerged at the Congress of Vienna, led to a paradigm shift that ended the hierarchical social systems of the preceding millennia. The nineteenth century brought about the emancipation of civic society, whilst the twentieth century saw the emergence of democratic mass society.

At the same time, the culture and civilization of Europe and beyond had finally become an urban culture and an urban civilization, a

Electric train by Siemens & Halske, Great Industrial Exposition of Berlin 1879, photo of a wedding party

process founded in a division of labor so incredibly diverse that only the close coexistence of a very large number of differently qualified and educated individuals makes the multitude of interactions possible without an intolerable loss of time and friction. This is true of production processes as well as in teaching and research, art and jurisprudence, politics, and in caring for the sick, the old, and the disadvantaged. Even the conceivable further development of telecommunications will not fundamentally change this.

This urban culture characterizes a social system that has achieved equality before the law, equal opportunities, and a reduction of the wealth gap to an extent never before seen in history. And all within the period of only a few generations. It is not the best possible world, probably not even a good world, but, at least in the West, it is better than all previous worlds.

Since the city represents, and will continue to represent, human habitat for the foreseeable future, it should meet our daily needs to the best degree possible—the needs of a society that, for the first time in history, is entirely democratic. Can this be?

There is no doubt that—even in democratic mass society—those privileged by ownership, education, and power have found satisfactory habitats in cities, spatially adequate living in "good" (a term that will have to be defined) locations. They practice professions that allow or require creative work, and enjoy recreational and stimulating leisure time. However, the majority of members of democratic mass society are people with limited income and opportunities who continue to have far less access. In fact, there is clear evidence indicating that not even their basic evolutionary needs are being met.

The first indication is suburbanization, or at least its increase, the exodus from cities into the surrounding region. Then there is the almost lemming-like flight from cities into what we call nature during leisure time, and the importance that holidays have gained, especially for employees, i.e. those with below average and moderate incomes. For many, vacations have become the focus of the entire year, just as the car has become a mobile second home, more than just a means of transportation, enabling people to escape from the urban world, which is apparently insufficient for human needs. In addition, housing market supply, although far from saturated, can no longer be implemented without difficulty. And finally, but no less significantly, the loss of votes for the traditionally urban parties, particularly in the last decade, indicates the fundamental inadequacy of urban living conditions—at least for broad swathes of the population.

However, those with a low and middle income are a compact majority, and have a decisive influence on the life and growth of cities. This influence is reinforced by the economic and political importance that this majority has acquired over the last century, which has resulted in unprecedented demands on the infrastructure of cities and the use of land reserves. I don't know of any city that has succeeded in executing these processes, which have a deep impact on economic, ecological, and sociological interrelationships, with a progressive design.

Indeed, it may not be tempting for a politician who is elected for a term of just a few years to initiate measures that will only take effect over a longer period of time. But apart from this example, the fact remains that urban planning has not yet truly attempted to trace human behavior back to its primal needs—to the needs of living beings predisposed to a particular habitat through the evolution of millions of years. The proof that these needs are common to all humans, regardless of the infinite number of variations, was provided by behavioral researchers decades ago—even if, on closer inspection, there are tiny differences and a statistically irrelevant number of exceptions. Apart from that, this is a fact that should be clear to anyone who observes their environment without bias or arrogance. Strangely enough, our self-image is so strongly influenced by the idealistic philosophy of the nineteenth century that we consider ourselves to be self-sufficient, monadic individuals instead of as members of an infinitely diverse yet nevertheless almost identical species—namely humans.

Our origin determines our being

In the course of our incarnation, we have not only acquired an ever larger and more powerful brain, but other changes that distinguish us among all animals have also occurred. In behavioral research, these processes are termed "domestication." It causes, among other things, a decrease in the intensity of certain innate instincts, as well as a phenomenon known as "persistent neoteny," or adolescent behavior that persists throughout adulthood.

"Instinctive certainty" is considered a positive ability, and is a revealing indication of our origins. In fact, weakening instincts are only apparently a loss. In almost all animals, instincts are so strong that they react to certain events in the outside world, so-called "trigger stimuli," completely automatically, almost compulsively, and in an unchangeable, pre-programmed way. In nature, this advantage allows us to act quickly and without thinking, in a process that has been tested over millions of years and, according to the statistics of the struggle for survival, has been proven to be effective in the overwhelming number of cases. But this instinctive strength certainty also has a disadvantage: it prevents us from perceiving and seeking alternatives that could be more advantageous for survival and development. These alternatives may not play a major role for most predators, but for the majority of animals they would be conceivable. In their early days, humans were undoubtedly primarily dependent on escape or hiding—it took quite a long time for humans to develop into predators themselves. And even this they could only do once they had developed substitutes for their small jaw, lack of claws, and minimal strength, compensating instead with artificial "organs," i.e. tools and weapons. However, it was the liberation from pre-programmed, automaton-like sequences of action that made possible the innovative intellectual achievements that became the basis for the rise of the human species. Take just the acquisition of fire alone, which arouses fear in all wild animals and would not have been possible otherwise.

A significant example of this is the wolf, the original and wild form of the dog, remains so closely related to dogs that to this day mating is possible. A mutation must have occurred in these animals 10,000 or more years ago that made it possible for some of these animals to join the "fire-guarding" people. It may have been young puppies. For in the juvenile phase of their lives, many higher mammals, especially those that we call predators in the broadest sense, show a specific and significant deviation from the pre-programmed courses of action that determine their adult life: they play. Here, too, the wolf/dog comparison is revealing: If a wolf and a dog pup are raised side by side, there are no noticeable differences in behavior until puberty. Through play, they practice the pre-programmed behavioral patterns of evolution. The differences only become apparent with sexual maturity: adult wolves cease to play, obeying for the rest of their live the pre-programmed behavioral patterns that force them to react to specific triggers in a certain way. They learn only through the experiences to which they are exposed, but which they no longer seek. Dogs, on the other hand, continue to play for life, or at least until old age, which, in dogs and humans alike, is often accompanied by the end of the mental ability that not only enables us to play, but also to invent, to discover, to seek new paths, and even to walk.

Eternal youth

Persistent neoteny, the continuation of the playful behavior inherent in the adolescent phase, allows us to use and develop the basic component of play, namely the capacity for abstraction. The stick, the ball, the bit of wool, every moving inanimate object becomes prey. War does not take place on the battlefield, but on the playing field. Abstract thought is the prerequisite for every higher intellectual achievement. Innovation requires thinking ahead—thinking in causal chains in order to create new, previously unknown phenomena from the targeted change of technical, organizational, and physical conditions. No adult wolf will run after a ball, but most dogs will. Domestication has deprived dogs of the intensity of many of their instincts—but in return has opened up a repertoire of alternatives which will ensure its survival as a species long after the wolf has ceased to exist except as an attraction or in nature reserves.

Domestication has worked in humans in a similar way and has had far reaching implications. The persistent neoteny that distinguishes us from all wild animals has enabled us to conquer the world. At the same time, it has enabled us to replace at least some of our destructive instincts with concepts like morality and ethics, which undoubtedly serve our conservation as a species. Thus domestication is the prerequisite of the ability and the need to change our world for the better, we believe, on a large and small scale, and to explore the limits of our possibilities.

But this urge, at least in our civilization based on the division of labor, has its limits: for the majority of people who are forced to make a living in a routine job, be it in a workshop, a factory, or at a desk, their own innovative, exploratory impulses are not only undesirable, but even forbidden. One should not underestimate the consequences of the resulting psychological strain. It is the same drive that impelled Amundsen to the North Pole and made Hannibal cross the Alps, that created cathedrals, great bridges, and railways, and gave humans wings. Art, as well, through which humans seek to represent what their minds cannot reach, our urge to try and grasp what is unseen, is driven by this power. Certainly, this power culminates only in certain individuals, but it is a collective inheritance of the species.

The seriousness of life, which adults occasionally warn young people about, means nothing less than they will soon have to renounce their instinct for play and exploration. If it were not a very strong, innate instinct, then the compulsion to suppress it would probably not be a punishment. This permanent, "persistent" desire to improve the world is as much the driving force behind all revolutions and social upheavals as it is the basic pattern of what we call the political consciousness of the individual. This is where our capacity for abstraction and innovation, our urge for exploration and progress, touches another aspect of evolution.

Social behavior

The being that stepped out of the deep forests into the green, sunny, fertile plains for reasons we do not know,[1] thus also relinquished the protection that these forests offered to their adapted inhabitants. It was therefore a condition of survival—and this condition has not changed to this day—that only groups could assert themselves and survive. In spite of numerous discoveries in the recent past, we know very little about the ways of life of our early ancestors, who after all lived, reproduced, and spread over several million years on earth, over vast distances, and over periods of time that are almost unimaginable for us. It is only from the comparatively recent epoch, which we call the Stone Age, that we can link ideas. These have become increasingly concrete since we know of people who, a few millennia ago in the Middle East, created communities from almost nothing, which had writing, hierarchical state systems, cults, architecture, visual, and literary arts. Apart from the technological gap, almost everything that characterizes modern cultures and civilizations. Each of these civilizations emerged from the organized interaction of large numbers of people. This would hardly have been possible if the ability and willingness to work together had not been present from the beginning.

The state is ultimately nothing more than an enlarged group, the most original form of human community. It sets standards of behavior, demands participation by all in the services necessary for common survival, and offers protection in return. Such social norms, the self-evidence of common action, and the protection of all for each individual, are also seen in herd animals. One can therefore assume that this social conditioning, the seeking of protection and acting in the community, is a very old hereditary trait, older even than humankind. This profound need for social integration in a manageable, familiar community should not be underestimated. Solitary confinement is a punishment. For centuries, exile has been the most severe sanction after death. Terms such as "loner," "recluse," and "loneliness" remain negatively connoted to this day.

What else we have inherited and the power of instincts

In addition to these three dominant hereditary aspects of evolution: the need for the spiritual call of nature, an innate desire for abstract planning processes, the drive for world improvement and world conquest, and the desire for the protection and security of the group, each of us still knows, feels, and experiences many patterns of behavior, preferences, and drives, all of which are inherited through evolution. For instance, the sensations evoked by open fire and warm light, our affinity for clear, flowing, and what at least appears to be drinkable water, the satisfaction and security of open views, the joy of eating together and the need to share meals with familiar people, the invitation to eat together as a gesture of friendship, flowers as gifts, but also the need to experience our physicality and to face challenges. In addition, there are countless rituals of facial expression and body language of which we are hardly aware, something we share with many higher animals, so that—taken together with other evidence—there can be no doubt that these are innate instincts and the result of evolution. All this—much of it already hypothesized by Darwin—is today part of behavioral research and regarded as anthropological constants.

But the humanities, especially human biology, teach us something else: Almost all these forces and instincts are innate, not learned, copied, or practiced, but present from the very beginning. Their effects are present in all cultures and civilizations, in variations that are only differentiated by constraints and the level of technology. They are particularly evident in the forms of living and lifestyles—at least as far as the living and lifestyles of individuals who, through possession and/or power are, or were, able to implement and live out their desires and ideas in their society and era without restriction or compromise.

Over millennia, countless people struggled merely to survive, a survival that depended more on fate than on the actions of the individual. It was only the social and political emancipation of the masses, the social developments of the last century that, at least in the western world, also enabled countless numbers of people to become aware of their evolutionary instincts and to demand their fulfillment.

The failure to acknowledge this emancipation of the masses, the most revolutionary event of recent centuries and perhaps of our entire history to date, more significant even than technological advancement despite its coincidental synchronicity, is the decisive cause of the problems. Not to mention the failure of housing and urban development that stubbornly clung to the ideals of the late nineteenth century, the last epoch before the final transition of hierarchical systems of rule to mass democracy.

The correspondence throughout all eras of the lifestyles and forms of living of the rich and powerful, who were able to realize and live out their ambitions and desires without restrictions, is a hardly refutable indication of the constancy of our evolutionary heritage, which manifests itself across all cultures and millennia. The way of life of a Roman patrician was very similar to that of a Chinese mandarin—although both had very little knowledge or experience of the other. It is therefore incomprehensible that the common man should have other desires and needs, but no claim to their satisfaction. This is not just about justice. Evolutionary drives, instincts, and behavioral patterns are compulsively lived out as soon as the material environment and social development make it possible. Not as generously and directly by the aforementioned "common man," but in many cases by substitutes, the consequences of which are to a great extent wasteful, even destructive, of our ecological resources.

It seems quite natural to us therefore that those who can live surrounded by green and abundant nature, close to friends and relatives, if possible with a wide view of the country, if possible by the water, or at any rate by artificial ponds, rivers, and wells, and exercise a profession or activities that involve planning, designing, and discovering in some form or another. Our streams of thought and emotion have indeed been narrowly laid out by evolution.

Our drives, needs, and desires, programmed over millions of years, arise endogenously within us. If they reach a certain intensity—the simplest examples are hunger, sex drive, and the need for exercise and fresh air—adequate stimulus or at least the possibility to fulfill them is required. When neither is present, the result is frustration—caused by unimaginably complicated chemo-electrical stimuli. In exceptional cases this pent-up energy can lead to spiritual or artistic expression, but as a rule it results in either resignation or aggression, both of which are harmful. One has immediate, the other longer-term effects, though mutual reinforcement and/or a combination of both can also occur. Primitive, rebellious, and vandalizing aggression may even, under certain circumstances, be less dangerous than the frustration arising from dull resignation, which is often the beginning of extreme, anarchic, and anti-social behavior.

Changed society and unchanged city

We must remember that the impact of the populace on the development of cities, our culture, and civilization, and our relationship with the environment results both from the masses themselves, but also from the changes that took place in the twentieth century. These resulted from the social changes that hark back to the thoughts and theories of the Enlightenment. It should not be forgotten that it was no coincidence that one of the schools of thought whose influence led to the French Revolution expounded "Back to Nature"—an appeal that many of the later victims of the revolution flirted with. The ideas promoted by the Enlightenment questioned, for the first time, the millennia-old hierarchical systems. They became common knowledge in the course of the nineteenth century and brought the old world to the point of collapse with the end of the First World War. Since then, democratic mass society has been, and remains, an irreversible social reality, as well as the basis of our economic system, which has been exceptionally successful compared to anything that previously existed. This development has been accompanied by the demand—anything else would be inhumane and disastrous for our economic system—by the great mass of the lower classes to share the living conditions of the upper classes for the first time in history. That is, to live in accordance with the phylogenetic inheritance of the species. It must be clear that quality of life, which is to be seen as a complex combination of environment and home, cannot be replaced by substitutes such as consumption, mobility, travel, and holidays, only, when necessary, during short phases of life, such as professional development or the search for a partner.

Remember, the transformation of society took place in two phases: first, during the nineteenth century, as the emancipation of the middle classes, which led to their participation in power, and later to the acquisition of power. This still meant a hierarchical and repressive society, albeit with an extended upper class. It was also the epoch of the explosive growth of European cities—which were again built according to the interests and ideas of a society that had changed, but remained hierarchical. They were different from the monarchical and autocratic models of earlier centuries, but nevertheless still oriented towards a social order based on the separation of the upper and the lower classes.

"Wanderer at the edge of the world," wood engraving from the book *L'atmosphere* by Camille Flammarion, Paris 1888

Industrialization offered an alternative existence to the younger sons and unmarried daughters of the rural population. It is well known what this alternative was like. Nevertheless, a new and ever-growing stratum of the population was created.

The twentieth century finally brought the emancipation of the masses and thus the legitimation for all to make life claims according to the law and the agendas of evolution. At the same time, the demands of the Enlightenment evolved into the socio-political principles of the Western world that, at least in theory, were no longer questioned.

The shape and conception of our cities, however, still date back to the nineteenth century and, especially in the last few decades since the end of the Second World War, cities have been built in the spirit of the latter half of the nineteenth century, for reasons that will be discussed later. They offer little or nothing in the way of meeting the needs of the countless numbers existing on low and median incomes. These cities do not, in other words, provide housing and environmental conditions that correspond to our evolutionary driving forces. Since countless numbers of people are if not underprivileged, then at least less privileged, even in democratic mass society they cannot create the habitats they desire, and are only capable of effecting change through slow democratic mechanisms. Release is sought out: escaping into leisure, relocating to the countryside, a second home that becomes the center of life, in long-distance travel, in the importance of the car as a means of escape and a mobile second home,

Jean-Jacques Rousseau, philosopher, naturalist and educator of the Enlightenment in his garden in Ermenonville in June 1778, colored etching of a portrait by Georges-Frédéric Mayer, 1778

and in the television as a substitute for the hidden horizon. The ecological, economic, sociological, and logistical fallibility of these substitutes need not be argued.

The facts are evident. They lead to the conclusion that those appointed and commissioned to convert the cities of the nineteenth century into habitats for the democratic mass society of the twentieth century, i.e. architects and urban planners, sociologists, housing and urban politicians, have not resolved their task. Indeed, they hardly even recognized it—evidently because they refused to acknowledge the changed society.

Urban planning—and architecture—have always served those in power and have followed a clear mission throughout the millennia, namely to secure power. Sometimes this involves merely representing it—building as an act of prestige and intimidation. This connection began to loosen with the Enlightenment and the French Revolution. The profession of architects sought a new self-image, finding it in the École des Beaux Arts, founded in 1817, which declared ostentatious and theatrical aesthetics to be an end in itself. The platitude "architecture is architecture is architecture" was coined at that time. Thus, since then, during two centuries of social upheaval and the associated change in almost all spheres, it has hardly been noticed that architecture and especially urban planning, regardless of the artistic and technological aspects, are still primarily social phenomena in a fundamentally changed, namely no longer hierarchical, society. These were phenomena of a completely new kind

View of Karlsruhe, copper engraving by Heinrich Schwarz, 1721

For most planning experts and politicians, urbanity, i.e. city life, consists of a combination of cultural and gastronomic venues with an upscale shopping district. Countless numbers of people, however, want nothing more than an undisturbed night's rest in a green environment, living space for children and the elderly, neighborly contact, and restful living in traffic and emission-free neighborhoods that include elements of nature.

It should be remembered that the harsh material and housing shortages of the post-war period and the decades of reconstruction are over. New generations have grown up who do not know the—comparative—narrowness and backwardness of the 1930s and 1940s, but rather an open, free world. This experience never even entered the minds of the older generation. The younger generation is making these demands, and rightly so, in a world that is constantly getting richer despite all the pessimism about progress. The only thing is that wealth turns into consumption and cities remain as they were. The quality of life in cities is becoming worse because developments are taking place that were unimaginable for their builders.

It is a favorite topic of the critics of civilization that we waste our potential on consumer goods instead of converting it into quality of life. The short-lived goods of superfluous consumption can be bought on every corner. But the prerequisites of an environment worth living in can rarely be created by the individual alone. Part of such consumption is therefore compensation for this impossibility.

Therein alone lies the decisive reason for the dramatic extent of suburbanization in recent decades, the flight to leisure time spent in traffic jams and the empty kilometers of weekend excursions. But at the same time, this results in the destruction of nature close to the city, an enormous, unproductive waste of resources, a myriad of most alarming ecological consequences, and, beyond the material waste, wasted time, where the specific goal is usually not even achieved. Furthermore, this development reduces the quality of the city, which we call urbanity, regardless of what any individual may understand by the term.

The escape from anonymity

One of the clichéd complaints about living in cities is their anonymity, the isolated coexistence of thousands, even millions of people. We know from behavioral research that every stranger we are not able to slowly get to know, and whose intentions we therefore cannot be sure of, is a stress factor. The unknown, whether human, animal, or force of nature, has been a stress factor throughout all eras of our history, and humans have tolerated it all the more readily because they could be sure of the support and protection of the group to which they belonged.

This search for support in a group or community, in addition to the need for contact with nature and the expectation of finding possibilities for personal enterprise, is another principal motive for the urban

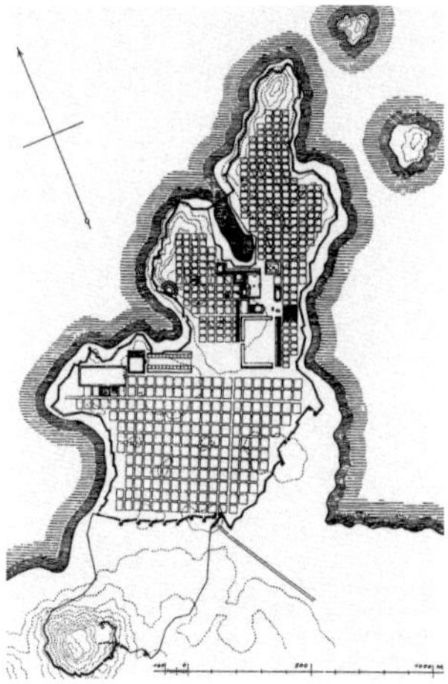

Plan of Miletus based on the grid system of Hippodamus of Miletus, 5th century BC (reconstruction)

Map of San Francisco, 1852

development or, more correctly, the urbanistic phenomenon of suburbanization. One should not underestimate the extent of the fear of anonymity, of being alone in a foreign world. If one replaces the "foreign world" with the "foreigner," then it becomes clear from the history of the last century what can arise from this archaic heritage.

The anonymity of the ever-growing suburban settlements is similar to that of apartment buildings that mono-functionally serve the functions of "living" in the narrowest sense: a space to sleep, cook, and store one's personal belongings, only connected to the world through a television cable. Nevertheless, housing estates are the dream of many, as it offers, or seems to offer at least in part, some of what we are conditioned for: A small patch of ground, a few fruit trees, the possibility to shape something "according to one's own ideas," and thus to evoke memories and expectations of a life close to nature in a small village community, where everyone knows everyone and help is near, where church, shopkeeper, and inn, in former times probably also the village well, represented "communal bonding situations" in the language of behavioral research. That of all this, in the disarray of settlements around our big cities, only the dispute over the garden fence would remain, is something that only emerged later.

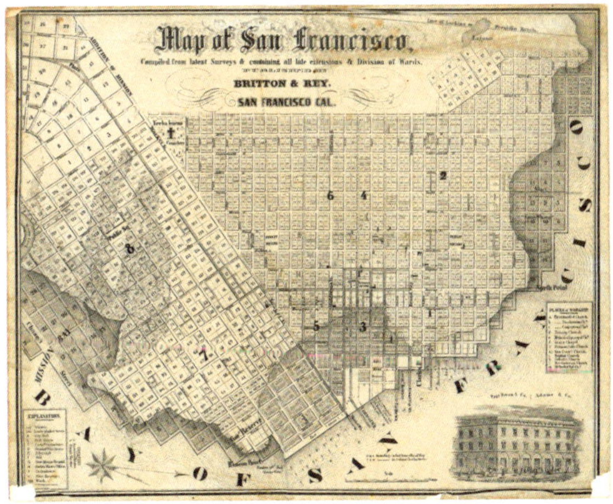

Town planning and housing since antiquity

Even the foundation walls of cities, which existed thousands of years before our era, were erected according to a plan. The name Hippodamus is known to us; he was the architect of Miletus, the grid city whose layout has been used time and again for over 2,000 years. It is the basic layout pattern of many rapidly developing cities in the New World. It is a clear system of organization that enables easy orientation and clear ownership, as in, for example, Manhattan and central New York. It has also proved its worth in the speculative division of suburbs and the undeveloped surroundings of Central European cities during the transition from the Biedermeier era to the *Gründerzeit* period in the second half of the nineteenth century, to the satisfaction of a large number of small investors, as one might call them today, who wanted to invest in real estate and become landlords. Interestingly, a large proportion of current designs for new housing estates today are based on similar configurations.

Parallel to this orthogonal parceling of urban land, which makes it easy to sell, there was a desire not to lose the psychological appeal of nature. With the overnight emergence of new cities lacking historical city centers, with no constraints except topography, but also as a result of the ideas developed primarily in England, landscaping became an important part of urban planning in the New World. The early capitalist maximum use of land was mitigated by "green lungs," such as Central Park in New York or the sequence of parks

Berlin tenements ca. 1900, from: *Berlin in Bildern*, ed. by Adolf Behne, Verlag Dr. Hans Epstein, Vienna and Leipzig, 1929

strung together in Boston, both projects of Frederik Law Olmsted, an influential planner of the era. To this day, in these and other cities, the neighborhoods bordering the parks planned by him and his successors are the finest and most expensive residential addresses, which were reserved for the economic and social elite. Housing of the lower classes, even if they represented the majority, was not a concern.

The urban design measures we are familiar with from the nineteenth century, the boulevards of Haussman's Paris or Vienna's Ringstrasse, did not follow an idealized plan, but were rather a consequence of the changes in the social structure on all levels, not least in military technologies. The feudal city, which had dominated until then, gave way to the self-representation of an economically and politically successful bourgeoisie. It was the transition to a society that was still hierarchical, but was now also determined by the owners, who lived on the new boulevards and villa districts, owned country houses, and spent holidays by the sea, in mountain hotels, and at spa resorts.

In the nineteenth and early twentieth centuries, however, it was not only the enterprising citizen who rose to power, but also the collecting, researching, and cataloguing professor, and with him the "educated" class. The educated citizen enjoyed historicism as an entertaining illustration of the science of art history "invented" by Johann Joachim Winckelmann at the turn of the eighteenth to the nineteenth century. At the same time, the arbitrary disposal over the

Courtyard of a tenement,
from: *Die Wohnung für das Existenzminimum*, ed. Municipal Building Office Frankfurt am Main and the International Congresses for New Building, Frankfurt am Main, 1930

wealth of past forms signified a kind of cannibalistic appropriation of its cultural substance.

In this era, cities were still relatively small, and their construction or reconstruction was possible in manageable periods of time, even with the technology of the time, with the help of what is today an almost unbelievable amount of human labor. Today, cities have grown to dimensions that make their conversion, even into green cities, only possible through selective projects, step by step, in the medium to long term—provided the fundamental political will to bring nature back into the city and thus keep people in cities is even there.

Jean-Baptiste André Godin, entrepreneur and utopian socialist, planned the Familistère in Guise, France for his factory workers in the mid-nineteenth century. It is considered to be the first social housing project. Courtyard in the central wing of the complex, photographer unknown, 1890

As a consequence of the Enlightenment, the ideas of the so-called Utopian Socialists emerged, parallel to, and in part in competition with, Friedrich Engels and Karl Marx, who developed residential projects for the lower classes, especially the emerging class of industrial workers of the time, the outer appearance of which ironically corresponded to the palaces of the High Baroque. It is unclear whether this stemmed from a fascination with the monarchy that made any other form of construction seem inconceivable, or whether it was supposed to express political aspirations. But the interiors revealed an almost ideal communist multifunctional concept. It was undoubtedly recognized that the miserable lives of these early industrial workers and their families required not only material improvement, but above all, the possibility of individual development. There were therefore to be schools, kindergartens, and halls for parties, dance, and music in these facilities, which Charles Fourier called a "*phalanstère.*" Fourier's *phalanstère* was never built. It was only in the second half of the century that Jean-Baptiste Godin, a philanthropic factory owner, built the "*familistère*"—in Guise sur Oise—implementing Fourier's ideas apparently so successfully that they continued to serve their original purpose until 1968 (!).

Both concepts more or less corresponded to that of several other workers' housing estates built in the nineteenth century, though Fourier's *phalanstère* and Godin's *familistère* were more like what we would today call an apartment block, perhaps even a superblock. In fact, by the beginning of the century, in 1824, a philanthropic—and

Westend Workers' Colony in Essen, the first Krupp company workers' settlement, built in 1863, photo ca. 1870

clever—textile entrepreneur, Robert Owen, had already founded New Lanark in Scotland. Workers there received comparatively good housing for their families and the factory owner also provided schools, crèches, a dance hall, playgrounds, and a church. Owen's competitors scoffed until they realized that he also made higher profits thanks to higher productivity. Owen later tried to transfer his ideas to the New World, but failed. Apparently, the people who emigrated with him across the Atlantic were not factory workers who were searching for better lives, but rather what we would now call "alternatives" who preferred debate to manual labor.

The basic idea was nevertheless born. In 1845, Benjamin Disraeli, later Prime Minister of England's Queen Victoria, described in his novel a philanthropist entrepreneur who built a village for his factory workers with everything that liberal thinking—bold and progressive for those days—could imagine for living, including also educational and development opportunities for the workforce. In addition to fresh spring water distributed and disposed of via a closed canal system, small houses and apartments, schools, crèches, baths, hospitals, and community facilities, dance halls and theaters were also supplied. This novel impressed a young industrialist named Titus Salt, so much so that he actually built such a facility, called Saltaire, in 1851. Other industrialists followed, including Alfred Krupp in Germany. These men were generally less idealistic and were more interested in the availability of a qualified foreman thanks to the proximity of the housing. Incidentally, similar facilities had already existed for specialists

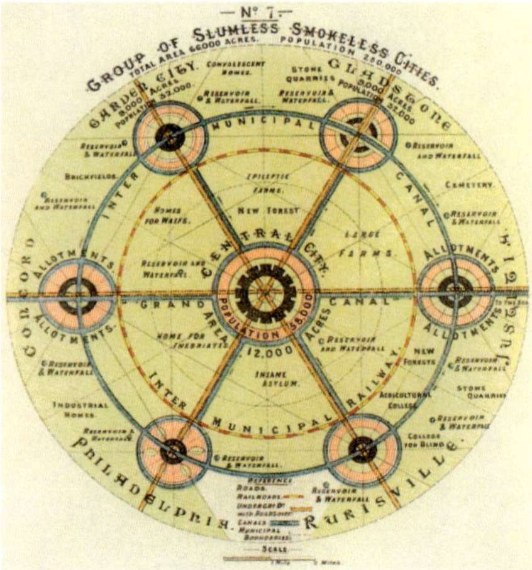

Ebenezer Howard, diagram of a garden city and its surroundings, published in *Garden Cities of To-morrow*, Swan Sonnenschein & Co., London, 1902

in the industrial era, such as Maria Theresa's Nadelburg near Wiener Neustadt, where a needle factory was built with the help of skilled workers brought in from abroad and settled there.

The enlightened humanitarianism of these factory owners cannot be denied. However, although their factory estates were undoubtedly an improvement, at least compared with the cramped quarters of big city tenements, it was of course a mutually beneficial business. After all, whoever ruled the house ruled the worker. Those who lost their jobs also lost the benefit of this comparatively decent living situation, which was a bonus, not a right.

Otto Wagner, ideal plan for the 22nd district of Vienna, 1911, model at the Otto Wagner exhibition in the Wien Museum, 2018

One of the most important ideas of the late nineteenth century was that of parliamentary stenographer Ebenezer Howard, the Garden City. London had expanded enormously due to the predominance of terraced houses. The later highly dense network of subways was only just beginning to develop. As a solution to the problems this created, Ebenezer Howard proposed a belt of overspill towns—although the term did not exist at the time—which were connected to each other by a ring road and to the metropolis by radial lines. Each unit was to consist of workplaces, a residential area, and an agricultural greenbelt to supply the population living there. Howard also developed financial plans and actually succeeded in creating three of these Garden Cities. However, he assumed that the social status of his time would continue and did not take into account the emerging and increasing need for freedom of choice of workplace, determined by individual interests. As a result, his concept was relatively short-lived. One could say that it lived on in the post-war overspill towns, also called satellites and new towns, in Scandinavia and England. The "development axes" that emerged after the war, i.e. dense construction along efficient mass transport lines, can also be tied in to Howard's ideas.

In the German-speaking world, the Garden City movement gave rise to the *Gartenstadtbewegung*, a literal translation of the English term. This combined allotment garden clusters, condensed low-rise buildings, and single-family house settlements to create a romantic, petit-bourgeois idyll, which appealed to important parts of our evolutionary heritage.[2]

Bernhard Hermkes,
housing for working women
in New Frankfurt, 1931,
photo 2013

Of course, there were also urban designs for the expansion of large cities, such as Otto Wagner's plan for the expansion of Vienna on the left bank of the Danube. However, these are entirely in the tradition of the grid city of the second half of the nineteenth century, and assume a society unaltered from the state in which the plan was drawn up in 1910. The early decades of the twentieth century brought the first impulses for the emancipation of the lower classes, not least due to the millions of people who had been affected by the war. Social housing during the years after the First World War in the Netherlands,[3] Germany,[4] and in its most fundamental form in Vienna was the result of a deep humanitarian conviction. These were the forerunners of new housing and thus a new city.

Le Corbusier's proposals for a conversion of the old quarters of Paris into a city of residential high-rise buildings along cruciform ground plans, separated by huge green spaces (Plan Voisin, 1925), are comparatively radical. These may have seemed realistic to Le Corbusier, who had Haussman's no less radical urban redevelopment in mind—after all, they were rational and modern, and technically not even overly utopian.

As early as 1922, Le Corbusier presented a two-story maisonette, placed one above the other, at the Salon d'Automne in Paris, calling them *Immeuble-villas*. Consciously or unconsciously, I have similarly described my first terraced buildings as "stacked single-family houses." Why Le Corbusier never considered the stepped terrace house I do not know,[5] as he certainly could have been familiar with

Gerrit Rietveld, Erasmuslaan residential complex in Utrecht, 1931, photo 2013

Adolf Loos' design for a terraced, pyramid-shaped hotel (see p. 69 f). He certainly knew of Henri Sauvage's Parisian stepped terrace building from the 1910s and 1920s, one of which even has a swim ming pool in its "belly" (see p. 67 ff).

The fact that completely or partially destroyed urban structures were rebuilt after the war does not always seem to make sense in retrospect. In many cases, it was a missed opportunity, but understandably so, after all one cannot demand vision from people who are trying merely to survive. There were—and still are—many explanations for housing development during the post-war period. To me, none seem entirely plausible, but what is certain is that there was an urgent demand. But instead of looking back at fascist barracks and apartment blocks for officers' families—as most of the small amount of housing built during these years did—we should have looked a mere ten years further back. Modernist housing in France, the Netherlands, and Germany would have made far better prototypes. The housing of Red Vienna was far ahead of its time in its concept and approach compared with most of what came after the war. The political minds whose fierce humanitarianism had developed a vision of decent housing in the 1920s, particularly in Vienna, were no longer to be found only two decades later. One justification—one is tempted to say excuse—for the housing construction of the post-war period was lack of money and the need to build cheaply. That said, this is equally true of the years after the First World War. But above all: what was built was neither very cheap nor at least economical in the sense

Sigfried Giedion, *Liberated Dwelling* [Befreites Wohnen], Orell Füssli Verlag, Zurich and Leipzig 1929, book cover

of a long-term cost-benefit calculation. Accommodation was built, nothing more.

Some overspill towns, now referred to as satellite cities, were created, such as Milton Keynes in England (from 1967) or Vällingby near Stockholm (1954), undoubtedly conceived according to Ebenezer Howard's concept, albeit without including his agricultural autonomy. But they repeated his misapprehension, namely the assumption of a fixed relationship between living and work. I recall the disappointment expressed by a Swedish study showing that this relationship proved attractive only to women with children working part-time.

Most of what was built outside the city centers, and thus the majority of new buildings, went up on greenfield sites which, however, were no longer green once built upon. This "satisfied" the living needs of the countless numbers of urban residents with low and middle incomes. Those with higher wages, as always, took care of themselves. Nor are they the subject of these considerations, since their housing is only of importance for urban design to the extent that it nevertheless becomes a prototype for those excluded from this possibility. Although—as a rule—this is by no means successful for the masses, as it leads to attempts that are highly damaging: The villa in the garden district becomes a settlement house in the urban hinterland, the lack of contact with nature is replaced by a hectic flight for leisure and second homes. Urban life in the sense of social communication, of leisure time that can be enjoyed with a minimum of time wasted in traffic, does not develop—and did not develop—in this manner.

Le Corbusier, Immeubles Villas, stacked "single family homes" with gardens as a densified form of urban living, 1922

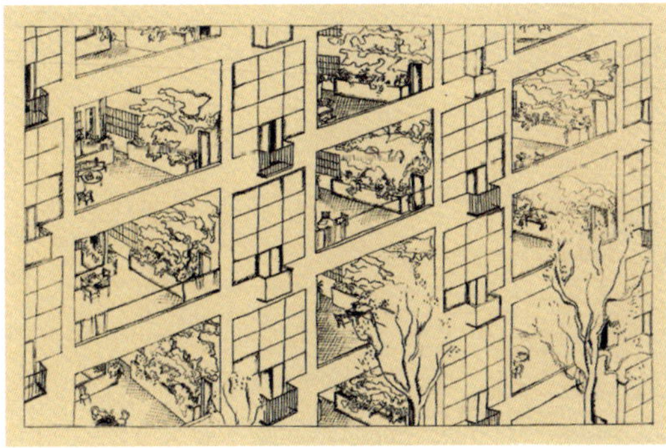

The real improvement in our quality of life, which is essential for the city's continued existence, lies in circumstances and changes that the individual cannot bring about on their own, not even through a few percentage points more pay. Living in the city, yet in harmony with nature, enjoying the opportunities arising from the city's diversity and freedom without the detrimental effects of anonymity, loneliness, and lack of relationships, but finding identification in the big city in a manageable way. And not losing the living universe in the civilized city: water and sky, the feeling of one's own body, as well as closeness and accessibility of other people. The ability to experience the immense, branched, yet single origin of all the drives, desires, wishes, and needs that have formed over millions of years of evolution. We have learned to limit them, to control them, to replace them with substitutes and release them only sometimes, for a short time, like unleashing a dog. We have resigned ourselves to living like this. The Green City is a concept that increases this scope—that "extends the leash."

Hugo Breitner, Vienna City Councilor of Finance 1919–1932

With 1,587 apartments and an extensive social infrastructure, the Sandleitenhof is the largest municipal housing facility in Red Vienna, 1924–1928, architects Schönthal, Hoppe, and others

Children's outdoor pool on Margaretengürtel, the so-called "Ring Road of the Proletariat" in Vienna, 1926

Red Vienna

The municipal buildings of Red Vienna were a declaration that decent housing is a fundamental right. Political objectives were directed towards the restructuring of society, and resulted in the reconstruction of the nineteenth-century city, a reflection of a repressive society that was still only marginally democratic.

The driving forces were bourgeois men, one could say of upper middle-class origin. Hugo Breitner, the person responsible for the City of Vienna's finances, had previously been the general director of the largest bank in the country, and university professor Julius Tandler, an important anatomist, was responsible for health. They were neither architects nor urban planners, but they set ambitious sociological goals for the architects—most of whom were conservative—the urban consequences of which led to the abandonment of the principles of urban and residential construction of the *Gründerzeit* period. In response to the cramped housing conditions of the past, they went above and beyond the usual requirements for air, light, and surrounding greenery that had emerged throughout Europe in the 1920s.

The unique urban—and socio-political—special aspect of the Vienna Model was primarily its dimensions: Many of the buildings were the size of entire districts. However, this did not result in blocks lined up along access roads, but was instead designed as a sequence of courtyards situated like parks, edged by the outermost boundaries of the property. These park-like courtyard landscapes were fundamen-

tally different from the rigid street grids of the *Gründerzeit* era, which had essentially only served to provide access to narrow, preferably rectangular sites, but also from the more schematic lines of residential construction in the rest of Europe. The goal of creating a small-scale, multifunctional, green city was achieved with a total of about 60,000 apartments in ten years, though only selectively, distributed throughout Vienna, and realized using various methodologies and exemplary approaches.

Though widely published, the Karl-Marx-Hof—not coincidentally for the neo-historical zeitgeist of recent years—is by no means a characteristic example of this objective. Its striking monumentality has far more to do with the "order" of the SS—its architect, Karl Ehn, was indeed a follower of National Socialism—than with the humane attitude and idealistic philanthropy of most other municipal buildings, such as the George-Washington-Hof, the Hof am Fuchsenfeld, the Rabenhof, the courtyard buildings in Sandleiten, and others.

Apart from the park-like greenery and the free series of spaces and buildings, the decisive objective of Red Vienna's municipal buildings, which distinguishes them from what existed elsewhere in Europe then and later, was its multi-functionality. This multi-functionality affected almost all areas of life and aimed for social and cultural self-sufficiency. As already mentioned, the discrimination of the lower classes, i.e. the working class and the lower middle class was, in the nineteenth century, not only a material but also and perhaps primarily a cultural and educational one. Therefore, not only were social facili-

George-Washington-Hof in Vienna, with spacious green courtyards, architects Karl Krist and Robert Oerley, 1927–1930, photo 2016

ties in the narrower sense, such as maternal counseling and nurseries, outpatient clinics, dental clinics, community baths, and affordable grocery stores integrated into the social housing projects, but also people's education centers, music schools, libraries, theaters, and cinemas featuring artistically or scientifically significant films. There were meeting places for the anti-alcoholic movement—"a thinking worker does not drink, a drinking worker does not think"—and, of course, there were also meeting spaces for the Social Democratic Party, known as "sections." It was therefore obvious that the political opponents saw the municipal buildings as fortresses and hotbeds of world revolution. The accusation may not even have been unjustified in the atmosphere of the time. In terms of urban planning and urban sociology of little importance, but the shared attitude of the inhabitants and the possibilities for joint activities in these courtyard buildings, *Höfe* in German, gave rise to communication and sense of belonging. At that time, this sense of belonging was not available in the modern cities and social housing built elsewhere in Europe, especially in Germany and the Netherlands, although they were mostly of a much higher standard in terms of formal architecture.

Because of their comprehensive aims, the Viennese buildings became symbols of the workers' cultural movement of the time, the expression and realization of a humanitarian vision that aimed to raise the living and cultural standards of a large, previously underprivileged swathe of the population—to let everyone participate in what a small privileged class had previously claimed for itself.

From today's point of view, it is hard to imagine how novel and outrageous for the supporters of the hierarchical past the social housing of Red Vienna really was. A social stratum which, despite it being in the majority, had never made an appearance, had never dared to present itself, now entered the urban stage. Not with buildings that, like the *Gründerzeit*-era tenements, were caricatures of the palaces of the ruling class, with miserable accommodation behind Potemkin facades, but with a call for a new way of life, in a new city, for new people. If living in a generous green environment, not divided into speculative plots, in buildings in the midst of tree-lined courtyards that merge into one another sounds lofty, it must be remembered that these were, and still are, for a large—probably the majority—of people the ideals of life, at least as far as housing is concerned. The fact that the multifunctional infrastructure of these buildings provided not only for daily needs, but also offered educational, social, and health care facilities, must today be supplemented and in part replaced by leisure, physical activity, and social facilities, is a consequence of emancipatory development. Even then, everything was traffic-free, because cars were still toys for the rich in those days. These buildings represented the vision of the dawning of a new era that had become reality. Their political success was great: although the epoch only lasted a decade, it emanated a signal whose influence reached into the recent past.

Historicism as a socio-political phenomenon

It seems that aesthetic debate always takes place when politics becomes unable to articulate the concrete development of improved living conditions. This was as true in the second half of the nineteenth century as it was in the last decades of the twentieth century. When the goal of social emancipation, which every person can define for themselves and which is by no means limited to material things, begins to blur, then this allows charlatans, populists, spin doctors, and swindlers from Andersen's fairy tale "The Emperor's New Clothes" to emerge. The objectives are lost: In all areas of life and politics, including urban planning, housing, and architecture, the development of which is limited to the formal but socially marginal.

The transition of power from the aristocracy and the military to the middle classes took place gradually. Therefore, following a notorious principle, the majority of the new upper class tried to follow the example of the social classes that still dominated the state, the aristocracy and the military. They tried to be accepted to a certain extent or at least tolerated in their circle through mimicry. Such behavior not only arises from human vanity, but is also an attempt to gain a higher, or at least more secure position in the horde through proximity to the "alphas."

As we learn in the second scene of the first act of Gotthold Ephraim Lessing's *Emilia Galotti*, "art follows bread," i.e. artists gravitate to the rich and powerful. And if they preferred the past to the present—it could be done. In this way, historicism became the self-representation of the citizen as nobleman.

In the second half of the nineteenth century, this also led to new building typologies that vividly demonstrated the masquerade. Even the richest citizen could never compete with the practically immeasurable wealth of some noblemen, who had, over centuries, accumulated assets and vast estates and castles with countless servants from the spoils of many wars and the toil of tens of thousands.

For the advancing middle classes, there could only be diminutives, and so the "Palace Hotel" was born, offering its guests the opportunity to live in castle-like buildings at a high price, but for a limited period of time. "Hotel" originally meant the seat of a nobleman or at least a very important family, around the clock service, delicious meals prepared by cooks at any time, and luxury wherever the eye looked. Concerts, balls, gambling rooms, and finally, as stage of the world, the theater of hotel entrance halls.

Another significant typology was the *Zinspalais*, buildings which lined the new boulevards, but no longer served as the seat of a single lordship and his retinue as before, but were instead divided into rented apartments and "villas." This concept was, however, a contradiction in terms even at the time. Today's speculators have further exacerbated the problem with the "city villa" crammed into a narrow street grid with a miserable front garden, its relative exclusivity resulting from the exorbitant building costs of the typology, which is neither, city nor country, nor villa.

Another new building typology emerging from the century of civil emancipation was the museum. Originating from the curiosity cabinets of wealthy aristocrats, museums became the first sign of the realization that the wealth of the world and human arts could not be restricted to the private property of a few. The myriad of new museums that have been created in recent years, but above all the overwhelming popularity that most of them have enjoyed, prove the fascination that emanates from the democratization of these treasures.

The large cities that developed in Europe in the second half of the nineteenth century were impressive manifestations of a social situation and their representation of new wealth was of great fascination. At least the lower classes were allowed to participate to the extent that their miserable quarters were furnished—mockingly—with facades reminiscent of the palaces of the bourgeoisie.

The urban planning of the second half of the nineteenth century manifested a social situation that was still hierarchical and, similar to previous epochs, was also blatantly stated: mansion districts and boulevards lined with parkways, stately gardens in between for the upper middle class, and a street grid with dense block development for workers and employees—i.e. the masses—designed without reserve to maximize economic profit. It is not easy to explain how in recent decades the urban planning and architectural ideologies for the masses, which have now been socially and economically emancipated, have provided nothing more than a street grid and building block, possibly even more confined than before.

Historicism as neurosis

The currents counteracting social emancipation undoubtedly also reinforced the fact that the change in society triggered by the ideas of the Enlightenment was accompanied and made possible by unprecedented development in the natural sciences, technology, and all kinds of machinery. For the people of that time, much of this must have been incomprehensible and thus mysterious—in truth, even today most of us don't have a true understanding of the nature of electricity. No wonder, then, that in the face of the emergence of previously unknown mysterious and therefore threatening forces, people sought refuge in an environment that superficially corresponded to an era of candlelight and horse-drawn carriages, and causes and effects were understandable and familiar. The belated cultural reaction in comparison to the turbulent development of science and technology was as much a neurotic symptom as a socio-political master plan like that designed by the Congress of Vienna, which included the restoration of the absolute monarchies and was enforced until the middle of the century at least, and in a marginally modified form for even longer.

The study of historicism should not be seen as an art history digression. Viewing it as a socio-political phenomenon with multiple origins can provide explanation for significant processes—and failures—in the planning of cities and housing estates today.

There is no doubt that, in the twentieth century, similar psychological mechanisms to a century before are at work. The functioning of steam engines and even combustion engines is now taught at school, and the younger generation is adept at using computers. Nevertheless, for many, if not most, of us, nuclear power and the electronically controlled world remain a mystery and are therefore threatening. This is why the entertainment industry presents us with fantasies played out in a fairy-tale past and history is valued and protected as never before. All this is probably also related to a search for stability in a world of frighteningly rapid development that seems to abandon everything familiar.

This is one of the reasons why historical, i.e. restorative urban planning and urban sociological concepts haunt almost all current planning concepts, competitions, and appraisals. Catchphrases such as "critical reconstruction" dominate everything from large and important building projects down to small and medium-sized ones. "Sustainable urban planning" is another such catchphrase, which, translated into common understanding, means that only urban forms from the past survive. Now one may see the reverent preservation of structures in connection with history. This can also be argued in city centers, which only marginally serve residential purposes, but above all the old function of the market place. But street grids from the *Gründerzeit* era with peripheral block buildings in residential areas can no longer meet the expectations of those seeking accommodation. With regard to their residential quality of life, the emancipation of the lower classes in the last decades of the twentieth century has progressed too far for this. It should be remembered that for a long time, only those who owned a house were considered citizens. Everyone else—if not family—was a servant. How they lived was of no interest, certainly not architecturally speaking. But these servants have become the countless members of democratic mass society, and regard themselves as citizens with the same entitlements and rights as the property owners before and—for lack of a better alternative—whose clothes and houses they want to claim even if this might only be possible on a far smaller scale.

The criteria of a green city

For me, one of the most beautiful pieces that has ever been written is Hölderlin's poem "Bread and Wine." It begins:

Town rests now, all around, the lit streets quietening;
Carriages leave in a flare of lamps with a rush.
Full of a whole day's happiness, people go home to their rest;
Shrewd men weigh profit and losses,
Pleased at home; empty the bustling market stands
Of grapes and flowers, and rests from works of the hand.
Distantly though, there is music from gardens; perhaps
Someone in love is playing or a lonely man
Thinking of distant friends or his young days; the unfailing
Fountains come with a rush through greenery, sweet.
Softly the rung bells ring on the dusky air and the watchman,
Mindful of time, calls out the counted hours.
Now comes a stir through the air and troubles the treetops,
And see, our earth's shadower, the moon
Comes too now, stealing in; the night comes, passionate night
Full of stars and not much concerned about us:
The astonishing night, the foreigner among humans, lifts
Over mountains, sadly, in glory, shining.[6]

Utopia Island, title woodcut from Thomas Morus's novel *On the Best State of a Republic and on the New Island of Utopia*, 1516

A more perfect description of the ideal city, I believe, does not exist. The Green City is a place where people live closely together, work, relax, have fun, enjoy leisure—enjoy all that our spirit has created, without renouncing the all-embracing nature from which we came, which formed us, which gave us abilities and needs, fears and desires, dreams and longings. We can renounce nothing in this universe—in us and around us—without suffering a loss.

The green city is a centuries-old dream—from Amaurotum the city in Thomas Morus's *Utopia* with its magnificent gardens full of wine, fruit, and flowers to Ebenezer Howard's Garden City. The Renaissance utopia was never realized and the Garden City only partly. The aim of the concept is to satisfy the needs and of the countless many with an urban, especially inner-city form of living, particularly when a single-family house surrounded by greenery is what is expected. However, the academic view of urban housing today is to regard this demand as romantic, contradictory, even simply nonsensical. Anyone who wants to—or has to—live in the city is just supposed to accept that the urban environment consists of streets and traffic, asphalt, noise, and dust. There could be avenues, and now and then a park, but not meadows and countryside, which incidentally are not found in most single-family housing estates either. The latter is true, but the former is only conditionally so: a green city is possible. Density without constriction, access without roads, and urban life in a green environment is possible. It is simply false to declare the renunciation of evolutionary basic needs resulting from a lack of urban planning and architectural imagination as necessary and their fulfillment as superfluous for the majority. To participate in nature, experience the seasons, have social interactions, experience creative, social, and physical activities, enjoy views and water—all these are innate psychological needs and therefore legitimate, at least in a society whose emancipation and material wealth are as advanced as ours.

A primary objective is eliminating traffic on sections made as large as possible by combining lots, made possible by accessing the individual developments underground via a system of subterranean garages. The streets, thus made superfluous, are converted into greenspaces, private gardens for the residents, and park-like, semi-public areas planted with large trees.

It is equally important to create green facades, not only for the quality of life within the individual apartments, but also to further embed the buildings in greenspaces with trees, by designing loggias, terraces, and verandas that can be planted. The sum of these planted loggias, terraces, and green roof will in most cases be equal to the floor space taken up by the building, so that this space, stacked vertically, will be reclaimed as recreational space. The value of designing open spaces which correspond to the apartments like this lies in their closeness to nature—as close to nature as is possible in the city. This is probably also perceived by most people as an improvement in quality of life, even if one could call a planted loggia or terrace merely a substitute for a garden. But just how much this means to most people, and how much can be achieved in the smallest of spaces, is shown in Japanese cities, where every little patch of earth produces greenery just a few steps away from the thunderous noise of traffic.

One of the most important criteria of a green city is access to water for all residents, through swimming pools that serve the purpose of recreation, physical experience, and last but not least, health. Added to this is the ability of water to impart us with the weightlessness we experience in utero. The swimming pools are surrounded by roof gardens, also used as sun and viewing decks, children's playgrounds, reading pergolas, barbecue areas, or simply a place to gaze up at the sky and the clouds. Roof gardens and swimming pools have been proven to be particularly conducive to stimulating communication and community activities.

A further objective is not only to significantly increase satisfaction with housing and life, but also to change behavior. That is, the decrease of the tendency towards suburbanization, less leisure time away and more leisure time in the residential area and thus an increase in communication and even cultural activities and better neighborly contact. The anonymity of the city is counterbalanced by the feeling of living in a small community at the same time, an important enrichment of psychological wellbeing for many people. The decrease in leisure time away from home decreases the ecological burden on the nature of the periphery of the city. This effect increases significantly if a decrease in the preference of single-family houses as a residential ideal is also achieved.

In addition, and this is one of the most important components of the Green City concept, is improved overall health, i.e. the psychological and physical benefits from experiencing water, views, wind, and sky on the communal roof garden, which has become rare in the city, and the recreational and creative function of the private open-air greenspaces, the spacious terrace or loggia assigned to each apartment, and the transition to semi-public, park-like greenspaces. The need to experience the changing of the seasons and the smell of the earth after the rain is not just a poetic cliché.

The prerequisite for this is, above all, a building structure that is superior to conventional models in the two most important parameters of economic efficiency, namely geometry and planning. Ideally, it should have a strict north-south axis, which allows apartments well lit by sun from the east and west. Because if one calculates the hours of sunshine multiplied by the sunlit area, this one-sided arrangement results in almost the same values as purely south-facing apartments and almost twice that of north-south apartments.

The economic efficiency of the construction and the geometry of the building is a decisive prerequisite for the concept of a Green City. After all, this should not be a habitat for millionaires, but one for the countless number of those whose economic capacity is limited. Only this economic efficiency makes it possible to equip the residential buildings with communal areas for socializing and hobbies, which are left to the residents, adults, adolescents, children, and elderly citizens to design freely.

The planning of dwellings with a central access configuration might be criticized by some, but this has not been proven to be

A

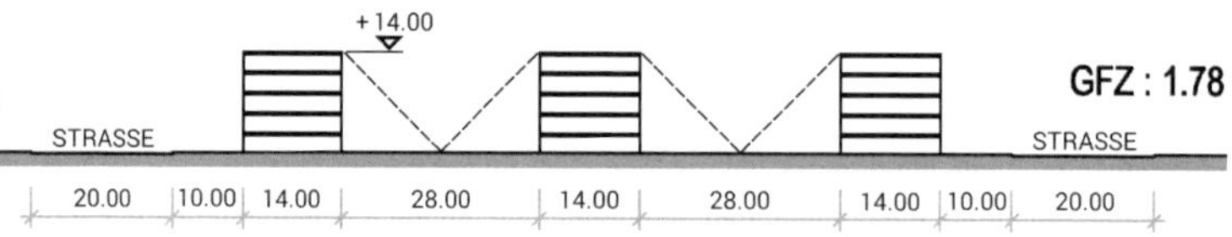

B

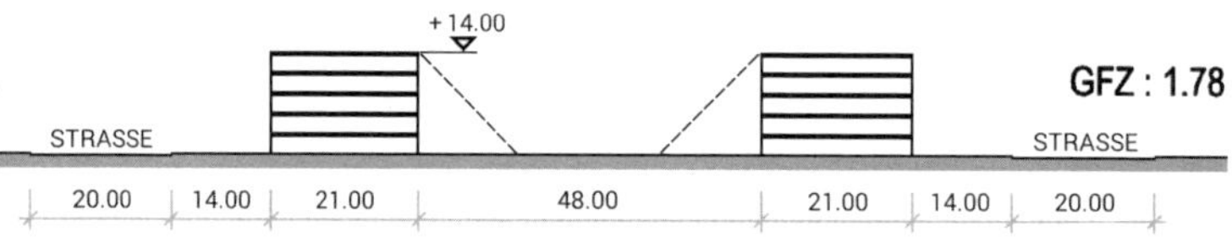

the case among residents. This planning system allows for the economical arrangement of staircases and lifts according to actual need. It allows, on the one hand, for spacious entrance halls because only a few are required and, on the other hand, large roof gardens, swimming pools, and subterranean garages. The fact that this compact building geometry is a prerequisite for low heating costs, as well as favorable operating and service costs of the lift systems, and above all 10–15 percent lower construction costs, is obviously not adequately recognized. For the inclusion of leisure and community facilities essential for quality of living in buildings for the masses, i.e. within a limited price segment, can and will be made possible in the future, and only to a limited extent, by savings in what we could call quality-relevant components. Likewise, the ecologically important positioning of the economical garages beneath the buildings is related to this concept.

In addition, this concept and the geometry of the buildings is also the prerequisite for developing densified but not cramped valuable urban land and the creation of a compact yet green city. A simple consideration illustrates this: Examples A and B have the same floor area density per level. The shorter distance between the facade in A(x) forces residents to live behind curtains. These same short distances allow only small plants that have no effect on the microclimate, do not provide privacy, do not create distance, and do not provide a nesting place for birds, etc. The ratio of facade to volume is one third more favorable in B than in A. A further advantage is that in B, the garages

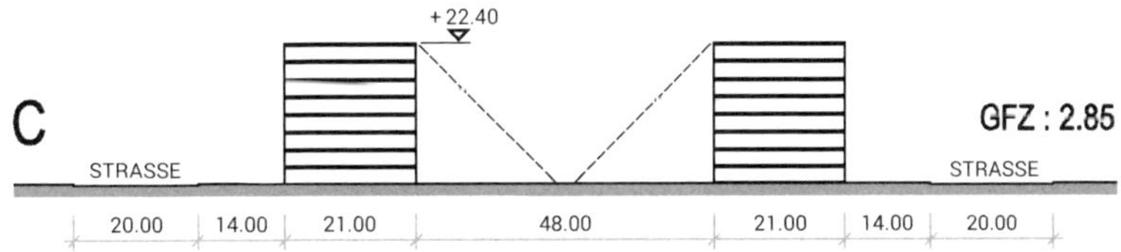

can be located beneath the buildings, while in Example A additional land must be paved over. Example C shows that a higher density is possible on the same plot of land without creating a sense of constriction, and the front garden is even widened. The buildings in A and B have five floors of 2.8 meters each, for a total of 14 meters of height. The distance of 48 meters in Example B, however, allows up to eight floors of 2.8 meters totaling 22.4 meters, i.e. up to twice the density at the same generous distance!

The building concept of Green Cities that allows for larger greenspaces through greater wing depths at the same density also has direct ecological effects, namely the possibility of surrounding the apartments with almost natural habitats. This is a necessary and desirable goal that will meet with resistance from the majority of architects and urban planners who, rooted in the nineteenth century, want to see nature in the city merely as "urban greenery," as décor on boulevards, or as punctual parks scattered amongst a sea of houses.

A Green City is a more compact city with shorter distances despite the return of nature, and thus, in addition to the reduction of costs for technical infrastructure, above all both a relative and absolute reduction of street area. On the one hand, because more densely built-up areas require a smaller proportion of roads than less dense ones, and on the other hand, because within the building sites, access takes place via the underground garages that accommodate both parked cars and moving traffic, allowing above-ground street space to be converted into green areas and gardens. As shown, the gain in greenspaces can be considerable. It is evident that by expanding the greened spaces of the city, the microclimate, dust filtration, and groundwater flow is improved. Furthermore, these greenspaces, freed from traffic, make children's playgrounds possible, offer recreation and communication for the elderly, improving the quality of life with a park-like urban landscape instead of a desert-like landscape covered in stony asphalt and concrete.

Of course, none of this saves energy directly on the building itself. But it is easy to see, although tangible studies are still pending, that the resulting energy savings could be considerable, in total even higher than anything achieved by optimized building physics. The concept is capable of reducing leisure time travel as well as lessening the preference for single-family homes as a residential ideal, i.e. leading to a reduction in suburbanization. Both leisure travel and commuting alone could mean a consumption—and waste—of energy that goes far beyond anything that can be achieved through thermal insulation, solar collectors, heat recovery, and thermal storage.

In other words, in a Green City, green building must not be limited to immediate energy and water savings but must also allow, and even encourage, behaviors that avoid the disproportionate consumption of energy and land. This in turn means that an ecological city must be a compact, extremely green city, one could say rather like a vacation hotel that is urban thanks to a variety of communal, playful, perhaps even cultural options.

A more compact city also leads to a general reduction in traffic, directly by shortening distances, and indirectly by increased incentives to cover these shorter distances on foot or by bicycle in a greener, traffic-reduced urban landscape. It is evident that a more compact city can also provide public transport more easily, more economically, and more appealingly.

The Green City concept also allows for smaller projects that are far greener than the surrounding city. It is always possible to reclaim traffic areas to create green pedestrian zones and climate oases within the rigid grid of the nineteenth century city. These can be measured in degrees of temperature and humidity, and biotope oases recognizable by birdsong in the city. With a size of about 200 apartments upwards, many of the economic and spatial features of larger developments can also be created, from rooftop swimming pools to party and hobby rooms, while still keeping below the budget of standard buildings.

The paradox of the Green City, which allows for higher densities and more greenery in conjunction with more options for leisure and personal development and as much social contact as desired, leads to the restoration of the relationship network that is necessary to mitigate the negative effects of feeling anonymous and social distress. The psychological and physical benefits obviously reach far beyond the apparent "luxury." Everyone benefits from an ecological, nature-friendly, and people-friendly city, not least the public sector.

Katsura Palace near Kyoto,
17th century, view of the tea pavilion,
photo 2007

A Green City for all

One can describe the city for all with Hölderlin's wonderful words, one can define it as a habitat in the sense of our evolutionary needs, and one can present the characteristics necessary for its functioning in a pragmatic way. Namely, as the type of city that best meets the logistical and ecological criteria recognized as indispensable—ecological in every sense, i.e. also in relation to humans, granting them the same rights as a rare amphibian. However, one can also demand, in a very banal and pragmatic way, that the quality of life in the entire city should be that of those neighborhoods where the privileged live, through property ownership and/or power. Any of these formulations or definitions, if fulfilled, could correspond to the emancipated democratic mass society at the beginning of the new millennium.

This approach has already taken place in many areas including medical care, access to travel, information and education, and equality in the eyes of the law. Living in harmony with nature remains a privilege. Reducing this gap by allowing the "poor" to live in the same city as the "rich" is the aim of the Green City.

It should be pointed out once again that the abandonment of this comprehensive urban and housing policy in favor of an aesthetically pleasing petty-bourgeois view of the city may also partly be due to a decline in favor for those politically responsible for it. After all, the attraction of traditional political parties was not only their vision of social justice, but of a better world in general. This in turn closely cor-

The Hanging Gardens of Semiramis, still image from a computer game

responded to our evolutionary ideals: To live in harmony with nature, in a green and peaceful environment, to have social contact without hostility, and therefore to live without fear. Work was, at least in a higher sense, creative and without drudgery, the body was not a burden or sinful but a joy, the future seen to be endless and promising. An essential factor of this future and this new world was better, yes even beautiful living.

Now the point of view can be taken that if the client does not request more than just a place to sleep and to watch TV, the architect doesn't do much more, because no discussion about planning is wanted. But this point of view, as shortsighted as it is, also shows that there are other parties involved. First of all, the client who is not the actual client, the actual client is the end user, the person looking for an apartment. As long as clients buy or rent without making any further demands, often due to a lack of alternatives, housing developers pay little attention to them.

The world, at least the western world, has become richer and, despite all skepticism of growth—and pessimism—is becoming richer every year. It is not mentioned that material growth destroys the ecological balance. It is only a question of directing the opportunities offered by prosperity in the right direction, of satisfying the innate needs of human beings directly by creating living conditions that correspond to our nature and thus limit the need for substitutes.

The city as a habitat is a complex task that neither the individual citizen nor the mechanisms of free enterprise, however one defines the term, is able to solve. Individual citizens can only leave a city that doesn't seem like a biotope either completely or in their leisure time. It is obvious that the building materials trade, building societies, and town mayors will help with this—even if it is directly and indirectly to the detriment of nature as well as to the city and thus to the detriment of us all.

"Innovative" forms of housing

Evolution has taken several million years to program our instincts, needs, and behavior. The expectation that the cordless phone and the previously unimaginable mobility that became possible within just a few generations would change our human genome is premature, as far as we have learned to understand these processes. In any case, our test group, i.e. those privileged thanks to ownership and/or power have hardly changed their forms of living, which were already developed thousands of years ago, not even in the last century during which the greatest technological and social changes in history took place. And, to say it once again, this group has created exactly the forms of housing and ways of life, and exactly the environment that corresponds to our evolutionary programming. In the twentieth century, for the first time, the majority of lower and middle classes have tried to do likewise, as best they could, albeit not with the same success. This has led to ecological, logistical, and urban consequences that are harmful to us all, and which may well lead to calling into question the tradition of European urban civilization, which is not entirely unsuccessful and which has become dear to our hearts.

In the history of living—as we understand it—recognizable to us from the beginning as a development that has emerged with an ever-increasing merging of inside and outside, an opening of the cave, and an attempt to reintegrate into the natural habitat as far as climate and the dangers from humans and animals will allow. The direction is clearly discernable from the hanging gardens of the Semiramis, to the country homes of the Roman aristocrats, to the palazzi and villas of the Renaissance, to Baroque palaces with their artificial garden landscapes merged for the most part into the open countryside, to the sequences of rooms by Frank Lloyd Wright, Richard Neutra, Ludwig Mies van der Rohe, and others that open into nature.

In reality, meaningful innovation can only consist of adapting housing forms more precisely to our evolutionary needs and to the respective ecological, economic, and sociological conditions. With the exception of certain niche projects, this will always consist of a constant core of functional spatial references that are varied only slightly conceptually, i.e. essentially only by economically determined parameters.

Television has certainly influenced people's lifestyles, mechanical kitchen appliances, frozen food, sanitary installations, and central heating—but none of this has required or brought about new forms of living. The same applies to our almost total global mobility, shorter working hours, entitlement to vacations, old-age provisions, everything that has changed social development and emancipation for the last generation. Variations in the functional relationships of housing are only the result of greater or lesser spatial possibilities and are not fundamental.

The lifestyles of people, as special as they may seem to the individuals themselves, are so similar in their functional needs that they are in fact identical. The great differences between individual living situations seen from close up, disappear almost completely when viewed from a distance. Innovation in the homes and lives of large numbers of people must, if it is to be meaningful, serve to optimize the quality of life and the ecological conditions that are recognized as being vital. Ecology, as the study of the interaction of the living, not only includes the treatment of land and soil, of nature in and around the city, but also everything related to it. This includes the logistics of transport and technical infrastructure, the sociological and urban consequences thereof, and the economic support of the necessary measures. This is such a complex task, in such tremendous dimensions and has such a huge impact on the quality of life of millions of people that there is no need for the spectacular innovation of clones with two heads and four arms. Optimization, to the greatest degree possible, is innovation. Contemporary housing and urban planning has by no means solved this problem, in fact, it is still far from doing so. Worse still, it is not even moving in this direction, but is rather harking back to the nineteenth century.

We are still creatures of nature—even in a mega-city. To exclude nature, to depersonalize social contacts, to offer no options for physical experience and play, inevitably leads to aggression, resignation, and meaningless consumption of what is easily and cheaply attainable.

Housing is essential, and if we see people at the center of our world, is the most vital component of urban planning and social and cultural policy. The demand to bring nature back into the city, to live in harmony with a sensitively developed form of nature in the city, is a far more realistic ideology than the urban romanticism that prevails in the intellectual bohemian world. These spheres are by no means mutually exclusive. In fact, only a compact and green city allows the possibility to create a living environment in which urbanity can develop. The phenomenon of "urbanity," like the concept of culture, can be seen in a far more differentiated and comprehensive way than is generally the case. This manifesto—not invented by me or any other architect, but rather by evolution—to realize, to complete, to improve, is the innovation that people are looking for in cities.

Notes

Harry Glück has written numerous essays on housing and the city during his professional career. Manuscripts have often been developed over the course of several years and are available in different versions. A 460-page collection of his writings was published posthumously in 2018: *Schriften zur Architektur für Menschen* (Writings on Architecture for People). The essay you read here has been shortened and illustrated by the editors of this book and essentially corresponds to the original manuscript. Beatrix Becker-Glück, copyright owner of the texts and Nikolaos Kombolis, Glück's long-time collaborator and co-author have read and authorized the version printed here.

1 The "savannah hypothesis" of anthropology is based on the assumption that human ancestors developed the ability to walk upright by shifting their habitat from the forest to the open steppe. Although this theory remains controversial today, studies continue to show that humans consistently find open, lushly structured landscapes with water to be beautiful.

2 The settler movement in Vienna after the First World War, with Garden City advocate Hans Kampffmeyer as its protagonist, was not a "romantic petty bourgeois idyll," but a grassroots, democratic, participatory, and green movement.

3 The Netherlands pioneered social housing construction in the interwar period. In Amsterdam, housing estates were built according to plans by Michel de Klerk from 1913 onwards; in Rotterdam, construction on the Justus van Effen Quarter in Spangen began in 1918, the Tusschendijken estate was built according to plans by architect Michiel Brinkman, and Jacobus Johannes P. Oud's Kiefhoek settlement was built between 1928 and 1930.

4 In "New Frankfurt," the urban planning program of the City of Frankfurt am Main under Mayor Ludwig Landmann and the city planning officer Ernst May, 12,000 new apartments were built between 1925 and 1930. The comprehensive New Frankfurt program set new standards in urban planning. In Berlin, Martin Wagner and Bruno Taut were the leading figures in social housing construction during the 1920s.

5 Le Corbusier did consider stepped terraced house after all: in 1933, in his project for the Durand estate in Algeria, see p. 68 f.

6 Translation by David Constantine, Bloodaxe Books, 1996.

The *Invention* of Stepped Terrace Housing

Gerhard Steixner, Maria Welzig

We are part of nature. Contact with nature is essential for our physical and mental health.[1] The experience of nature establishes a deeper understanding of life: change, growth, blossoming, developing, and passing away. Smells, sounds, the variety of colors and shapes, the humming of insects, the singing of birds, the wind in the leaves and grass, the taste of fruits. Nature activates all our senses.

Opportunities to move freely in a natural environment and discover oneself in the process have been radically reduced for children over the past decades. What does growing up without the possibility of these everyday experiences do with these developing beings?[2]

Another interpretation of urbanity

It is necessary to arrive at a new understanding of urbanity and to dissolve the alleged contradiction between city and nature: from a city of representation, hierarchy, military considerations, and traffic to an eco-solar city radically oriented towards those who use it.

This book brings back into view a prototype that was planned and realized in the 15 years around 1968 as a solution to the challenges of housing and urban development, namely the stepped terrace apartment building. The protagonists of this residential typology re-envisaged the city, offering an alternative to the car-centric, mono-functionally structured cities of the 1950s and 1960s. Stepped terrace housing fulfilled the desire of a large majority of the population for contact with nature, for a sufficiently sized outdoor space with privacy,

Harry Glück, Inzersdorfer Strasse residential complex, 1974, photo 2014

that can be planted, nurtured, and cared for. At the same time, these (large) compact structures offer the advantages of the city and a dense mix of housing and infrastructure. Stepped terrace housing replaces the principle of the facade with a categorical focus on the users. By individually appropriating and planting their terraces, the residents become co-designers of the city.

Balconies, on the other hand, do not usually offer protection from view or privacy. They are regarded as formal elements of the facade and often cannot be altered to suit one's own needs, and in some cases even growing plants on them is prohibited.[3]

The densely overgrown stepped terrace housing estates of the time we are looking at here herald a paradigm shift in the scale of aesthetic urban perception. The terrace vegetation, a vertical green space, merges almost seamlessly into the spacious communal green spaces. By separating traffic, public and semi-public spaces can be kept car-free. The stepped terrace structures also provide a new interpretation of urbanity in terms of privacy and community. Space for communication and community, for movement, for social and urban life are all part of the stepped terrace living concept. The terraced structures planned during the era are mostly conceived as hybrids: housing, urban infrastructure, and (stationary) traffic.

Stepped terrace housing as an *invention* in the early twentieth century

Around 1900 and then especially in the 1920s, answers were systematically sought for the first time to the question of mass housing as a central challenge for society. New urban typologies were developed, new construction methods were made usable for housing, "air, light, sun" were seen as basic needs to which everyone is entitled.

The public sector and politics became actors and the social, urban planning, and architectural programs could thus be implemented on a larger scale for the first time in the 1920s. In Rotterdam and Amsterdam, in Vienna, Berlin, and Frankfurt, true alternatives to previous housing and urban development practices emerged on a larger and, in Vienna on a very large, scale during the 1920s. This included apartment buildings with courtyards and housing estates with generous green spaces instead of the highly densified perimeter block pattern. Apartments were tailored to the needs of the residents, and facilities for community, education, and personal hygiene were integrated. The prerequisites for this were the corresponding fiscal, legal, and land policy reforms that made subsidized housing possible in the first place.

One can say the invention of stepped terrace housing also took place during this time and in this context. Apart from the mythical Hanging Gardens of Babylon, this type of terrace is without precedent in the European architectural tradition. The impulses that led to its

Henri Sauvage

Metropolis project, 1928

Social housing with swimming pool, Paris, Rue des Amiraux, 1916–1927, cross-section and overview, photo 2016

development in the twentieth century did not come purely from the discipline, as is so often the case with significant developments in architecture. In this instance, the medical and health sector provided the impetus. Air and sun were needed to cure the widespread disease of tuberculosis. The physician David Sarason therefore proposed the terracing of sanatorium buildings in the early twentieth century, calling in a next step for the application of knowledge on healing tuberculosis in housing and urban planning.[4]

The pioneer in the development of the stepped terrace typology for residential construction based on medical knowledge is undoubtedly the architect Henri Sauvage.[5] Together with Frantz Jourdain and others, he founded the Society for Hygienic and Affordable Housing (*Société anonyme de logements hygiéniques à bon marché*) in 1903.

During several years of study and practical experience in worker housing, Sauvage developed stepped terrace housing as a solution to the pressing problem, aiming to build healthier cities by bringing more light and air into the apartments and streets, providing residents with their own private garden, increasing green in the city, and providing communal facilities and infrastructure. Sauvage designed entire blocks of houses and streets with stepped terrace worker housing.

Sauvage was able to build terraces for the first time in the Rue Vavin apartment building (1909–1912). The client for the experiment was the Society for Stepped Terrace Housing (*Société anonyme des maisons à gradins*), founded shortly before by himself and others. Even in this early example, an essential element of the 1960s and

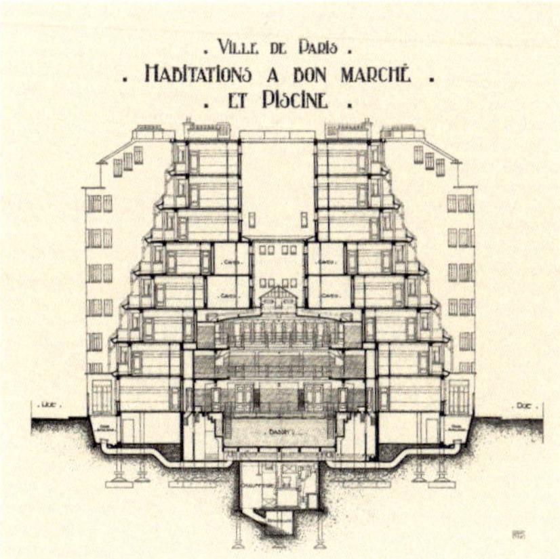

1970s facilities was in place, namely the planter, used with the dual purpose of preventing looking down at the terraces below.

Sauvage and his business partner Charles Sarazin were so certain that the stepped terrace principle was the future of urban architecture that they patented it in 1912.[6] Sauvage and Sarazin built the first subsidized stepped terrace apartment complex between 1916 and 1927 as part of the City of Paris housing program (*Habitations à Bon Marché*), The 7-story, 78-apartment complex is constructed in reinforced concrete and fits into an existing block development on the Rue des Amiraux. It is terraced on three sides and each apartment has a terrace. The "belly" of the building, its interior, is used for social spaces and facilities. Sauvage had originally planned a cinema, but the City of Paris wanted an institution in place to help improve the poor health situation. And so the complex was designed with a swimming pool, still in operation today and now open to the general public. The windowless interior, problematic from a traditional point of view, was seen as an opportunity to integrate additional uses.[7]

Important impulses towards harmonizing density and quality of living (light, air, sun, and garden) also came from Le Corbusier, who, incidentally, wanted to solely claim the pioneering achievement of using reinforced concrete assemblies in housing construction at the founding congress of CIAM in La Sarraz in 1928, rather than Sauvage.[8] Le Corbusier developed the method of stacked single-family houses from 1922 onwards with his Immeubles Villas (see p. 39). In 1933, he tested the principle on a large scale in the Durand Apartments for

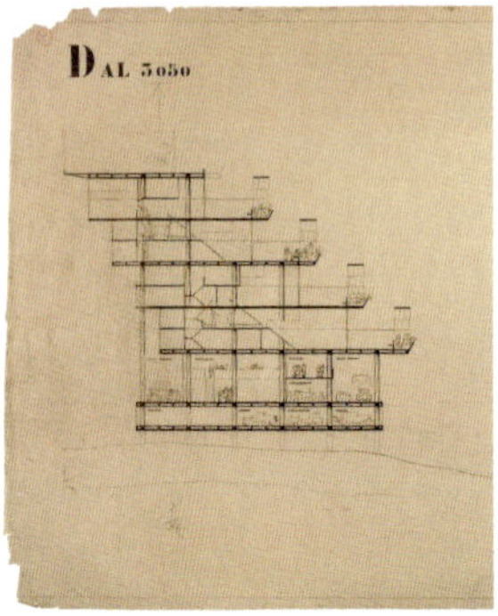

Oued Ouchaia in Algeria. The project has rows of 300 apartments each, stepping back to create generous terraces on the longitudinal sides and correspondingly overhanging on the other side, where the access cores and balcony walkways are also located. Each block contains communal service facilities and all four are situated in a landscaped park with sports facilities, walking paths, and swimming pools that merge into the hilly terrain. Vehicular traffic is at ground floor level and pedestrian traffic is at first floor level.[9] With the Durand project, Le Corbusier designed the classic principle of a linear building stepped back with terraces along one long side, a profile that can be continued virtually endlessly.

Adolf Loos—possibly inspired by Sauvage's buildings and stepped terrace concepts for subsidized housing during his numerous stays in Paris after 1918[10]—became intensively occupied with stepped terrace structures in 1923. Three of these were characteristically planned for France: the most fully developed was the Grand Hotel Babylon for Nice in 1923, in which the interior is used as an impressive hall naturally lit from above. He also designed a sports hotel for Paris, and a house with a stepped structure in the affluent "20 Villas for the Cote d'Azur" sector.[11]

Loos likewise saw the stepped terrace model as a possible solution for dense social housing. In 1923, he proposed stepped terrace buildings for two locations in Vienna, at Inzersdorfer Strasse and Winarskyhof, both projects developed for the Vienna Association for Settlement and Allotment Gardening. Unlike Sauvage, however, Loos's

Le Corbusier, Durand stepped terrace housing, Algeria, 1933, cross-section and sketch

Adolf Loos, project for the Grand Hotel Babylon, Nice, 1923, overview and cross-section

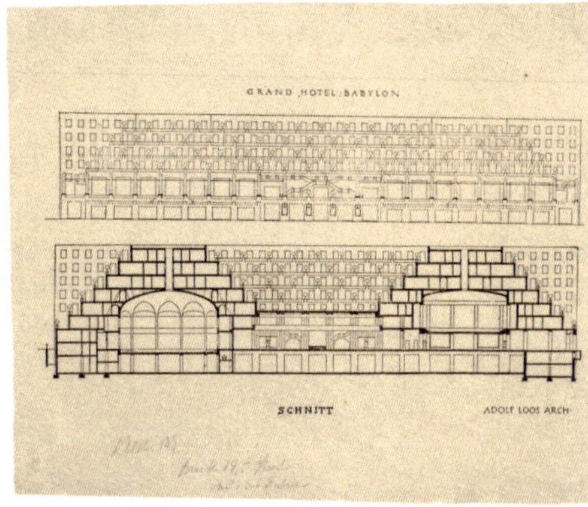

terraces are not private open spaces, but instead form "elevated streets"—actually access balconies to the apartments that are intended for shared use. However, Loos was met with skepticism from the city for this new type of planning. In the same context as Loos, Oskar Strnad and Peter Behrens also planned a stepped terrace apartment complex at Inzersdorfer Strasse for the Vienna Association for Settlement and Allotment Gardening in 1923 (part of a proposal for a master architectural plan for Vienna).

The revolutionary housing programs of Red Vienna and New Frankfurt came to an end in the early 1930s. Not least because key protagonists were Jewish and were deported or murdered.[12]

Stepped terrace structures as a housing and urban development approach in the 1960s

As if in the wake of a major traffic jam, new social approaches developed over the course of the 1960s. Fair distribution was a political stipulation: Everyone should have a share of the prosperity. Until the mid-1970s, the rising productivity curve followed parallel to the wage curve. The simultaneous technological developments made anything seem possible.

Resistance to car-centric urban development geared to the interests of the construction industry, the economy, and technology has been active in Europe since the 1950s, although criticism did not primarily come from architectural and urban planning circles.

Since the 1930s, the US historian, sociologist, and philosopher Lewis Mumford had been criticizing technocratic urban development that ignored human beings and human nature,[13] pleading for urban and architectural development in harmony with the conditions of the human body in the sense of "organic humanism." The sensational photograph of the Earth rising across the lunar horizon, taken from the Apollo 8 spacecraft in 1968, became an image of the epoch. Suddenly the beauty and vulnerability of the blue planet and the interconnectedness of its inhabitants was made visible.

In 1965, the psychoanalyst Alexander Mitscherlich published the book *Die Unwirtlichkeit unserer Städte* (The Inhospitality of Our Cities), influential in the German-speaking world, writing: "One crams the employee behind uniform glass facades and then into the uniform monotony of apartment blocks. One has created a state of affairs that makes any planning for democratic freedom illusory." Mitscherlich thus criticized both capitalist and socialist construction practices. He pleaded for citizen participation. Mitscherlich was appointed special advisor for the planning of the Olympic Village in Munich in 1968.

In the 1960s, architects and urban planners developed densified stepped terrace structures throughout the industrialized world. These structures, which were designed a great deal yet realized in small numbers during those years, made use of industrial construction methods and were generally planned as large structures in order to conserve land resources. However, at the same time, they developed as a reaction to purely technocratic urban development, a departure

“Earthrise,” taken from the Apollo 8 spacecraft on 24 December 1968

from the mainstream of car-centric cities, and as an alternative to mono-functional urban expansion. The planned stepped terrace structures were based on the idea of separating traffic levels and mixing uses—as long as these do not interfere with each other. The result was traffic-free shared (green) spaces.

The ecological concerns of the era played an important role in the development of stepped terrace concepts. Our current environmental situation was forecast with clarity 50 years ago.[14] The emerging housing concepts were also founded in the increased opening of architecture to other disciplines, such as behavioral research, sociology, environmental research, traffic engineering, demography, and others. Above all, the idea of participation began to enter the debate. With their private terraces and gardens, the complexes provide space for the individual needs and the nature of humans.

Ideas for new, democratic ways of creating housing and urban development for the masses circulated in the 1960s not only as theoretical constructs within a circle of experts. They influenced the building policies of nations and cities. However, no clear attributions to specific political parties can be made. In France, the Gaullist state under Georges Pompidou realized social architectural concepts just as innovative as those in communist-led cities. In Austria, the Christian Democrat government initiated the *Wohnen Morgen* (Living Tomorrow) series and the Social Democratic leadership of the City of Vienna came closer than ever before to fulfilling the demand for “luxury for all” in subsidized housing with an entire series of stepped

Georges Candilis with Shadrach Woods and ATBAT-Afrique, residential complex in Casablanca, Morocco, 1954

Kenzo Tange, Tokyo Bay Project, 1960

Paul Rudolph, superstructure project for the Lower Manhattan Expressway, New York, 1967–1970

terrace apartment buildings. In Italy, the Christian Democratic government implemented the largest social housing plan in the country's history. Socialist Yugoslavia experimented on a large scale with highly diverse housing typologies and neighborhood concepts. Creating housing for the masses requires the will and commitment of public authorities. Stepped terrace housing is an indicator of political will: "The greatest possible happiness for the greatest possible number."[15]

As in socio-political and philosophical matters, France was also a trendsetter for architecture and urban development in the 1960s. A line can be drawn from Sauvage and Le Corbusier to Georges Candilis and Jean Balladur. The Marxist architect and urban planner Georges Candilis had been associated with Le Corbusier since the fourth CIAM Congress in Athens in 1933. From 1945 into the 1950s, he was one of his main collaborators and responsible for the realization of the Unité d'Habitation in Marseilles (1947–1952). From 1951 to 1952, Candilis and Shadrach Woods planned housing estates in Casablanca for the French civil engineering firm ATBAT Afrique, attempting to adapt modernist architecture to the climatic and cultural conditions there. Taking up on local tradition, they stacked courtyard houses to form a *Cité Verticale*, or vertical city, an adaptation and development of Le Corbusier's Immeubles Villas.

Also influenced by these experiences in North Africa—where the struggle against French colonial rule was taking place at the same time—Candilis and others founded Team X at the 10th CIAM Congress in 1953. They were in opposition to the universalist dogmas of

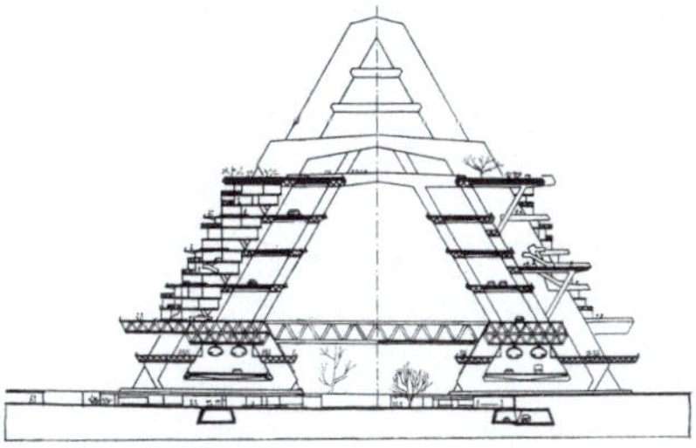

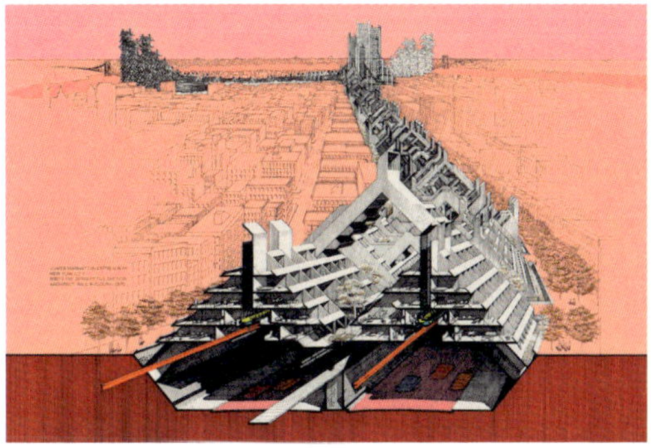

CIAM and particularly against the dogma of separating functions in urban planning. However, Candilis also continued to be a bridge to Le Corbusier.

In France, in partnership with Shadrach Woods and Alexis Josic, Candilis built tens of thousands of subsidized housing units, entire districts based on social mixing, radical equality for all, and having a multitude of functions within walking distance of the city center.

Candilis was probably the most influential protagonist in urban planning and housing for the masses after the Second World War.[16] He was also an architect in France's state planning enterprise for the coastal region of Languedoc-Roussilion. Instead of the highly economized sprawl of hotels, as on the coasts of Spain, a holistic and social approach to the new phenomenon of (travel) holidays for the masses was sought. Five new (holiday) cities with harbors and traffic infrastructure emerged out of nowhere.[17] The most remarkable achievement of this massive project is undoubtedly the town of La Grande Motte, built starting in 1963 as an entirely stepped terrace town.

In Japan, impacted by the complete annihilation of the atomic bomb, new concepts of architecture and the city emerged from the rubble: growing, large stepped terrace structures with individual modules that could be inserted and removed (plug-ins), bionics—the transfer of phenomena from nature to technology and architecture, the connection between humans and nature. With these ideas, with their projects and manifestos, the Metabolist group of Kenzo Tange,

Moshe Safdie, Habitat 67 at the Montreal World's Fair, under construction in 1966

DP Architects for the Singapore City Council, Golden Mile Complex, Singapore, 1967–1973, circulation, photo 2017

Noboin Kawazoe, Kisho Kurokawa, and Kyonori Kikutake began to inspire architects in Europe and the USA in the late 1950s.

In the USA, projects for superstructures on transport axes and master plans on previously unimaginable scales were created. Kenzo Tange's urban expansion on Tokyo Bay and Paul Rudolph's superstructure project over the planned Lower Manhattan Expressway in New York (which would have, in line with a car-centric city, cut a path through Manhattan) were both designed as stepped terrace structures. A 1962 project for San Francisco shows parabolic stepped terrace towers 60 stories high with a thousand apartments in each one. The usual hierarchy of high-rise residential buildings is compensated for: The apartments on the lower floors don't have views, but do have large terraces. Alt-Erlaa, Graz-St. Peter, and Schlangenbader Strasse are all based on a comparable concept.

Habitat 67 at the 1967 World Expo in Montreal was the first realization of a stepped terrace apartment complex on a very large scale. The Israeli-American architect Moshe Safdie combined single-family homes with gardens horizontally and vertically to form a representative urban structure. Each of the generously sized apartments had at least one terrace ranging from 20 to 90 square meters in size. Pedestrian, cycling, and automobile traffic levels were separated. However, consisting of individual prefabricated housing modules, Habitat 67 is not a prototype for low-cost housing, as it lacks the necessary compactness. The focus was on the sculptural effect and on creating an image at the world exhibition. Subsequently, however,

stepped terrace housing was hardly realized in North America and Japan, but was instead built predominantly in Europe and Israel.

As in France, the three decades after the end of the Second World War were a time of investment in social and cultural emancipation. Social goals were the driving force of politics and municipal administrations. In the 1960s, the London City Council built two stepped terrace housing estates that reinterpreted the relationship between city, street, and home, namely the Brunswick Centre and the Alexandra Road Estate, both built by the progressive Building Department of the London Borough of Camden. A sector of the huge Thamesmead urban development area in Greater London was also built up with four to five-story stepped terrace complexes, with the building style drawing international attention to the project.

The Golden Mile Complex (1967–1973) at the center of the former British colony of Singapore is, like the Brunswick Center, a hybrid experiment. Initiated and carried out by the state as an urban revitalization project, it primarily houses shops and offices, as well as apartments on the floors with terraces. As in the Brunswick Centre, circulation is given high design significance, filling the belly of the terraced structure across several stories. The Golden Mile Complex is a "collective form."[18]

In Italy, the biggest campaign to improve housing for workers in the late 1940s was initiated by the Christian Democratic government. The driving figure was Amintore Fanfani (1908–1999), Minister of Labor and Social Affairs among other positions, and advocate of state

Cesare Blasi, Gabriella Padovano stepped terrace housing complex Via Airolo, Milan, 1966–1971, part of the INA-Casa program of the Italian government, photo 2010

housing construction. His many years of involvement with the housing conditions of workers was rooted in the principle of Christian charity. The so-called Fanfani Law made the INA-Casa housing plan possible, which built 355,000 apartments in Italy between 1949 and 1963 following a principle of individual neighborhood establishment. The industrialist Adriano Olivetti was an important advisor in the implementation of INA-Casa and probably the most important private client of social architecture in Italy in the 1950s, a pioneer in urban and regional planning,[19] embodying the model of "democratic or participatory paternalism."[20] As an advisor to INA-Casa and as president of the *Istituto nazionale di urbanistica*, or National Institute of Urbanism, he played an essential role in public building. Within the framework of Olivetti's architectural initiatives around his company headquarters in Ivrea, the experimental intervention of the superhybrid *Centro di Servizi Sociali e Residenziali* (Social and Residential Services Center) in Ivrea was created.[21] The stepped terrace complex in Via Airolo in Milan, built in the second phase of INA-Casa (1966–1972), was designed as an urban renewal project consisting of rows and infill structures inserted into the perimeter edge of the block, with a commercial area on the ground floor.

In 1965, the book *Neue urbane Wohnformen* (New Urban Dwelling) by architects Ot Hoffmann and Christoph Repenthin gave an impulse to the German-speaking world for a new interpretation of urban planning schemes using buildings with garden courtyards, carpet settlements, and stepped terrace buildings. The idea behind the

Ot Hoffmann tree house,
Darmstadt 1968-1972, photo 2011

stepped terraces is derived genealogically from the densification of carpet settlements: "With further densification, the dwelling levels begin to slide over each other and we can then speak of a stepped terrace building."[22] Ecological aspects already played an important role in the book. Ot Hoffmann's own terraced tree house in Darmstadt (1968–1970) can be understood as a green statement in this regard.

The hill housing concepts, which emerged from the late 1950s as a special type of stepped terrace housing,[23] were in response to the massive urban sprawl and destruction of the countryside by single-family detached homes. Starting in 1965, four residential "hills" were built in Marl, Germany. Cars are routed into underground garages, thereby creating open, car-free communal spaces. Each apartment has a terrace or a garden. Hermann Schröder, one of the architects of the Marl apartment buildings, built an early stepped terrace building in Germany together with Peter Faller, namely in Tapachstrasse near Stuttgart from 1965 to 1973. It followed along the lines of the model developed by Le Corbusier in his Durand project, namely a row of buildings with terraces along one long side and cantilevers protruding on the opposite side, where the vertical accesses and balcony access corridors are located.

The City of Munich took the risk of planning the prestigious project of the Olympic Village for the 1972 Olympic Games as a green stepped terrace city—a remarkable social and architectural act. Today, the self-sufficient district is one of the city's most popular residential areas. Its planning and realization within an extremely short period

of time between 1968 and 1972 has influenced other large-scale stepped terrace projects in central Europe.

The earliest built stepped terrace housing estates in Austria, and one of the earliest in Europe, is Hans Puchhammer and Gunther Wawrik's Goldtruhe settlement in Lower Austria (1966–1969). In 1969, a research project by Puchhammer and Wawrik looked at the possibilities for constructing stepped terrace housing within the framework of Vienna's building regulations.[24]

An important initiative for Austria was the "*Neue städtische Wohnformen*" exhibition, or "New Urban Housing," in 1966–1967, organized by the Austrian Society for Architecture, which had been founded the previous year. The title is probably a reference to Hoffmann and Repenthin's book *Neue urbane Wohnformen*. The projects shown in the exhibition were almost exclusively stepped terrace structures. A manifesto-like catalog of demands for residential construction was published in conjunction with the exhibition.[25] How much was truly possible in the period around 1968 is shown by the consequences of the exhibition: the City of Vienna commissioned the exhibition organizers to design a housing complex, the Schöpfwerk, with over 2,100 apartments. Furthermore, in 1968, a municipal housing cooperative commissioned one of the largest experiments in Viennese housing construction for the same urban expansion: the Alt-Erlaa residential park. Planning for Alt-Erlaa as stepped terrace high-rises began in 1970, with the number of apartments roughly equivalent to the number of stepped terrace dwellings in the Olympic Village in Munich.

ANPAR
Michel Andrault, Pierre Parat

Pyramid-shaped apartments, Créteil, 1979
Les Pyramides Evry, 1973–1980, photo 2014

Jean Renaudie, Renée Gailhoustet
Jeanne Hachette Center Ivry-sur-Seine, 1969–1975, photo 2014

Vienna is the only city in the world that was able to establish stepped terrace housing by building a great number of projects, with Red Vienna's housing program of the 1920s creating the foundation upon which the Viennese stepped terrace housing phenomenon could be built.[26]

The French firm ANPAR (Michel Andrault and Pierre Parat) worked on the stepped terrace typology for decades. Following in the footsteps of their compatriots Sauvage and Balladur, ANPAR continued to develop pyramid-shaped stepped terrace buildings, taking it all the way to pyramidal forms stepped on all sides, called a *Hügelhaus* in German, or "hill house". These buildings had, in addition to the interior circulation, exterior paths that also led to the apartments, and were either stand-alone or joined together to form a network, as in the 2,000 apartments of the Pyramids of Evry, a new town in the belt around Paris.

Ivry-sur-Seine is one of the communist-governed towns in the Paris region which, from the 1950s onwards, pushed for the construction of new housing estates, often based on the Soviet model of multi-story prefabricated concrete slab buildings. As part of this housing offensive, but as an alternative to the slab buildings, from 1970 onwards Jean Renaudie and Renée Gailhoustet built star-shaped stepped terrace "hills" in the midst of the historic city center and 1960s high-rises. Their approach was a dense mixture of apartments, offices, shops, and a cinema, linked by a winding network of pedestrian paths and (semi-) public squares. No two apartments were alike and each had a private terrace garden. While the most prominent

Stepped terrace development in Novi Beograd, 1970s, photo 2011

example of Soviet-style concrete slab buildings in the *banlieus rouges*, the Yuri Gagarin Estate in Ivry-sur-Seine completed in 1963, was demolished in 2019, the stepped terrace buildings of Gailhoustet and Renaudie are now completely overgrown with greenery and remain sought-after places to live.

Formerly socialist Yugoslavia emphasized its special position as a non-aligned state through distinctive and independent modernity in architectural and urban planning. The district of Novi Beograd, started in 1948, was a veritable urban planning laboratory in the 1960s and 1970s. Highly diverse residential and other typologies and community models were tested here. The stepped terrace typology was implemented in a prime location on the banks of the Sava River, in a cluster of four to five-story stepped terrace blocks, each arranged in an open U-form.

Features of stepped terrace housing

The construction method of the stepped terrace scheme is cross wall construction. The loads are transferred by slabs positioned at a distance of around five to six meters. There are no load-bearing outer walls. This makes room-high and room-wide wall openings possible. Industrialized production, repetitive construction, and the sequencing of similar modules are all means of building economically. Circulation options are manifold: balcony access corridors, cluster access, central corridors in various combinations, and direct access via external staircases. Maisonette and split-level apartments are frequently used as an alternative to single-level apartments. On the one hand, this saves on construction costs by reducing overall access areas, and on the other, it provides a living experience more similar to that of a single-family home.

The material is concrete, often exposed. For a number of buildings, however, architects and developers have chosen a white painted finish and, if necessary, insulated industrial panels made of sheet metal or fiber-cement panels.[27] The main characteristic of the complexes is of course the terraces: an outdoor space usually the size of a room. "The balcony or loggia as demanded by past ways of life no longer meet our living requirements," wrote Viktor Hufnagl in 1968, co-initiator of the "*Neue urbane Wohnformen*" (New Urban Dwelling) exhibition and architect of the Schöpfwerk in Vienna.[28] Terraces, on the other hand, provide both privacy and contact with nature.

The use of simple planters is extremely effective. When a planter is made available, the probability of planting by residents increases. Such large trough-like planters also make it possible for deep-rooted shrubs and trees to flourish. Hanging gardens can be cultivated, creating visual protection. Through a personal terrace, people have the opportunity to reveal their individuality visibly to the outside.

An important feature of the stepped terrace structure is its mixed use, the idea of combining dwelling with additional urban and social functions. The facilities have rooms for communication and community: youth clubs, hobby rooms, swimming pools, saunas, community centers, schools, etc. They expand the residential function, for example, by adding guest apartments and workrooms. A wide range of spatial possibilities is used for this purpose, transforming above all the "belly" of a stepped terrace building from a problem zone into an opportunity to provide shared spaces. Another possibility is an entire community floor, as in Graz-St. Peter, or a continuous walk-through meeting zone with communication areas and hobby rooms, as in the Schlangenbader Strasse, which also has community terraces. The ground floor zone is used for business premises, and large facilities often have their own shopping centers.

Cars are routed into garages below the apartment blocks. This allows for extensive greenspaces and semi-public spaces within walking distance. These greenspaces are not schematic, low-maintenance greenery, but landscaped terrain with hills and hollows and a variety of trees and shrubs. Here, landscaping is designed to create intimate and protected areas. The terracing of the buildings and the openness to the urban space prevent the cramped kind of situation that can occur with courtyards that are enclosed on all sides. The park-like terrain of larger facilities also provides space to move around—even to toboggan in the winter. Movement and physical exercise are likewise made possible by the swimming pools, an important part of Harry Glück's residential buildings. The swimming pool is also a place where social contact can easily be made. Even the first social stepped terrace housing in the history of the typology, built in the 1920s, is equipped with an indoor pool.

Selection of examples

The selected examples are all experimental stepped terrace housing projects built in Europe around 1968. The selection illustrates how such structures can be implemented in a variety of urban conditions and different typological variants. The examples cover the field of urban planning to a great degree and are fundamentally prototypical for housing and urban development. Further selection criteria were building site size, urban location, positioning along traffic arteries, and clustering of various urban functions.

Five urban development categories can be identified: autonomous districts, along the edge, shaped by traffic, density in block grids, and inner-city hybrids.[29] The examples for each category also show different interpretations of the topic.

Autonomous districts The Olympic Village in Munich and Alt-Erlaa residential park in Vienna are, with over 3,000 terraced apartments each and corresponding infrastructure, facilities that can be defined as self-sufficient urban districts. Alt-Erlaa follows a strictly modular concept with a consistent east-west orientation of the apartments and central corridor access throughout. A superstructure, Alt-Erlaa defies conventional European urban concepts. In contrast, the Olympic Village has approximately the same number of apartments, but is based on an organic urban idea. Staggered buildings unfold in a wing-like arrangement. The terraces are primarily south-facing and the apartments are interspersed and accessed via circulation cores and balcony access corridors. The density is far lower than in Alt-Erlaa. Both share the achievement of making a "small town" completely accessible by foot. In Munich, this is done starting with the second upper floor.

Along the edge The Koseze stepped terrace housing estate near Ljubljana, the Nittel-Hof in Vienna, and the St. Peter estate in Graz are all prototypes for dense neighborhoods on the outskirts of the city, ranging in size from 500 to 1,500 apartments. Koseze and the Nittel-Hof both have around 1,500 apartments and, like Alt-Erlaa, both demonstrate an emphatically rational, unsentimental, and urban approach. In Koseze, each module is an autonomous building, with 34 identical modules arranged in 10 parallel rows. Each row has its own underground car park; cars drive down into the garage at the front end of each row. The rows are arranged in a strict north-south direction, making maximum use of the irregular building plot.

With 530 apartments distributed across four blocks, the St. Peter stepped terrace estate in Graz is likewise modular in design. However, the architects of St. Peter were keen to create a certain design excitement between the buildings by breaking them down into smaller parts. The individual blocks were designed with special front buildings. The modules were staggered in height, allowing for far-reaching views for the apartments in the rows vis-à-vis.

With its characteristic structure and size, the Nittel-Hof can even be recognized from an airplane. Its meandering ribbon-like structure defies all contextual demands.

Shaped by traffic One of the major issues of twentieth-century urban development is the question of how to deal with express traffic and the emissions it produces. The Alexandra Road Estate in London (522 apartments) deals with its location directly on the railway by turning away from it. Its rear façade follows the line of the tracks and is virtually hermetically sealed, looking somewhat like the outside of a stadium. In contrast, the Viennese complex on Hadikgasse (210 apartments), an arterial road, faces the street to the south. The design reacts to the context by shifting back and staggering the buildings, with structural soundproofing that also acts as an architectural element, and with a dense filter of greenery. The Schlangenbader Strasse complex in Berlin goes a step further: the motorway disappears into the belly of the 600-meter-long stepped terrace strip (1,064 apartments). So far, it is the only superstructure above a motorway worldwide.

Density in block grids The Inzersdorfer Strasse and Wohnen Morgen residential complexes in Vienna, with 200 to 300 apartments, illustrate how stepped terrace housing with greenspace can function within a block grid. One of the complexes reinterprets a courtyard (open to the south), the other the pattern of greenspace—street—greenspace. The greenspaces of both designs open towards the urban space, thus extending it and vice versa.

Inner-city hybrids The *Centro di Servizi Sociali e Residenziali*, or Social and Residential Services Center (later the Unità Residenziale Est, then Hotel La Serra) in Ivrea (55 temporary apartments) and the Brunswick Centre in London (560 apartments) both have a dense mix of uses that emanates even beyond the district. The Brunswick Centre combines apartments with a pedestrian zone, shops, offices, and a cinema. The Olivetti Social and Residential Services Center is a hybrid with a swimming pool, cinema, restaurant, auditorium, shops, offices, and plug-in capsules for short-term living. The complex creates a bridge between the historic city, Olivetti's modern company premises, and a park. Part of Adriano Olivetti's architectural offensive, its spaceship-like forms have a more advanced architectural language than the public buildings. Super-hybrids are rare.

At the same time, similarities across categories can also be found. Alt-Erlaa and Schlangenbader Strasse are based on a similar concept: a linear structure with terraces on the lower floors, above which is a high-rise with loggias, central corridor access, and an access tower every sixty meters. The street or square as a space for meeting is the theme of Alexandra Road Estate, the Brunswick Centre, Wohnen Morgen in Vienna, and the Social and Residential Services Center in La Serra. In both Wohnen Morgen and Alexandra Road Estate, a number of apartments are accessed via external staircases directly from the street. Some of the schemes are experimental building projects accompanied by research projects.

In almost all examples, the client is the public sector. Only the Social and Residential Services Center is privately owned by the Olivetti company.

Not all schemes consist of rental apartments. The stepped terrace complexes in Graz and the Olympic Village both have owner-occupied apartments, but are in the lower, i.e. subsidized, price

Neave Brown
Alexandra Road Estate London,
rear, photo 2013

range. Vienna occupies a special position when it comes to subsidized stepped terrace housing: In no other city have so many facilities been built with such high-quality infrastructure. For this reason, the selection here includes five examples from Vienna.

The reaction: the media, critics, and residents

Most of the schemes were condemned by the media and professional critics after completion, which roughly coincided with the advent of postmodernism. The large structures disrupted the conventional idea of the city and abandoned the familiarity of facade and street. However, by the twenty-first century at the latest, this assessment had been reversed, with structures receiving late recognition by experts and now largely protected as historic monuments.[30]

The residents, on the other hand, reacted positively to the complexes from the very beginning. Various studies confirm a high level of approval. Identification with the residential complex is also reflected in community activities and residents' initiatives. For example, applications for the preservation of Alexandra Road and Schlangenbader Strasse both came from the residents themselves. Today, the complexes have a kind of cult status, with a remarkable number of artistic projects and film documentaries about the complexes.

With this Europe-wide synopsis of stepped terrace housing, an idea for better living, this book aims to raise awareness of what is possible and provide insight as a basis for future action.

Notes

1 This was the latest finding of an interdisciplinary study at the Central Institute for Mental Health in Mannheim in 2019. See https://doi.org/10.1038/s41593-019-0451-y (9 September 2019).

2 A 2019 study from Uppsala University shows that the presence of green spaces in residential areas during childhood is associated with a lower risk of mental disorders from puberty to adulthood, see: https://www.pnas.org/content/116/11/5188 (17 September 2019).

3 https://www.derstandard.at/story/2000108308651/wenn-die-schilfmatte-am-balkon-verboten-ist (8 September 2019).

4 Sarason, David. "The open-air house, a new construction system for hospitals and residential buildings." Awarded the Golden Medal of the International Tuberculosis Congress in Washington 1908, Lehmann 1913. For more on the development of stepped terrace housing in the context of health see also Pierre-Louis Laget, *L'invention du système des immeubles à gradins. Sa genèse à visée sanitaire avant sa diffusion mondiale dans la villégiature de montagne et de bord de mer,* put online 18 July 2014, http://journals.openedition.org/insitu/11102 ; DOI : 10.4000/insitu.11102 (28 September 2019). A series of stepped terrace hospitals were built in France and Switzerland in the 1930s. In Germany, the architect Richard Döcker worked on the stepped terrace concept for hospitals in the 1920s and 1930s.

5 Cf. especially Loyer, Francois, Hélène Guéné, and Henri Sauvage. *Les Immeubles a Gradins*. Set Back Buildings, Brussels: Institut Francais d'Architecture, 1987. David Sarason gave a lecture in Paris in 1902, which Sauvage also attended.

6 "Système de construction de MM. Henri Sauvage et Charles Sarazin demandé le 23 janvier 1912, délivré le 3 avril 1912, publié le10 juin 1912, N°439.292 (procédé de construction à gradins)," see https://archiwebture.citedelarchitecture.fr/pdf/asso/FRAPN02_SAUHE_BIO.pdf, 10 (10 September 2019). See also: F. Loyer, H. Guéné. Henri Sauvage: les immeubles à gradins, Paris/Liège, IFA/Mardaga, 1987. In the 1920s, Sauvage applied for further patents for reinforced concrete structures and modular construction methods in residential buildings. Minnaert, Jean-Baptiste, and Henri Sauvage. "Les brevets et la construction rapide." In *Revue de l'Art,* 1997, 118, 41–55; doi: https://doi.org/10.3406/rvart.1997.348359 (10 September 2019).

7 Sauvage set up his own studio in the "belly" of the Rue Vavin building.

8 Minnaert, Jean-Baptiste, and Henri Sauvage. "Les brevets et la construction rapide." In *Revue de l'Art,* 1997, 118, 41–55; doi: https://doi.org/10.3406/rvart.1997.348359 (09 August 2019).

9 In clear emulation of Le Corbusier's stepped terrace housing project for Algeria, his former employee, Antonio Bonet, realized a stepped terrace project in Mar del Plata in Argentina in 1957–1958—one of the first and rare stepped terrace buildings in South America.

10 The spectacular stepped terrace building on Rue Vavin had been there since 1912, and the subsidized stepped terrace housing on Rue des Amiraux was under construction and had already been published in 1922 and 1923—among others in the well-known magazines *L'Architecture* and *L'Architecture Vivante*.

11 Adolf Loos's essay on the subject, "Eine neue Hausform. Terrassenhaus." In *Die Neue Wirtschaft. Wiener Organ für Finanzpolitik und Volkswirtschaft*, 1st ed., Vienna, 20 December 1923. On the development of stepped terrace housing in Vienna see De Chiffre, Lorenzo. *Das Wiener Terrassenhaus. Entwicklungsphasen und Aktualität eines historischen Wohntypus mit Fokus auf den lokalspezifischen architektonischen Diskurs*, dissertation at the TU Wien, Faculty of Architecture and Spatial Planning, Vienna, 2016.

12 The revolutionary Vienna City Councilor of Finance Hugo Breitner and City Councilor Robert Danneberg, responsible for the housing program of Red Vienna, and City Councilor for Welfare and Health Care Julius Tandler were all of Jewish descent, as was Ludwig Landmann, who as Lord Mayor was responsible for "New Frankfurt" between 1924 and 1933. Not to speak of all the planning architects.

13 Lewis Mumford published *Technics and Civilization* in 1934 and *The Condition of Man* in 1944. *The City in History* was published in 1961.

14 Cf. Robert Jung and Werner Filmer, *Terrassenturm und Sonnenhügel. Internationale Experimente für die Stadt 2000*. Düsseldorf: Schwann Verlag, 1970, 8 and 82–136. 1972 saw the publication of a study on the future of the world economy commissioned by the Club of Rome and carried out by the Massachusetts Institute of Technology titled "The Limits to Growth."

15 Jeremy Bentham and Stuart Mill developed the utilitarian idea of a welfare state in the course of the Enlightenment, whose laws were supposed to guarantee "the greatest possible happiness for the greatest possible number."

16 Viktor Pust, the architect of the stepped terrace complex in Koseze near Ljubljana, had worked for Candilis Josic-Woods.

17 The megaproject was able to function due to the establishment of an inter-ministerial commission, spanning five ministries, which lasted for twenty years.

18 A term coined by Japanese Pritzker Prize winner Fumihiko Maki.

19 In cooperation with INA-Casa, Olivetti also acted as a builder of social housing.

20 As defined by sociologist Franco Ferrarotti.

21 Created after Adriano Olivetti's sudden and early death in 1960.

22 Hoffmann, Ot, and Christoph Repenthin. *Neue urbane Wohnformen. Gartenhofhäuser, Teppichsiedlungen, Terrassenhäuser*. Berlin: Bertelsmann, Gütersloh, 19693 (1st edition 1965), 101. "From terraced garden courtyard to stepped terrace housing. Student apartments in New Haven, USA, Paul Rudolph, New Haven."

23 In 1959, Ot Hoffmann planned one such "hill" as a carpet settlement (Wiesbaden). Roland Frey and Hermann Schröder developed hill housing concepts in 1959.

24 Puchhammer, Hans, and Gunther Wawrik. *Terrassenhausbauten, Studie zum Terrassenhaus im Rahmen der Wiener Bauordnung*, 1969.

25 "New Forms of Urban Living," exhibition organized by the Austrian Society for Architecture, Hufnagl, Viktor/Czech, Hermann, Vienna 1967

26 On the phenomenon of Viennese stepped terrace housing, cf. De Chiffre 2016, see note 12.

27 The terrace typology of cross-wall construction can also be implemented in brick, as shown by a scheme in Norrebro, Copenhagen (1974–1978) (Murergade-karreen, Niels J. Holm).

28 Hufnagl, Viktor. "Neue städtische Wohnformen," exhibition organized by the Austrian Society for Architecture, Hufnagl, Viktor, and Hermann Czech, Vienna, 1967.

29 The categories are a result of the research project "Evaluation of milestones of European and non-European post-war modernism 1958–1978" since 2010 at the Research Department of Structural Engineering, Construction and Design at the Faculty of Architecture of the TU Wien/Prof. Gerhard Steixner. La Grande Motte is a stepped terrace (holiday) town that does not fall within these categories.

30 Today, the Brunswick Centre, the Alexandra and Ainsworth Estate, the Olympic Village in Munich, Wohnen Morgen Wien, Schlangenbader Strasse motorway development, La Grande Motte, and La Serra are all listed buildings.

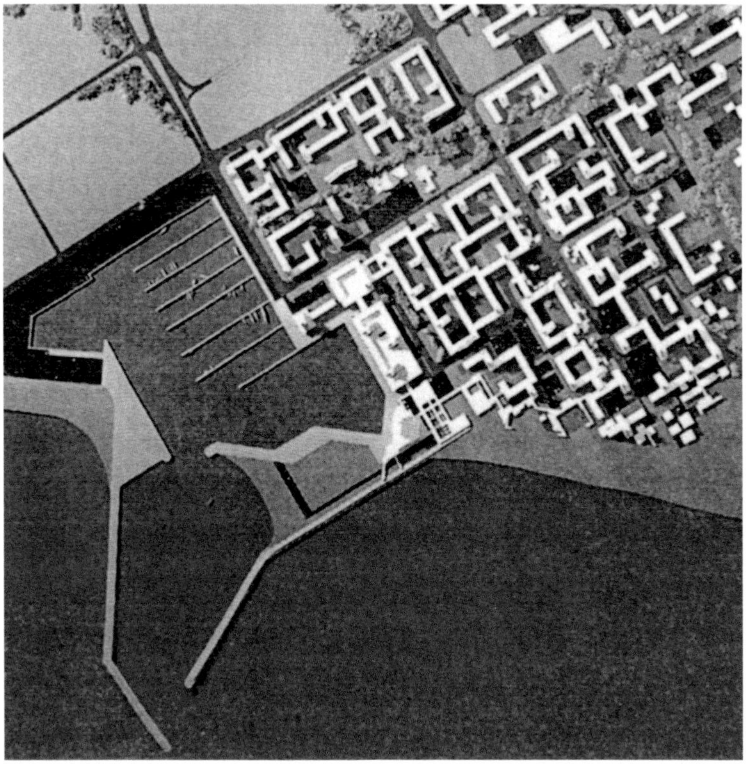

Site area 1,200 hectares
Greenspace 70 %
Apartments ca. 25,000 (110,000 beds)

Architecture
Jean Balladur with a team of 60 architects

Landscape planning
Pierre Pillet

Project steering committee
Mission Racine

Public art
Joséphine Chevry, Michèle Goalard, Albert Marchais and others

La Grande Motte, France
on the coast of Languedoc-Roussillon region (now Occitania)

Client
Republic of France

Start of planning 1963
Start of construction 1966
First holiday guests arrive 1968
Construction completed ca. 1983

Site plan 1:10,000

“Sundecks for All” — La Grande Motte

Maria Welzig

The urban space of La Grande Motte springs from a philosophical observation of human nature.

Jean Balladur[1]

The Democratization of Vacations

Just as the quality of housing for the lower to middle social classes is the driving force behind the residential buildings presented in this book, La Grande Motte addresses another domain previously reserved for the wealthy classes, namely vacation travel, which from the 1950s onwards became something also enjoyed by the middle and working classes. Vacations became a commodity for everyone, offering free time for relaxation, contact with nature, physical recreation, and new impressions.

In Spain and Italy, the response to this new demand was unbridled, with a reckless development of nature and beaches. France, however, in its *Trente Glorieuses*[2] period, developed a concept for the appropriate urban and architectural response to the democratization of vacations.

In an unprecedented large-scale project, the state first acquired land in the marshy and mosquito-infested coastal section of the Languedoc-Roussillon region, and made it arable. Five new port cities were built on the formerly undeveloped land.

George Candilis, a pioneering architect in social housing of the time, played a key role in the overall concept of these new resorts for

La Grande Motte, photos 2019

L'avenue de l'Europe

View from the Acapulco residential complex

the greatest number. The planning group developed a *Doctrine pour la Ville de Loisir du Plus Grand Nombre*[3] (Doctrine for the Vacation Town for the Greatest Number).

An egalitarian terraced city

The representative project of the initiative was the port city of La Grande Motte, planned from 1963 onwards by Jean Balladur. As a young man, Balladur moved in the same circles as the philosopher Jean-Paul Sartre and worked for Sartre's magazine *Les Temps Modernes* (The Modern Times) during his studies. In this highly important public forum for French left-wing intellectuals, Balladur later published repeatedly on architectural topics. His article *Urbanisme et démocratie*[4] (Urbanism and Democracy) appeared in the January 1956 issue.

La Grande Motte is based on a new conception of the city, one that is egalitarian, green, and focused on people rather than cars. The latter in particular is noteworthy given the time of its creation. In keeping with the idea of a democratic, classless society, there were no grand hotels, luxury resorts, or exclusive areas on the sea front.[5] Accommodation consisted mainly of small apartments in apartment blocks.

The apartment complexes are equal in terms of their location and their respective advantages. While the first planning for La Grande Motte still featured conventional blocks, a second planning phase from 1963 developed all residential buildings as stepped terrace develop-

ments to create an entirely stepped terrace city, where all apartments have terraces and loggias.

An autonomous city

This was indeed a vacation settlement, but from the onset it was laid out like a permanently inhabited city. Jean Balladur planned all the relevant facilities: school, town hall, church, synagogue, sports facilities, cultural venues, exhibition hall, congress hall, swimming pool, health center, restaurants and cafés, cinemas, market square, main square, and cemetery. Resolutely not conceived as a satellite of nearby city Montpellier, La Grande Motte thus also presented an alternative to the dormitory towns of the *banlieus*, or suburbs.

Consequently, La Grande Motte was elevated to a separate municipality in 1974. The facilities of a holiday resort and those of a "normal" town complement each other. One benefits the other as the substantial infrastructure would not have been created specifically for seasonal guests, nor would it have been created for a few thousand inhabitants.

The plan was to cater to 4,000–6,000 permanent residents and about 60,000 vacationers per year. The number of permanent inhabitants should be, according to the example of the historical bathing resorts St. Tropez or Deauville, approximately ten percent of the number of annual vacation guests. Today, 9,000 people live year-round in La Grande Motte and the city attracts two million vacationers per year.

Courtyard of the Acapulco residential complex

Architecture and landscape planning are equally important

Balladur saw the dominance of moving and parked vehicular traffic as a major cause of failed urban development. Contrary to what has been usual in seaside resorts, in La Grande Motte vehicular traffic is kept completely away from the coast, where there is no road. The main vehicular traffic is concentrated on separate roads outside the city center. On the remaining streets, pedestrians have luxuriously wide sidewalks, with carefully selected ground surfaces, seating, and shady trees. There are no, or only slight differences in level between the street and the promenades. The boulevards are interspersed with small green areas. La Grande Motte also has a network of unpaved pedestrian paths beneath the trees, parallel to the streets.

Balladur saw architectural and landscape planning as being equally important at La Grande Motte. Pierre Pillet was the congenial landscape designer. Seventy percent of La Grande Motte is green, making it one of the greenest and most pedestrian and bicycle-friendly cities in Europe.

The first two stepped terrace buildings, Le Grand Pavois and La Provence, completed in 1968 according to Balladur's plans, created the typological model: pyramids on an almost square floor plan with stepped terraces on two sides. This was a bold reference to the (four-sided) stepped terrace temples in Teotihuacán. In preparation for the project of his lifetime, La Grande Motte, Balladur had made a trip to Brazil in 1962 and also visited the temple complexes in Mexico.[6]

The February 1971 edition of the German travel magazine *Merian* was dedicated to the new holiday destination in Languedoc-Roussillon Cover: Le Grand Pavois apartments in La Grande Motte

Though Balladur's concept was functionally and chronologically closer to his fellow countryman Henri Sauvage's pioneering plans and buildings for stepped terrace workers' housing, to which Balladur also explicitly refers. Sauvage's concept of "hygienic living with light, air, and sun for all" in stepped terrace housing was realized in La Grande Motte, albeit in the context of a vacation town.

A total of sixty architects worked on La Grande Motte, following Balladur's clear stipulations on the inclination angle of the terraced pyramids to the number of apartments, everything was specified. Most of the buildings followed the prototype of the first two pyramids planned by Balladur, with stepped terraces on two sides. But some pyramids were terraced on all sides, like the Les Incas complex by Lucien Guerra, built in 1975 with 240 apartments. The layout of the buildings within the urban concept is particularly interesting and applicable to mixed-use (residential) districts as well. The roughly ten-story stepped terrace buildings are connected by lower horizontal "bridges" to form complexes with, for example, 200 apartments. This creates dense urban structures that are staggered like landscapes. The complexes are accessible to the public through carefully designed, green courtyard-like open spaces. The ground floor areas are often open and designed as arcade zones for shops and restaurants. The apartments are small and simple, some are just studios with an integrated kitchen.

In the La Grande Motte du Couchant district, which was begun in the 1970s, the crystalline pyramids are transformed into softly

Lucien Guerra
Les Incas residential complex, 1975

curved stepped terrace complexes that extend like wings into the dune landscape. The compact, low-rise settlements of La Grande Motte can also serve as a prototype for general residential housing.

From "concrete monster" to national cultural heritage

In the 1980s, the media and critics reacted extremely negatively to the *ex nihilo* city. After forty years, however, its image has changed completely. As Balladur and Pillet's concept envisaged, nature is now doing its part and also contributes to this change in perception. The trees have grown and the greenspaces have evolved. The qualities of the unusual architecture are now also being recognized; indeed, have reached cult status. In 2010, France declared La Grande Motte to be a "twentieth century national heritage site."

In 2018, on the occasion of the 15th anniversary of the arrival of the first holiday guests, many consistently enthusiastic reports about La Grande Motte appeared throughout Europe. "Sun decks for all" read one apt headline in the *Süddeutsche Zeitung*.[7] While *die Welt* wrote, "Half a century after its foundation, the 'Cité des Pyramides' looks neither old nor worn out."[8] A Swedish design magazine asked architects for articles on inspiring vacation destinations: NL Architects chose La Grande Motte.[9]

Today La Grande Motte is a lively, functioning city, accepted by its short-term and permanent residents (although housing prices there no longer correlate with the original idea of "vacations for all").

Jean Balladur, Jean-Bernard Tostivint residential complex Les Jardins de la Mer in the Motte du Couchant district, 1974

In its uniformity as a completely terraced residential town, in its rejection of the dominance of traffic, and in the equal status of its landscape and architecture, La Grande Motte remains unique to this day.

Of the complexes presented in this book, La Grande Motte is, on the one hand, an exception as a vacation town, and on the other hand, it is archetypical and by far the most comprehensive and largest example of a green terraced town—an ideal city. La Motte is also one of the earliest realizations of a terraced housing scheme.

The fact that La Grande Motte caters to the countless numbers of vacationing people makes it significant among social terraced housing. Regarding the summer lifestyle in London's Brunswick Centre, resident Stuart Tappin said: "It's like being in the south of France."[10] The question of what people need in order to feel comfortable, relaxed, and in contact with nature, with themselves and with others, i.e. ideally in a vacation-like state, lies at the very root of the stepped terrace housing concept. The aim is for residents to spend more of their leisure time in their immediate living environment, thus reducing leisure mobility, conserving resources, and strengthening social contacts.

Notes

1 "L'espace urbain de La Grande Motte résulte d'une conception philosophique sur la nature de l'homme." Quoted from Ludwig, Wolfgang. "La Grande Motte, die ideale Stadt am Meer." In *Wiener Zeitung*, 13 July 2019, https://www.wienerzeitung.at/nachrichten/reflexionen/vermessungen/2018018-La-Grande-Motte-die-ideale-Stadt-am-Meer.html?em_cnt_page=1

2 The three decades after the Second World War, from 1945 to 1975, are known as the *Trente Glorieuses*. Formative statesmen were Charles de Gaulle as president and Georges Pompidou as prime minister and president.

3 The megaproject was able to function through the establishment of a commission spanning five ministries under the leadership of Pierre Racine, which eventually lasted 20 years.

4 In 1967, Balladur discussed "L'Urbanisme aujourd'hui: Mythes et réalités" with Henri Lefebvre and Michel Ecochard. In *Les Cahiers du Centre d'Etudes Socialistes*, No. 72–73, September 1967.

5 Not only are there no luxury hotels or resorts, but the few hotels do not have grand, but rather unobtrusive and modest entrances.

6 Balladur also took another formative impression from Oskar Niemeyer's sculptural handling of concrete from his 1962 trip to Brazil, paying careful attention to every design detail. Until 1983, i.e. over a period of 20 years, the planning team met every Friday. Balladur owned an apartment with his family in La Grande Motte and it was his wish to be buried in the city's cemetery.

7 Rössler, Antje. "Sonnenterrassen für alle." In *Süddeutsche Zeitung*, 11 July 2018, https://www.sueddeutsche.de/reise/la-grande-motte-in-frankreich-sonnenterrassen-fuer-alle-1.4049555

8 Schlömer, Hans. "La Grande Motte – die perfekte Stadt am Meer." In *Welt*, 22 August 2018, https://www.welt.de/reise/staedtereisen/article181249264/Frankreich-La-Grande-Motte-die-perfekte-Stadt-am-Meer.html

9 "La Grande Motte." NL Architects Blog, 25Jun2009, https://nlarchitects.wordpress.com/2009/06/25/la-grande-motte/

10 Stuart Tappin on the Brunswick Centre terraces in summer. Beckmann, Karen. *Urbanität durch Dichte? Geschichte und Gegenwart der Großwohnkomplexe der 1970er-Jahre.* Bielefeld: transcript Verlag, 2015, 408.

Bibliography

Direction régionale des affaires culturelles (DRAC) du Languedoc-Roussillon (eds.). *Jean Balladur et La Grande-Motte. L'architecture d'une ville, Monuments historiques et objets d'art du Languedoc-Roussillon.* Montpellier, 2010.

Prelorenzo, Claude, and Picon, Antoine. *L'aventure du balnéaire. La Grande Motte de Jean Balladur*. Marseille: Éditions Parenthèse, 1999.

Ragot, Gilles. *La Grande Motte, Patrimoine du XXe siècle*. Paris, 2016.

Milestones in European Stepped Terrace Housing

A Catalogue

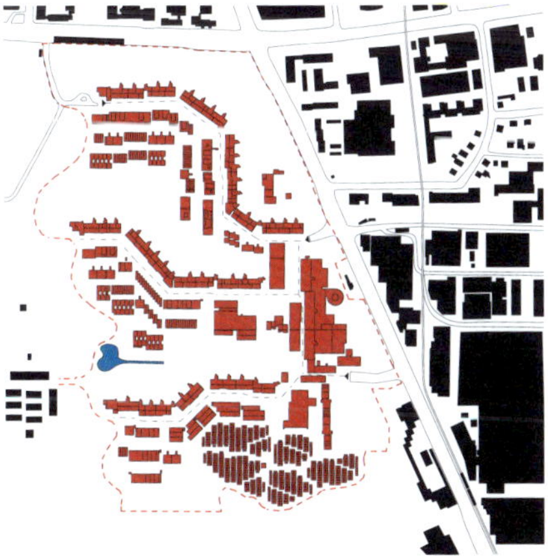

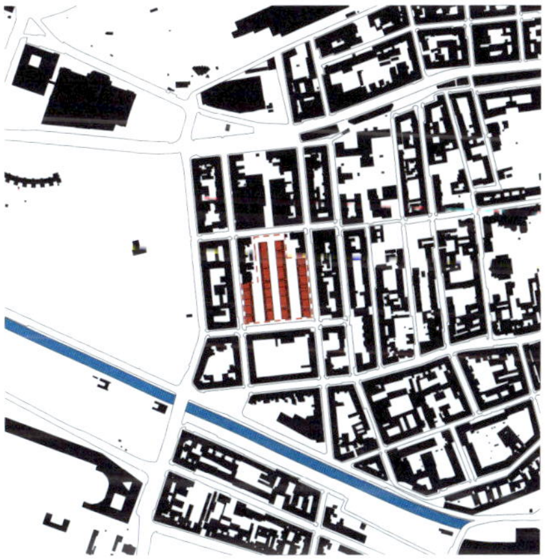

Along the Edge

St. Peter Housing Estate, Graz
Werkgruppe Graz
1965–78

Koseze Housing Estate, Ljubljana
Viktor Pust
1968–81

Heinz-Nittel-Hof, Vienna
Harry Glück & Partner
1973–83

Shaped by Traffic

Hadikgasse Residential Complex, Vienna
Harry Glück & Partner
1970–76

Alexandra Road Estate, London
Neave Brown
1967–79

Autobahnüberbauung Schlangenbader Strasse, Berlin
Georg Heinrichs, Gerhard Krebs, Klaus Krebs
1971–80

Autonomous Districts

Olympic Village, Munich
Heinle, Wischer und Partner
1968–72

Alt-Erlaa Residential Park, Vienna
Harry Glück & Partner
1968–85

Density in Block Grids

Inzersdorfer Strasse Residential Complex, Vienna
Harry Glück & Partner
1969–74

Wohnen Morgen, Wien
Wilhelm Holzbauer
1973–80

Inner-City Hybrids

Brunswick Centre, London
Patrick Hodgkinson
1967–72

La Serra, Ivrea
Iginio Cappai, Pietro Mainardis
1967–75

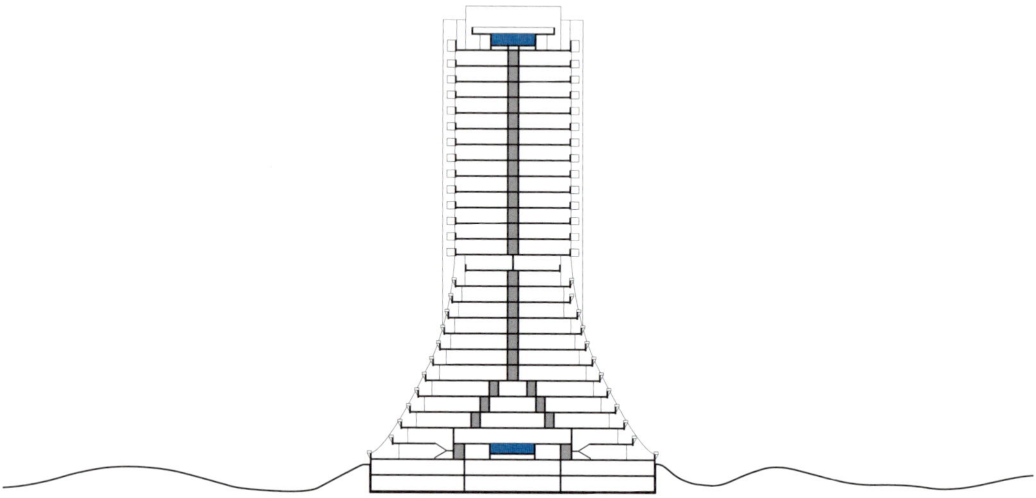

Alt-Erlaa Residential Park, Vienna

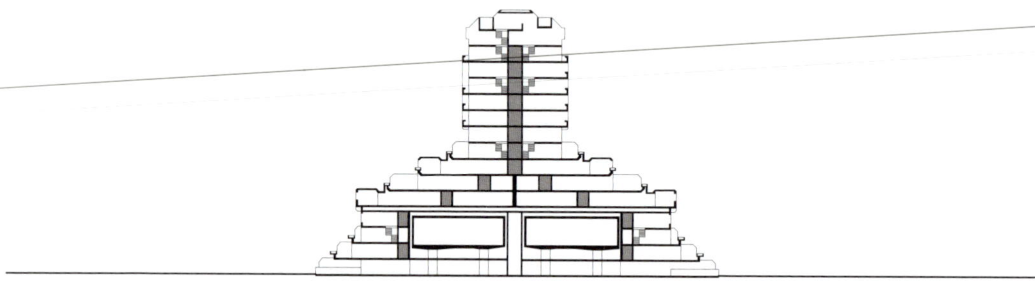

Autobahnüberbauung Schlangenbader Strasse, Berlin

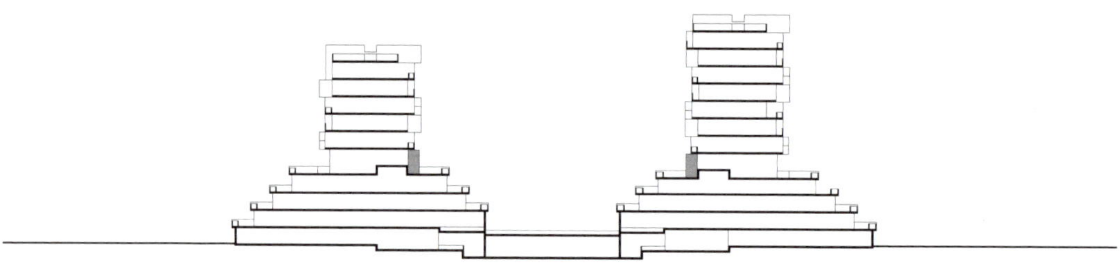

St. Peter Housing Estate, Graz

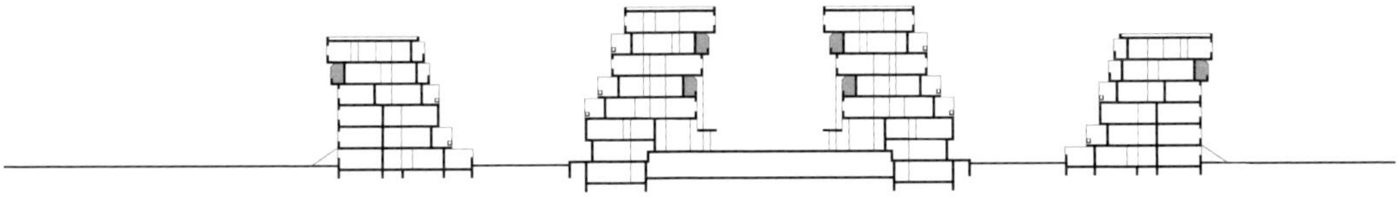

Wohnen Morgen, Wien

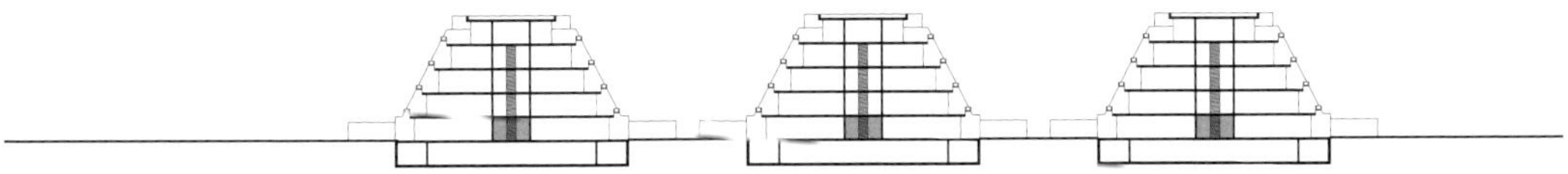

Koseze Housing Estate, Ljubljana

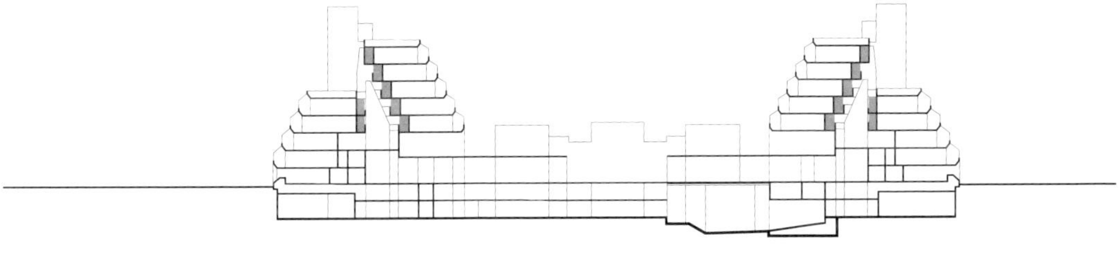

Brunswick Centre, London

Living spaces facing east/west

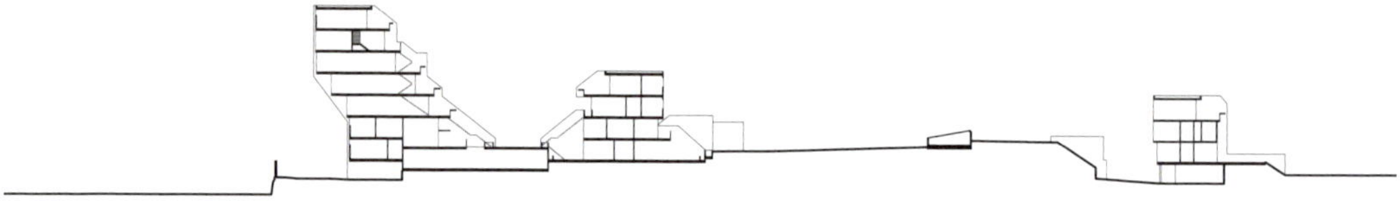

Alexandra Road Estate, London

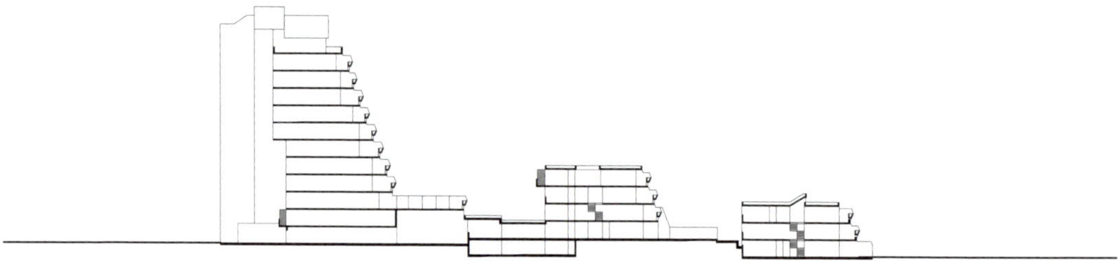

Olympic Village, Munich

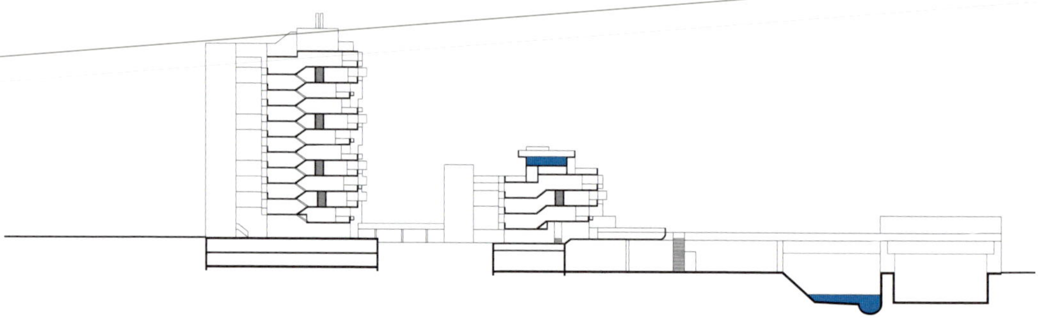

Hadikgasse Residential Complex, Vienna

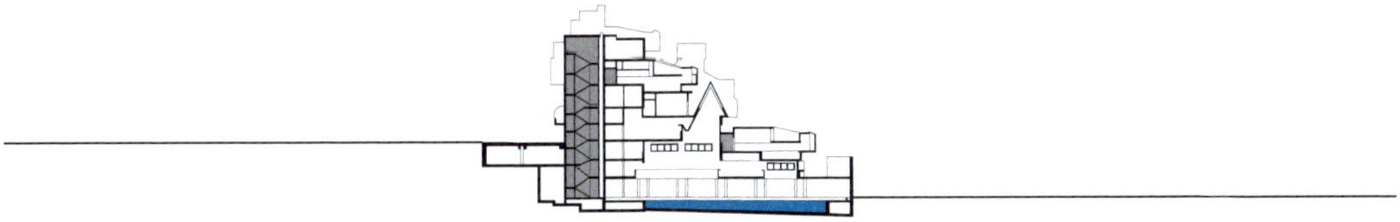

La Serra, Ivrea

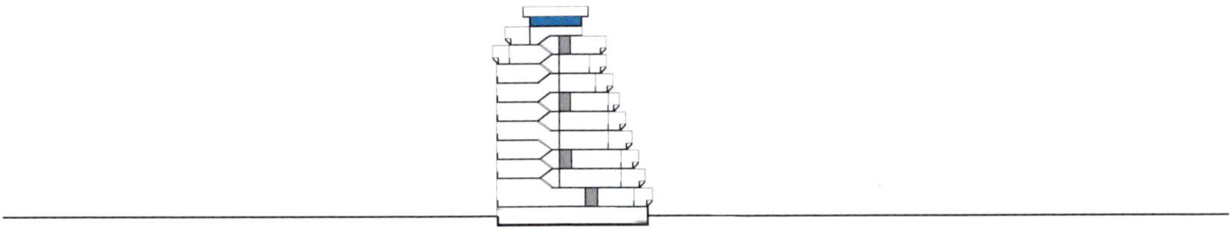

Inzersdorfer Strasse Residential Complex, Vienna

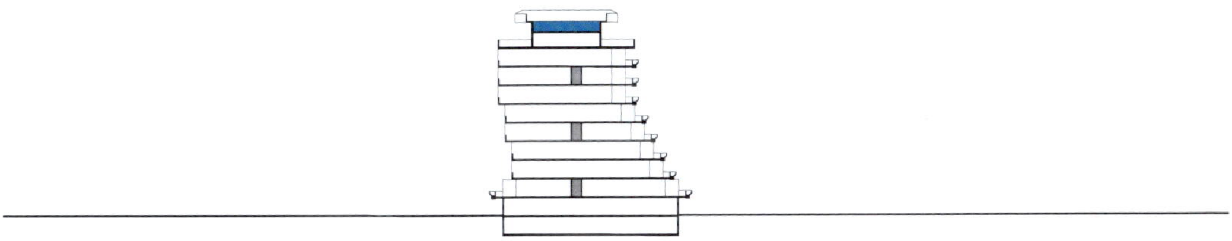

Heinz-Nittel-Hof, Vienna

Living spaces facing south

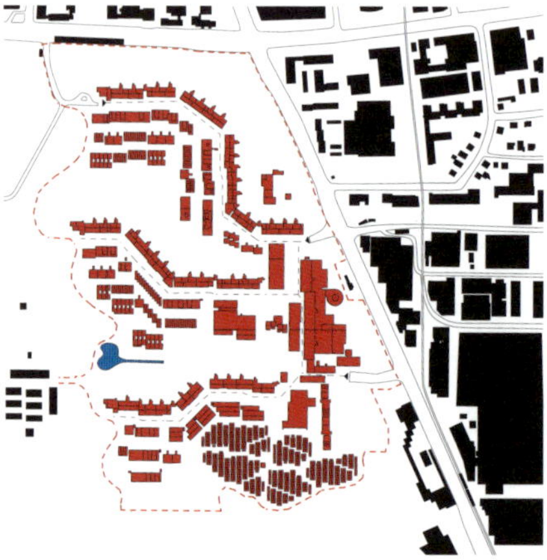

Autonomous Districts

Olympic Village, Munich
Heinle, Wischer und Partner
1968–72

Alt-Erlaa Residential Park, Vienna
Harry Glück & Partner
1968–85

Apartments ca. 5,000
Floor space index
Residential 1
Center 2.4
Built area ratio 39 %

Site area ca. 399,000 m²
Built area ca. 156,000 m²
Terrace apartments ca. 3,000

Collective facilities, infrastructure: Shops, offices, churches, schools, kindergartens, cultural institutions
Special technical equipment: Pneumatic waste disposal system, "Media Lines" guidance system by Hans Hollein

Munich, Germany
Lerchenauer Strasse, Mossacher Strasse, Georg-Brauchle-Ring

Architects
Heinle, Wischer und Partner

Client
Olympia Bau-GmbH, later Olympiadorf Maßnahmeträger-GmbH & Co. München

Planning and construction
1968–72

Site plan 1:10,000

Olympic Village, Munich

Heinle, Wischer und Partner
1968–72

The Hanging Gardens of Munich

Natalie Heger

"The history of this settlement," wrote architectural critic Manfred Sack, "is like a fairytale: At the beginning, it is bombastically and angrily doomed [...], then, seized by a miraculous transformation, at the end cheered and transformed into a paradise dwelling that has now become almost priceless and unattainable. This fairytale should make the builders of all post-war settlements envious."[1]

Among the large housing estates of post-war modernism, the Olympic Village in Munich plays a special role. Due to the context of the Olympic Games, the project was driven by a particular euphoria and ambition and, at the same time, was realized under difficult conditions and extreme time pressure. However, the specific situation of the time contributed to the fact that an urban planning experiment could be realized that created the framework for a very high level of satisfaction among the residents. Opinions about the quality of living in the Olympic Village could hardly be more esteemed. The scheme is referred to as a "paradise" and an "idyll," and it has been said that the "immense living quality" promotes social commitment in an ideal way.

A very active population lives in the estate, highly involved, among other things, in the Residents' Interest Group founded in 1973, which is currently working on a quality revitalization of the shopping areas in the center. Part of the Olympiapark ensemble, it has been a listed

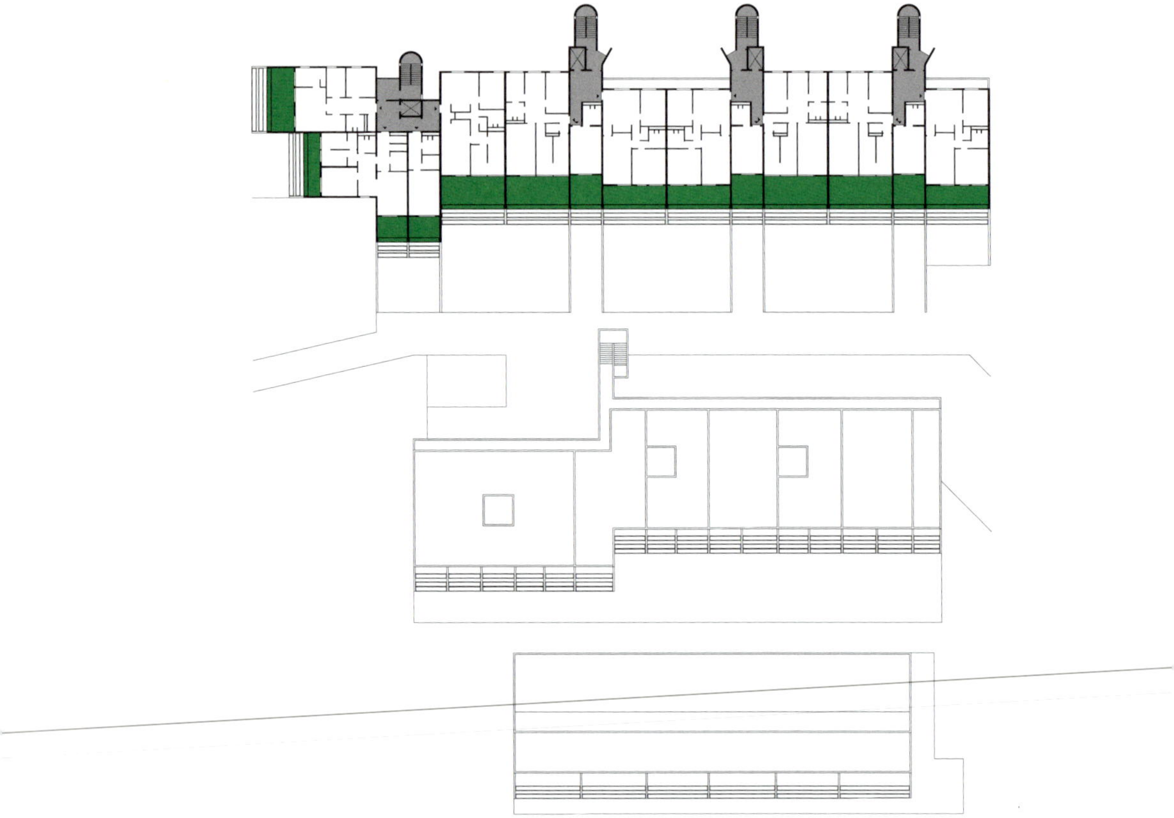

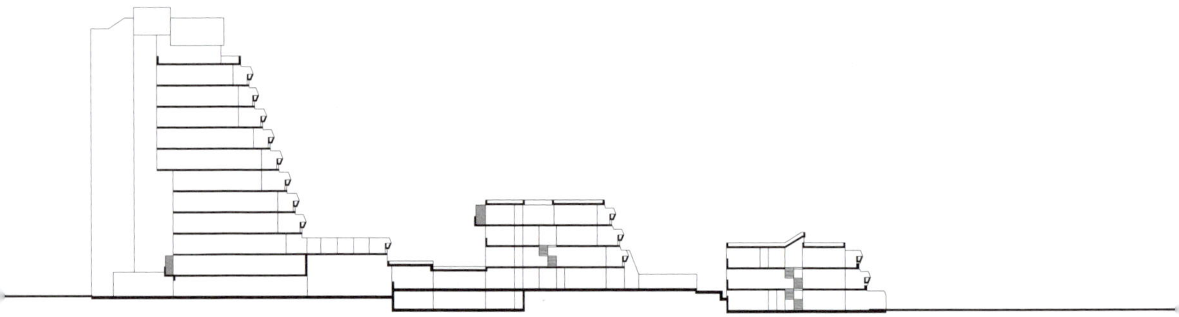

Floor plan 4th upper floor, Cross-section, 1:1,000

building since 1998 and an application for World Heritage Site status for the entire complex is being actively pursued. Thus, 50 years after its completion, the Olympic Village is one of the most sought-after residential locations in Munich.

If you look back to the early years immediately after the Olympic Games, when the approximately 12,000 athletes, coaches, supervisors, and officials had moved out and the freshly renovated apartments were up for sale, the situation was quite different. The image of the new city was at the time rather negative—headlined in the media as a "concrete fortress" and "ghost town"—which resulted in a high vacancy rate for years.[2] The rather inhospitable surroundings, such as the industrial area to the east and north, the still sparse greenery of the open spaces, and the gloomy reports on crime in the settlement contributed to the rather sluggish sale of apartments, which continued for years. Living in this "test-tube city" was initially unattractive to most people. Over the years, this changed fundamentally, with more and more "villagers" enjoying the advantages of living here. When the 1979 Olympic Village was presented as an exemplary project in the exhibition "Transformation in Modern Architecture" at the Museum of Modern Art in New York, previously critical experts were finally able to reconcile with the residential city.

Olympic games site

The background for the cautious acceptance of the planned city also lies in its planning history. The "Olympics of Short Distances" were to be held on the 280-hectare site of a former airport about four kilometers north of Munich's city center. The 1967 competition for the Oberwiesenfeld Olympic site was one of the largest and, due to its political dimension, one of the most important of its time, with around one hundred participating offices.[3] Stuttgart firm Günter Behnisch with Jürgen Joedicke won the first prize. After reworking the stadium roofs of the first and third prize winners, the Olympic construction company commissioned Behnisch with the sports facilities in the entire southern area and the Stuttgart firm Heinle, Wischer und Partner, third prize winners, with the planning of the Olympic Village, the Olympic press center, and the outdoor facilities (later to become a central university sports facility). As a result, no competition was held for the Olympic Village—a decision that triggered massive protest in

Olympic Village Munich, a "street" of greenspace, 1979

A five-meter high access road runs under the front gardens on the ground floor, lit by a gap between the front yards and the living street.

the architectural world. Five architects' associations joined together to form the Aktion Olympia der freien Architekten Deutschlands or "Action Olympia of Germany's Free Architects." Publishing telegrams, statements, and personal letters, they vehemently expressed their concerns, reaffirmed the advantages of the German competition system for the achievement of forward-looking housing construction concepts, and ceased to participate in any Olympic committees and bodies.

Design experiment in a large team

With high expectations and only five months to develop a sustainable concept, Heinle, Wischer und Partner started the first conceptual and planning phase for the men's Olympic Village.[4] They developed a special design process, which they called "multi-stage optimization," that was based on experience with systematic planning from previous projects and methods from systems engineering, cybernetics, and operations research.[5]

First, an interdisciplinary committee of 16 expert consultants was appointed to review and evaluate the urban planning studies of the 22 architects from their own office in five stages. The main aim was to produce the greatest possible variety of concepts and, by means of measured evaluation and gradual reduction, to finally obtain the best design. In doing so, shielding against traffic noise from the north and east had to be taken into account, the apartments had to face the park to the south, and central access to the residential city from the underground station had to be ensured. In the first stage, 57 different urban planning concepts were developed, which were then gradually reduced to 20, seven, and three alternatives, and finally to an end result.

The idea of the "street"

In addition to the urban development maxim of urban densification combined with nature (green and inhabited hills), the Olympic Village is based on the guiding criteria of humanity, diversity, vibrancy, and leisure. The basic urban structure fits into the morphology of the "Olympic landscape" of the entire complex with the sports facilities. The orientation towards the Olympic Park located to the south is an essential aspect of the living quality and ensures a positive image and identity in the residential city. Programmatically, spatially, and in its architectural formulation, the Olympic Village thus references its interior and the park. A contextual reference to the urban surroundings (traffic arteries and industrial areas) is largely absent. Three basic areas can be distinguished from each other: the men's and women's Olympic Villages (high-rise and low-rise schemes), and the "village center."[6]

With the idea of the "street," as the winning design for the area of the former men's village was titled and which resulted from the optimization process, access becomes a structuring component of the entire complex. Pedestrian and vehicular traffic are horizontally separated from each other, so that the entire above-ground residential quarter is accessible exclusively on foot and by bicycle, while all motorized traffic on the east side of the residential city is directed into the three main lanes in the level below. The three pedestrian streets are bordered by highly densified, south-facing residential clusters and are accompanied by a guidance system of colored tubes (media lines).[7] The different color and design concepts in the respective residential clusters is formative and creates a sense of identity. The densely populated residential areas interconnect with spacious public green spaces, which are enriched with leisure facilities such as playgrounds and water facilities. Narrow paths and cross-connections between the residential buildings add spatial contrast to this landscape expanse, and make a significant contribution to the spatial qualities of the immediate living environment.

The village center as an urban hub

The central area, the "backbone" of the residential city, was given particular attention in planning. During the Olympic Games, what was called the Forum was the central meeting point that held all the necessary facilities for the athletes. Subsequently, it became the central landmark of the residential city with a concentration of infrastructural facilities. The broad pedestrian platform connects all main routes and bundles the additional uses. The pedestrian access to the entire residential complex is connected to the underground station via this central area. From here, paths lead to the three residential clusters, to student housing, to the social and cultural facilities (primary school, kindergarten, churches, and cultural forum with cinema), as well as to the three public green spaces in between. Shops for everyday needs, restaurants, a medical center, and a hotel can be found in a partially covered arcade. Despite high ambitions in the design planning, the dark shopping arcade, the spatially unclear expansion of the square, an overall undifferentiated formulation of the exterior space, and problems with store occupancy make the center the weakest part of the residential city today.

Housing diversity

The urban residential structure with around 5,000 units (of which about 2,000 are now in the former women's village) ranges from one-room apartments, to penthouse apartments in high-rise locations, to single-story atrium row houses with gardens. A total of about 70 different floor plans (one to five-room apartments) are distributed throughout seven different types of residential buildings. The building typologies are arranged in combinations to help establish relationships between the different residents and their housing needs. A pronounced profiling of the facades on the terraced south sides contrasts with the simply designed north sides. This is particularly evident in the up to 14-story, stepped terrace tower buildings. High, vertical staircase towers and bands of windows contrast with the fully glazed south facades, ground-level private gardens, and upper-floor terraces that extend the living space outwards ("green rooms"). Concrete planters create a boundary for the terraces and were designed in such a way that it is neither possible to see in from the side nor from the

Living street and swimming pond in the Olympic Village, 1977

apartments above or below. They can be planted by the residents as desired and create a characteristic overall image of a "hanging garden." The separation of the individual residential units and simultaneous demarcation from the respective neighboring apartments was coupled with a modular cross-wall system, designed to be visible from the exterior. 20-centimeter-wide, cantilevered cross-walls sloped on the underside and set at an axial distance of 3.9 or 7.8 meters articulate the outer appearance of the southern elevations of the entire former men's village. The massive concrete planters and continuous floor slabs structure the facade horizontally while simultaneously providing views of the landscape from the upper floors and of the public outdoor areas from the lower levels.

The interior lighting of the relatively deep floor plans of the apartments is ensured by full glazing to the south and skylights set at strategic spots. The floor plans are characterized by flowing spatial transitions. Arranged in the core areas are the bathrooms, kitchens, storerooms and, in the case of the multi-story stepped terrace buildings, the internal access as well. The original idea was to have mobile wall and window elements to create more flexible apartments by reducing the terrace areas and extending the living space outwards or the ability to change the living space inside. However, in the end, only the possibility of connecting wall elements to the facade to divide double bedrooms into single bedrooms could be realized.

The division of the apartment floor plans into clearly defined common areas and flexible individual rooms takes into account contemporary living requirements. At the same time, the basic idea of combining private and public, individual and community is transferred from the urban planning principle to the small scale of the individual apartment. The fact that the architects focused on social aspects when planning the Olympic Village and built for an open, free society is clearly visible in the spatial design. In the early 1970s, the era of growth, major planning, and thus also of large housing estates, gradually came to an end. In addition, urban planning and architectural leitmotifs shifted towards new issues and social demands on housing. As a result, the Munich Olympic Village has remained a unique prototype for living and housing to this day.

Notes

1 Heinle, Wischer und Partner Freie Architekten. *Eine Stadt zum Leben. Das Olympische Dorf München.* Freudenstadt: Heinrich Müller Verlag, 1980.

2 On the history of the use of the Olympic Village see also Beckmann, Karen. *Urbanität durch Dichte? Geschichte und Gegenwart der Großwohnkomplexe der 1970er-Jahre.* Bielefeld: transcript Verlag, 2015, 365 ff.

3 For further information on the competition, see Heger, Natalie. *Das Olympische Dorf München. Planungsexperiment und Musterstadt der Moderne.* Berlin: Reimer, 2014, 47 ff.

4 Heinle, Wischer und Partner consulted the Munich architects and 4th prize winners in the overall competition by Gordon Ludwig, Franz Raab, Gerd Wiegand, and Wolf Zuleger.

5 The optimization process and its methodology is described in detail in: Heger, Natalie. *Das Olympische Dorf München. Planungsexperiment und Musterstadt der Moderne.* Berlin: Reimer, 2014, 113 ff.

6 For the planning of the women's Olympic Village, the Munich architects Werner Wirsing and Günther Eckert had already received a contract from the Munich Student Union for the planning of new student apartments on the site before bidding on the 1961 Olympic Games. In 2010, replacement new buildings were completed for the low-rise housing area by the Werner Wirsing bogevischs buero consortium. See: Domschky, Anke, Stefan Kurath, Simon Mühlebach, Urs Primas. *Stadtlandschaften verdichten. Strategien zur Erneuerung des baukulturellen Erbes der Nachkriegszeit.* Zurich: Trieste Verlag, 2018, 72–89.

7 Designed by Hans Hollein, the media lines are a system of different colored tubes crisscrossing the main paths of the Olympic Village. They were designed as a lighting and guidance system for sound, spatial separation, shelter from sun and rain, heating, and cooling. However, the system was used only to a very limited degree during the 1972 Olympics.

Bibliography

Beckmann, Karen. *Urbanität durch Dichte? Geschichte und Gegenwart der Großwohnkomplexe der 1970er-Jahre.* Bielefeld: transcript, 2015.

Domschky, Anke, Stefan Kurath, Simon Mühlebach, and Urs Primas. *Stadtlandschaften verdichten. Strategien zur Erneuerung des baukulturellen Erbes der Nachkriegszeit.* Zurich: Triest Verlag, 2018.

Heger, Natalie. *Das Olympische Dorf München: Planungsexperiment und Musterstadt der Moderne.* Berlin: Reimer, 2014.

Heinle, Wischer, Partner Freie Architekten: *Eine Stadt zum Leben. Das Olympische Dorf München.* Freudenstadt: Heinrich Müller Verlag, 1980.

Hennecke, Stefanie, Regine Keller, and Juliane Schneegans. *Demokratisches Grün Olympiapark München.* Berlin: Jovis Verlag, 2013.

Bauten der Olympischen Spiele 1972 München. architektur wettbewerbe, 1st special edition, Stuttgart/Bern: Karl Krämer Verlag, 1969.

Olympische Bauten München 1972. architektur wettbewerbe, 2nd special edition: Bestandsaufnahme Herbst 1970, Stuttgart/Bern: Karl Krämer Verlag, 1970.

Olympische Bauten München 1972. architektur wettbewerbe, 3rd special edition: Bauabschluss Sommer 1972, Stuttgart/Bern: Karl Krämer Verlag, 1972.

24

127
137

Apartments 3,180
Floor space index ca. 2.5
Built area ratio 31 %

Site area 240,000 m²
Built area ca. 74,500 m²
Gross floor area ca. 600,000 m²

Number of apartments 3,180
Block A 1,004
Block B 1,034
Block C 1,142

Vienna, Austria
Anton-Baumgartner-Strasse 44

Architects
Harry Glück, Kurt Hlaweniczka,
Requat & Reinthaller working group
Landscape planners
Marija and Wilfried Kirchner

Client
GESIBA – Gemeinnützige Siedlungs- und Bauaktiengesellschaft

Start of planning 1968
Start of construction 1973
Completion 1976 (Block A), 1978 (Block B), 1985 (Block C)

Site plan 1:10,000

Alt-Erlaa Residential Park, Vienna

Harry Glück & Partner

1968–85

Alt-Erlaa, Residential Park

Silke Fischer

"The discomfort that accompanies almost all realized projects in the field of urban housing, not only in Austria, is becoming ever more noticeable every day. Solving the problems related to this is a question of our very existence."[1]

Wolfgang and Traude Windbrechtinger began the publication for the 1967 exhibition "New Urban Housing" with this pronouncement. The catalogue indirectly reports on serious deficits, calling for alternative urban models: a mixed city, a city of community, a pedestrian city, and a general awareness that high-quality housing is the most responsible architectural undertaking of our time.

Stepped terrace housing is ubiquitous and, in Vienna, Harry Glück has a large number of projects to design on his desk. In 1974, Glück completes his first schemes, including the Inzersdorfer Strasse residential complex[2] in Vienna's 10th district. This is his first completed prototype and successfully demonstrates[3] high-quality, high density living (a floor area index of up to 4 for additions in the *Gründerzeit* area of the city), with proximity to nature. This is the urban equivalent of the classic single-family home, exactly what so many need and desire, yet within the framework of subsidized housing.[4]

The Alt-Erlaa Residential Park is the embodiment of this principle as a large-scale alternative model for future urban expansion. Open space, housing, and infrastructure facilities are creating a new

Collective facilities

2 tennis halls with a total of 3 courts, badminton hall with 4 courts, 7 indoor pools, 20 sauna facilities, 3 solariums, 2 sports fields, 7 rooftop swimming pools, 7 playgrounds, 7 weather-protected playgrounds, a youth center, numerous rooms for shared use

Furthermore

Tenant Advisory Board, residential park TV show, residential park magazine (WAZ)

Infrastructure

2 elementary schools, secondary school, 3 kindergartens, church, medical center, gymnasium, municipal library, Alt-Erlaa shopping center with ca. 45 shops, personal transport: above-ground car-free residential complex, integrated garage system, structurally a high-rise garage (beneath the apartment blocks, each garage with two floors) with ca. 3,400 parking spaces

Special facilities

In-house property management and maintenance (team includes electricians, welders, carpenters, painters, plumbers, ventilation technicians, gardeners, pool service, waste transport and waste collection system and recycling center technicians)

Pneumatic waste disposal system

Artwork

Residential joint stock company

Subsidized housing, rental apartments, all tenants hold one share each of the non-profit Alt-Erlaa residential park joint stock company (tenants and supervisory boards hold 34 % of the shares and 66 % GESIBA, as of 2016)

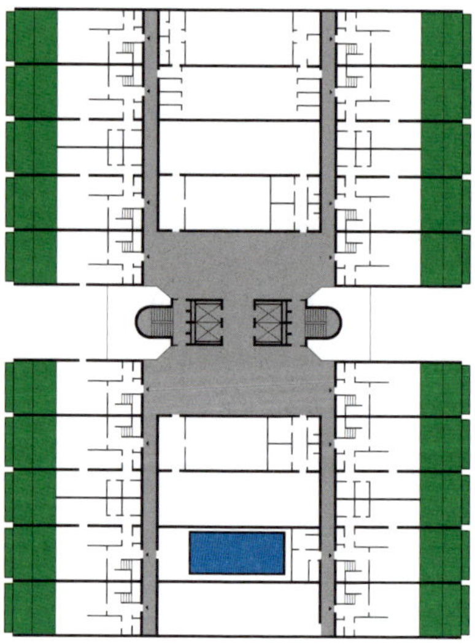

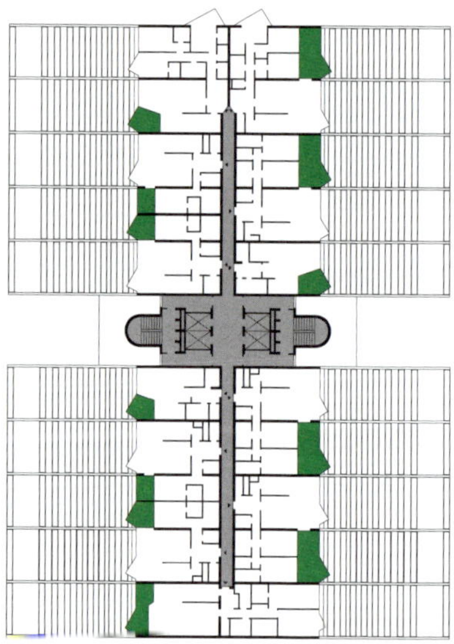

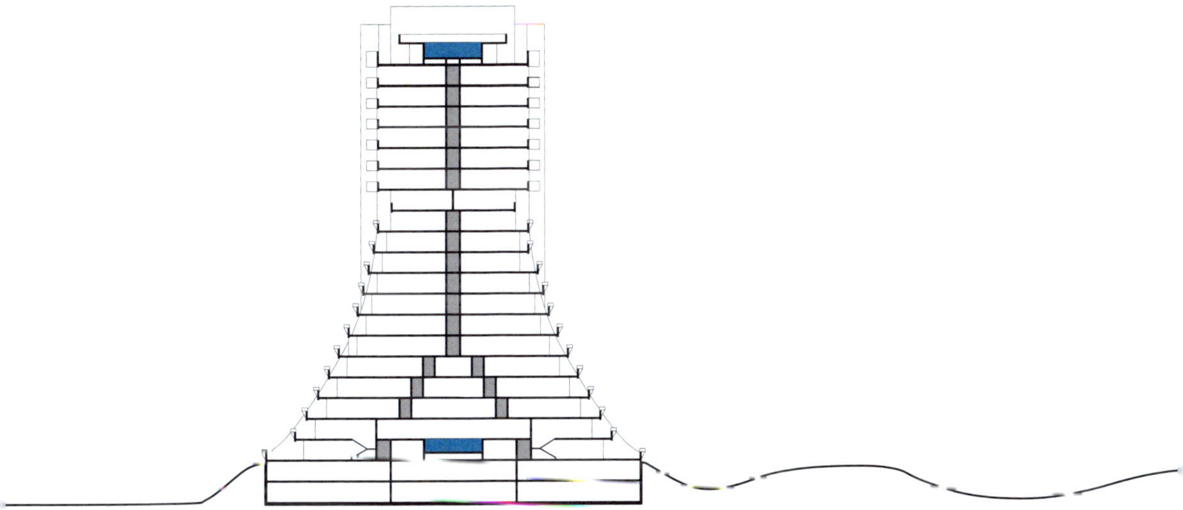

Floor plan ground floor and 14th upper floors, Cross-section, 1:1,000

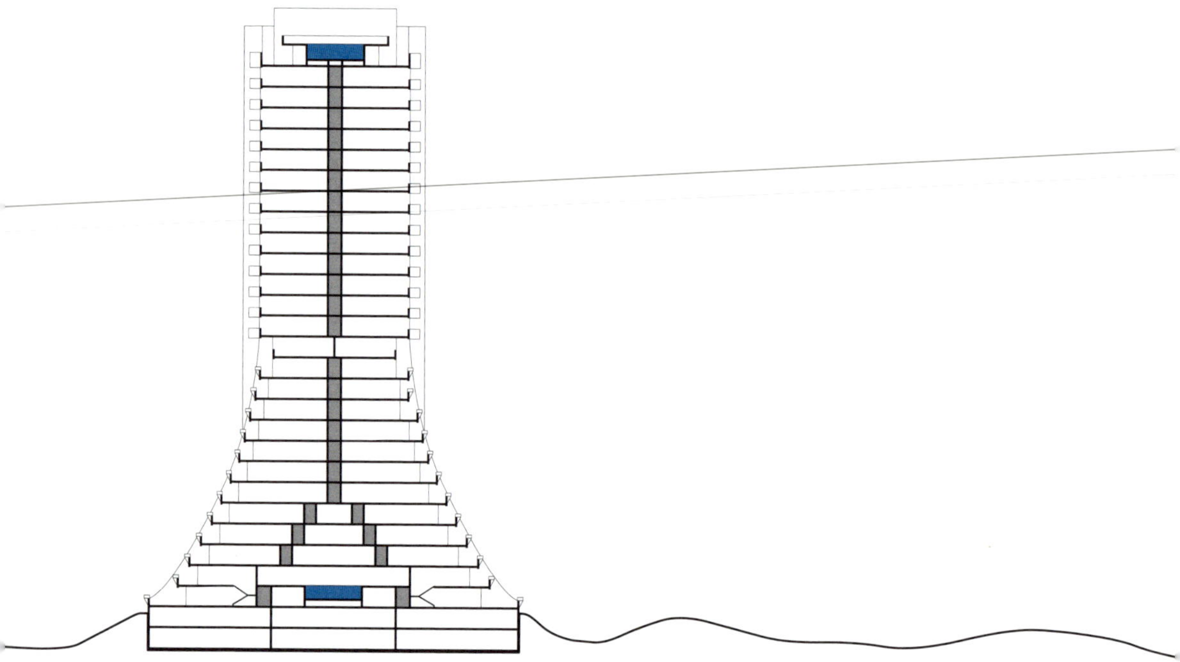

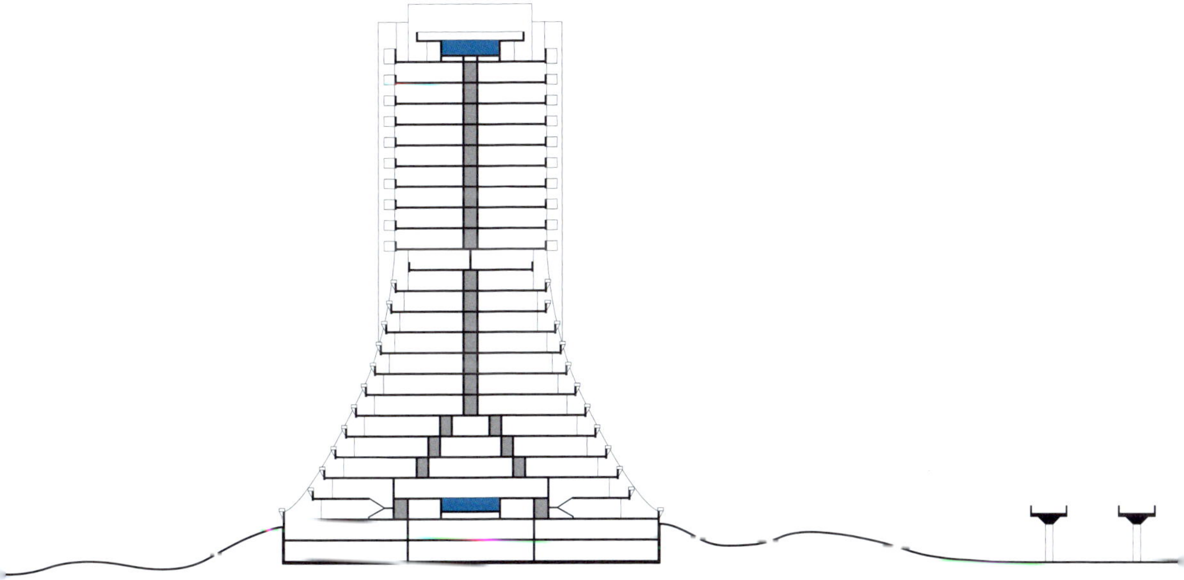

Cross-section 1:1,000

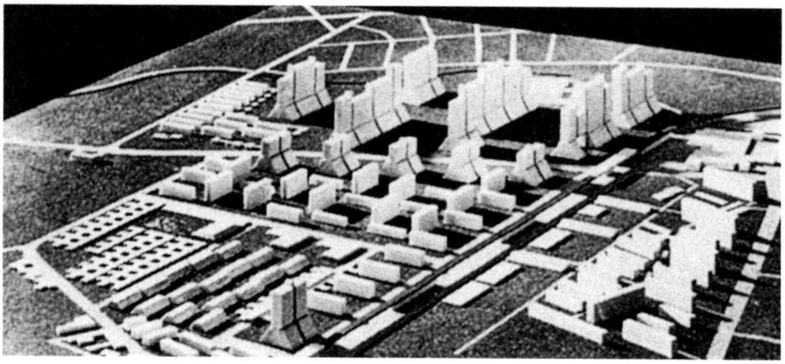

standard, indeed a new possibility: the achievement of the next level of quality in housing culture. For Harry Glück, subsidized housing is the only relevant field for accomplishing this, which, in turn, calls for urban solutions and working with large numbers. With approximately 10,000 initial inhabitants, the Alt-Erlaa Residential Park is the size of a small town.[5]

The Context: Vienna, 1968

Planning commences in 1968, the year in which GESIBA[6] acquires the property in the suburban, predominantly agricultural 23rd district of Vienna and, after a small invited competition of three teams, merges the competition participants into a design team, which is commissioned as a group to continue with further development.[7]

In those years, Vienna was thinking big: the 1969 international competition for the Vienna International Center (UNO City), the 1971 international urban development competition for Wien Süd (South Vienna, an urban expansion area for 60,000 inhabitants), and the 1972 construction of the New Danube, a relief channel providing flood protection, that brought with it the construction of the 21-kilometer-long artificial Danube Island, Vienna's most popular bathing beach.

Due to the stagnating and even declining population,[8] housing development in Vienna at this time consists primarily of *urban regeneration*. Conditions continue to be inadequate: too small, too

Alt-Erlaa urban planning model for the exhibition Urban Development Axis Meidling—Siebenhirten, 1969.

Alt-Erlaa always had its own public transport station. Rapid Tram 64 has run from Westbahnhof to Alt-Erlaa since 1979.

overcrowded, and a high prevalence of substandard units. An unacceptable state for a prosperous society. The urban development strategy of the era is that of the *urban development axis,* meaning dense housing on a large scale along efficient public rail transport routes. A prototype for the controlled and systematic development of the area between the city center and the city limits is the Meidling—Siebenhirten urban development axis, which envisages 20,000 new residential units for the southern part of Vienna: districts Meidling (12th) and Liesing (23rd). The planning formulates five principal points, namely the extension of the U6 underground line to the outskirts of the city as an access artery and infrastructural spine, and the adjoining large-scale housing projects Schöpfwerk, Alt-Erlaa, Wiener Flur, and In der Wiesen.

A planning exhibition in 1969 already showed the characteristic residential buildings with the terraced base and "normal" upper floors, but in an extended urban development formation. The typology had been invented, but was flexible. The number of floors went on to vary, as did the number and position of the rows on the site, the size of which was changed. While the urban development of the Alt-Erlaa Residential Park was only fine-tuned,[9] other planning projects were banished to typological banality (the Wiener Flur) or to the distant future. The planned extension of the U6 underground line to the extent that we know it today was not fully completed until 1995, however, the traffic axis was serviced by the Tramway 64 rapid transit line at frequent intervals as of 1979.

Alt-Erlaa, Block A–B 180 meters. The city of the future must be a Green City. The space between buildings is a park-like landscape, free of motorized traffic.

In its final stage of development—and as it remains today—the 3,180 residential units of Alt-Erlaa were divided into three rows of north-south oriented apartments of equal length (approximately 300 meters) and considerable height (70 and 80 meters), which—going from right to left when looking north—were designated as blocks A to C. The building plan was divided into three phases, each comprising approximately 1,000 apartments. This, which could be seen as a more construction-friendly format, was validated as the final construction schedule. The groundbreaking ceremony for Block A took place in 1973 and the building was completed in 1976. Block B was finished in 1978, with Block C following in 1985. The apartment rows themselves are linked to each other and to the city by public infrastructure facilities such as a shopping center, school, church, and leisure amenities as well as by an underground parking system. The park is also part of the program: the ratio of built-up area to open space is approximately 1:3. Alt-Erlaa is an urban development concept and a prototype of a Green City.

Alt-Erlaa, 1,000 apartments in Block A after completion in 1976. Fundamentally, every (true) stepped terrace building is a social manifesto: The diagonals invalidate the usual hierarchy of top and bottom, aiming for the equivalency of all apartments.

Typology of a high-rise

According to the architect, Alt-Erlaa is primarily the result of logical thinking:[10]

- Future housing is housing for an emancipated and democratic mass society.[11]
- Only through the extreme densification of residential space by means of an efficient high-rise typology can extensive open space, indeed even a natural landscape, and thus a Green City be realized.
- Only through the targeted economization of residential construction can additional spatial programs (supplementary communal spaces and private areas such as terraces) and thus a high quality of life be financed and realized at city, building, and apartment level.
- Only large building sites allow both. An atypically high number of facilities and a car-free design scheme based upon underground garages with connecting roads requires a critical mass.

The high-rise building is a means to an end. Rising upwards into space favors the preservation of ground surface area. The park like landscape is freed from motorized traffic. The distance between the blocks is a decisive dimensional factor. The distance of about 180 meters between the buildings (comparable to Vienna's Stadtpark) creates a generous feeling of space. Here, size becomes relative. The terracing of the lower floors also enhances the properties of the exterior space. Walking through Alt-Erlaa is like walking through a green valley. *How a house is anchored in the ground* takes on new meaning here.

In interviews and in his writing, Harry Glück strongly resisted the hasty use of the terms "tower" and "high-rise" and was against the "banalization" of his project. And indeed, the characteristic layout of the residential park typology is a stroke of genius. The volume is centrally divided into "above" and "below." The nine or 13 stories of the upper part of the building benefit from their elevated position, the views making them a certain success. The ever-disadvantaged lower floors, however—in the case of Alt-Erlaa anywhere below the twelfth floor—are upgraded by adding terracing.[12] The resulting open space is a positive addition to the individual apartments, and the additional space the terracing creates within the building becomes an area for community (indoor swimming pools, saunas, club rooms) and practicality (all kinds of storage rooms).

The module

Glück extrudes 786 linear meters of housing from his characteristic cross-section, in equal parts of 22 and 26 stories. Although the complex is divided into three rows, seen from an urban planning perspective it is actually modular, with 12 standardized cross-wall construction modules. Each module has a central circulation core, equipped with four elevators, two staircases, and vertical supply

Alt Erlaa, Block A 1976, detail
Equality without uniformity. The variety of apartments can be seen here: The depth of each apartment and/or terrace varies depending on its type. Without exception, all apartments on terraced floors have planters: two steel concrete brackets hold a fiberglass-reinforced plastic planter.

shafts (building services, garbage), serving on two sides four axes with central corridor apartments and one axis along the edge, which—depending on how the module is positioned—is either located centrally or at the front with additional incoming light. The axial dimension is 5.8 meters. On average, there are 250 apartments per stairwell, i.e. 60 apartments per elevator. The vertical access cores have entrances to both the east and west at ground floor level and are connected via the roof and the lower levels.

The (12) modules can be placed seamlessly in a row or be freestanding (individually). Alt-Erlaa is one variation of urban planning options and the arrangement must be understood as being tailored to the site. Blocks A and C are arranged in rows of two by two modules each, thus interrupting the row at the center. The distance between the blocks is joined on the ground floor with tennis halls. Block A has additional facilities, including a medical center and kindergarten in the east, and property management and another kindergarten in the west. Block B is also comprised of a total of four modules, with one module remaining freestanding and a further three modules aligned side by side. The in-between space is a public corridor and the entrance to the school complex.

Carefully metered deviations, shifts, variations—including a simple yet irregular staggering of heights—and individual design measures prevent severity and are to be understood as urban planning freedom. This creates similarity without uniformity, and discipline and resolute efficiency without being monotonous.

Housing

The (12) modules are identical in construction, but not identical in program. Variation is created not through exception, but is instead an integral part of the system. Alt-Erlaa offers the entire range of apartment types commonly used in subsidized housing in Vienna, including sizes (A to E)[13] and various typologies: multi-story apartments facing either one or two directions and maisonettes. Though not subsidized, a few penthouses are also included in the repertoire. The circulation determines the basic arrangement, beyond which the housing is an additive system within a carefully placed grid.

The bulk of the apartments are single-story flats accessed by a central corridor and oriented to the east or west. Towards the edges of the buildings, larger apartments with additional rooms have been created by utilizing the additional light coming in from the front facade. Maisonettes are strategically positioned (vertically): the two lowest floors merged with a staircase to ensure the "heightened feeling of a single-family house."[14] A further "layer" of maisonettes is located in the transitional area between the 12th, 13th, and 14th floors, thus completely eliminating the need for circulation access on the 13th floor.

The organization of the private living spaces logically follows the basic layout of the building. The adjoining rooms (cupboards and storage rooms) and mechanically ventilated bathrooms are situated to the rear, in the less well-lit area of the apartment, while the living area and bedrooms are arranged between the axes depending on the size of the apartment. The living area in combination with the "Glückian" walk-through kitchen deserves special mention. It is spatially independent, with a partition wall separating it from the living room and allowing for a compact and efficient working kitchen, which opens to a dining veranda with enough space for a family dining table and connects from there to the living room.

The facade is freed from its structural obligations and, on the terraced floors, opens completely to the room-sized loggias and terraces. Two planters per axis and side (east and west) provide, without exception, a planting area of around 5 square meters (two planters at 1 meter by approximately 2.6 meters each). The apartments on the upper, non-terraced floors have loggias (a half or full axis, depending on the size of the apartment), and one bay per axis extends the view to the north and south.

Housing as an urban system (Vollwertwohnen)

Housing is urban development, which means that quality does not stop at the front door. The term *Vollwertwohnen* translates literally to "full-value living", well illustrating a holistic claim that includes everything from living comfort (extensive technical equipment, e.g. pneumatic waste transport system, underground parking), to contact with nature (public in parks and privately on terraces with planters), to equipping complexes with amenities and communal facilities.

Glück presented the mathematical model for this in his dissertation.[15] By intelligently adjusting the economically relevant parameters of wing depth (increasing the wing depth from 12 or 15 to 18 meters) and circulation (central corridor instead of multiple units per stairwell), it is possible to achieve a cost advantage of 10–15 percent.[16] In contrast, the costs for the construction of a rooftop swimming pool with sauna and associated ancillary rooms are a moderate two percent of the construction budget.[17]

Already in 1974, the Inzersdorfer Strasse housing estate showed how, in subsidized housing of approximately 200 units plus, a well-sized pool (8 by 24 meters) can be accommodated by both the construction budget and the operating costs. A simple extrapolation results in 15 swimming pools including sauna and ancillary rooms for a complex with 3,000 residential units. Alt-Erlaa has seven rooftop swimming pools, seven indoor pools, and 21 saunas.

Glück was aware of the power of water in combination with the advantageous rooftop positioning and the benefits it created in terms of neighborly contact and distributed the seven rooftop swimming pools equally throughout the three apartment blocks. Six of them have lanes that are 23–25 meters long and all are combined with a sauna facility and relaxation area. The rooftop swimming pool is a place where community can develop naturally. Of course, this is a residential community: like in a club, the leisure facilities within the complex are available to residents only (guests can be invited). Additional sauna facilities, small indoor swimming pools, clubrooms, and numerous sports and covered playgrounds are located in the inner areas of the lower terraced floors, which have no natural lighting. With its additional indoor tennis courts, badminton, outdoor sports and play areas, the residential scheme is also a leisure park. The size of the complex also requires the integration of public infrastructure and makes short distances possibly by having a shopping mall, medical center, church, public library, three kindergartens, and two elementary schools nearby. The public facilities are also the interface to the city.

Reception

Alt-Erlaa is a high-performing residential model that looks good and is well-liked. An exceptionally high level of resident satisfaction was determined shortly after the initial settlement of Block A (1978) and has since been confirmed in subsequent studies (1982/1983, 2004).[18] The high scores for the views, communal facilities, playgrounds, sports, and greenspaces[19] are not surprising, but the resulting effect perhaps more so: The high recreational value of the complex encourages residents to spend more time at home. Some see this as the end of urbanity and the city; for others however, a staycation, or "holiday on balconia" is once again a valid ecological argument.

The complex is certainly in a good state, with renovations and upgrades taking place continuously. Extensive property management and upkeep ensure that the complex is always functioning, tidy, and clean. Only in the shopping center are vacancies sporadically an issue. Thanks to its medium size, it goes beyond just fulfilling daily needs (groceries from Billa and Spar, as well as a bakery and butchery) and a wide range of products are also available (stationery, drugstore, travel agency, textiles, health care), but—a child of the times—has to fight for survival due to nearby larger-scale competition. Issues that affect residents can be read online in the monthly *WAZ*.[20] A surprising suggestion was made in the 11/2019 issue with the proposal that Alt-Erlaa could counteract climate change with a green facade, namely planting *Parthenocissus tricuspidata*, or ivy,[21] from floor to roof on the front elevations. Clearly the inhabitants of Alt-Erlaa do not realize that they already live in a sustainable climate model. The 5,760 private planters on the lower 12 floors amount to a verdant 1.5 hectares of planted space. Biodiversity instead of green as an image would mean however exchanging the dull evergreen for more usable plants. This, however, seems to be one of the easier exercises in the reassessment of the housing model.

In the late 1960s, a sense of discomfort became the catalyst for numerous astonishing visions of a better urban life. Most of them, however, remained on paper and were never realized. One can only marvel that Alt-Erlaa did not meet the same fate. The residential park is in fact a built alternative, utopian not only due to its immense scale. Achieving high quality of living is rare, and contemporary housing design must strive to measure up to the standards set up by Alt-Erlaa.

Notes

1 "New Urban Forms of Housing." Exhibition organized by the Österreichischen Gesellschaft für Architektur. Curated by architects Viktor Hufnagl, Wolfgang and Traude Windbrechtinger. Catalogue: Hermann Czech, Vienna 1967.

2 Inzersdorfer Strasse stepped terrace housing complex: 222 residential units, plan submission 1971, completed 1974, developer: GESIBA. For more, see chapter by San-Hwan Lu, p. 321.

3 Housing Value Study 1975 with accompanying sociological research led by Kurt Freisitzer. Summarized in: Eibl-Eibesfeldt, Irenäus, Hans Hass, Kurt Freisitzer, Ernst Gehmacher, and Harry Glück. *Stadt und Lebensqualität. Neue Konzepte im Wohnbau auf dem Prüfstand der Humanethologie und der Bewohnerurteile, DVA Stuttgart and Österreichischer Bundesverlag GmbH, Vienna 1985.*

4 Glück, Harry. "Die Analyse des Problems. Die Wohnpräferenzen der Privilegierten als Indikator." In Harry Glück, Kurt Freisitzer. *Sozialer Wohnbau. Entstehung. Zustand. Alternativen.* Molden Verlag. 1979.

5 In Austria, the size is often compared to Eisenstadt, the capital of Burgenland.

6 GESIBA (gemeinnützige Siedlungs- und Bauaktiengesellschaft) is a non-profit corporation (the largest shareholder is the City of Vienna with 99.97 % of the shares) committed to upholding the Non-Profit Housing Act as applied to subsidized housing construction. The beginning of stepped terrace housing construction in Vienna by Harry Glück (and partners) coincides with the 1968 assumption of office by Director Dr. Anton Muchna, who was clearly the right man in the right place at the right time.

7 Gemeinnützige Siedlungs- und Bauaktiengesellschaft (ed.), *75 Jahre Bauen für Wien. Die Geschichte der GESIBA*. Vienna, 1996.

8 After the end of the war, the population remained stable at around 1,600,000. In the mid-1970s, it began to shrink, reaching a historic low of an estimated 1,484,885 in 1987, corresponding to the status quo around 1890. In 2019, Vienna had nearly 1,900,000 inhabitants.

9 The original plan included 4,500 residential units. In *Der Aufbau*, Vol. 25, 1971, Nos. 1–3.

10 Interview with Harry Glück. Seiß, Reinhard: Häuser für Menschen. Humaner Wohnbau in Österreich, Müry Salzmann: Salzburg-Vienna-Berlin, 2013.

11 Approximation of statement by Harry Glück in an interview with M. Welzig and G. Steixner in: Welzig, Maria and Gerhard Steixner (eds.): *Die Architektur und ich. Eine Bilanz der österreichischen Architektur seit 1945 vermittelt durch ihre Protagonisten.* Böhlau Verlag: Vienna-Cologne-Weimar, 2003.

12 Only too rarely does architecture use its inherent power to politically express in this way, to bring a social vision into a real shape. Alt-Erlaa becomes the better high-rise, by adding a humanistic component to the typology.

13 Viennese system: A = one-room, B = two-room, etc. A C-type apartment has two bedrooms and a living room or open plan kitchen. The average apartment size without loggia and/or terrace is 75 m² (see *Architektur.aktuell*, Vol. 10 (1976), No. 56).

14 Harry Glück, Kurt Freisitzer. *Sozialer Wohnbau. Entstehung. Zustand. Alternativen.* Molden Verlag. 1979

15 Glück, Harry. "Höherwertige Alternativen im Massenwohnbau durch wirtschaftliche Planungs- und Konstruktionskonzepte." Dissertation, Innsbruck 1982.

16 Ibid.: Glück enumerates a 10–15 % cost savings in a multi-page calculation that identifies the relevant parameters for economic efficiency in residential construction and records these pro rata, relative to the total cost of construction. He puts the costs for facade, circulation, and mechanical access (elevators) into a typological matrix consisting of 2 times 3 cases: Wing depth 12 m, 15 m, and 18 m in the access variants of two units per stairwell, three units per stairwell, and a central corridor.

17 Ibid., p. 76 shows a letter from WIBEBA announcing total construction costs for Glück's Arndtstrasse housing estate of 128 million shillings (1981), with the swimming pool (including sauna and ancillary rooms) reported at 2.5 million shillings, or 1.95 %.

18 The 1978 Living Quality Study is an expansion on the 1975 Living Quality Study and includes the Alt-Erlaa Residential Park. In 1982–1983, the Austrian Ministry of Construction commissioned the IFES and Dr. Fessel+ GfK institutes, under the scientific direction of Kurt Freisitzer, to research more than 20 residential complexes. Residential buildings in Vienna, Linz, Innsbruck, and Munich were included. The comprehensive housing value comparisons serve to review the results of 1975 and 1978 and to extend the scope. The 2004 Vienna Housing Study is a comparative study of Viennese housing estates (e.g. Alt-Erlaa) as well as "green housing forms" (e.g. compact, low-rise buildings) commissioned by MA18. More recent housing studies no longer include Alt-Erlaa as a comparative structure.

19 Stadtentwicklung Wien MA18 (ed.). "Wiener Wohnstudien. Wohnzufriedenheit, Mobilitäts- und Freizeitverhalten." In a series of workshop reports, Vienna, 2004.

20 *WAZ* (*Wohnpark Alterlaa Zeitung*): http://www.porter.at/

21 Grape ivy: robust, low maintenance, inedible.

Bibliography

Silke Fischer, PDF S. 156

Architektur.aktuell. Vol. 3, 1969, No. 12 ("Terrassenwohnbau").

Architektur.aktuell. Vol. 3, 1969, No. 14/15.

Architektur.aktuell. Vol. 10, 1976, No. 56.

Der Aufbau. Vol. 25, 1971, No. 1–3.

transparent. Vol. 7, 1976, No. 2/3.

transparent. Vol. 14, 1983, No. 7/8.

Eibl-Eibesfeldt, Irenäus, Hans Hass, Kurt Freisitzer, Ernst Gehmacher, and Harry Glück. *Stadt und Lebensqualität. Neue Konzepte im Wohnbau auf dem Prüfstand der Humanethnologie und der Bewohnerurteile.* Vienna: Österreichischer Bundesverlag, 1985.

Freisitzer, Kurt, and Harry Glück. *Sozialer Wohnbau. Entstehung. Zustand. Alternativen.* Vienna: Molden Edition, 1979.

GESIBA, Gemeinnützige Siedlungs- und Bauaktiengesellschaft (ed.): *75 Jahre Bauen für Wien. Die Geschichte der GESIBA*. Vienna, 1996.

Glück, Harry. "Höherwertige Alternativen im Massenwohnbau durch wirtschaftliche Planungs- und Konstruktionskonzepte." Dissertation, Technical University Innsbruck, 1982.

Glück, Harry. *Die Möglichkeit einer grünen Stadt.* Vienna: manuscript, 1980s.

Gruber, Stefan, Antje Lehn, Lisa Schmidt-Colinet, and Angelika Schnell. *Big! Bad? Modern: Four Megabuildings in Vienna.* Zurich: Academy of Fine Arts Vienna and Park Books, 2015.

Schöft, Gerhard. "Industrielle Bauverfahren im Hochbau, Der Wohnpark Alt Erlaa–Block C." Diploma thesis at the Institute for Construction Management and Construction Economics at the TU Wien, 1983.

Seiß, Reinhard. *Häuser für Menschen–Humaner Wohnbau in Österreich* (film). Salzburg-Vienna-Berlin: Müry Salzmann, 2013.

Seiß, Reinhard. *Harry Glück Wohnbauten*. Salzburg-Vienna-Berlin: Müry Salzmann, 2014.

Stadtentwicklung Wien MA18 (ed.). "Wiener Wohnstudien. Wohnzufriedenheit, Mobilitäts- und Freizeitverhalten." Series of reports, Vienna, 2004.

Weber, Stefan. "Der Wohnpark Alt-Erlaa im Kontext von sozialem Wohnbau und utopischer Architektur." Master's thesis in art history, University of Vienna, 2014.

Welzig, Maria, and Gerhard Steixner. *Die Architektur und ich—Eine Bilanz der österreichischen Architektur seit 1945 vermittelt durch ihre Protagonisten,* Vienna-Cologne-Weimar: Böhlau, 2003.

B4 WEST B3

BIPA

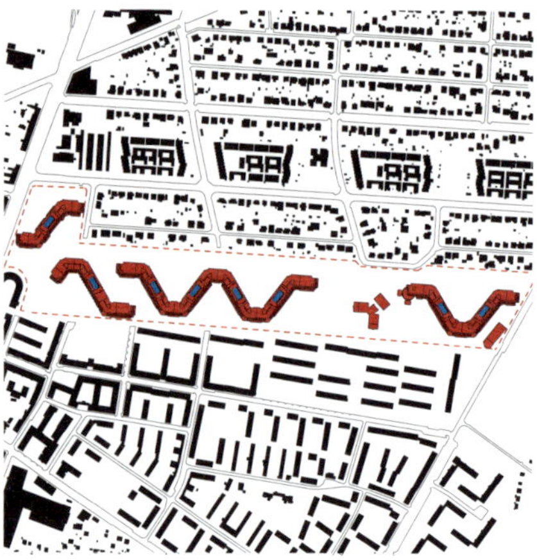

Along the Edge

St. Peter Housing Estate, Graz
Werkgruppe Graz
1965–78

Koseze Housing Estate, Ljubljana
Viktor Pust
1968–81

Heinz-Nittel-Hof, Vienna
Harry Glück & Partner
1973–83

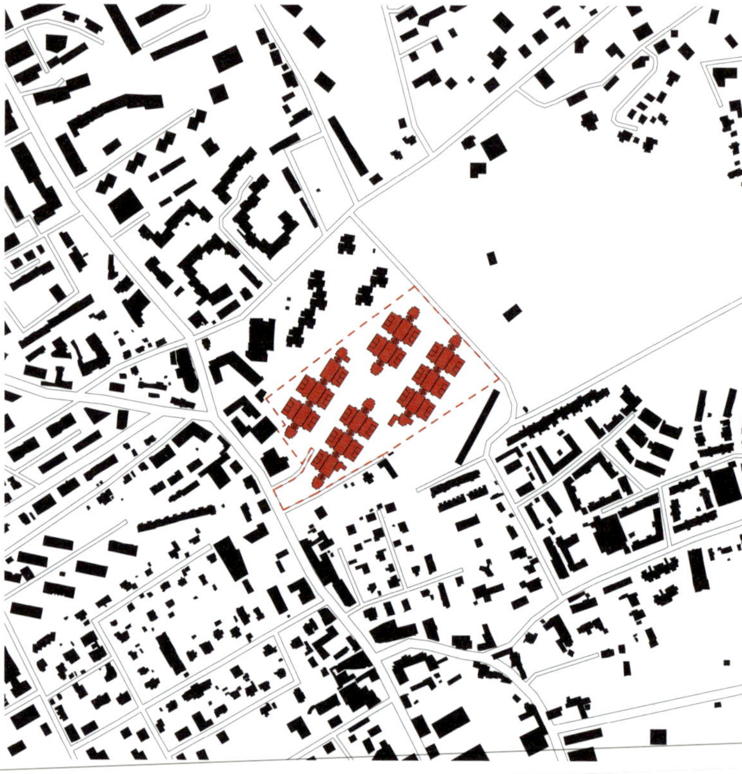

Apartments 531
Floor space index 1.8
Built area ratio 49 %

Site area 45,000 m²
Built area 22,000 m²
Gross floor area 80,000 m²

Collective facilities, infrastructure: Graz-St. Peter Interest Group rooms, medical practices

Graz, Austria
St.-Peter-Hauptstrasse 29–35

Architects
Werkgruppe Graz (Hermann Pichler, Eugen Gross, Friedrich Gross-Rannsbach, Werner Hollomey)

Client
Gemeinnützige Wohnbauvereinigung GmbH

Start of planning 1965
Construction 1972–78

Site plan 1:10,000

St. Peter Housing Estate, Graz

Werkgruppe Graz

1965–78

Individuality and Community—How Architecture Shapes Life in the Graz-St. Peter Stepped Terrace Housing Estate

Karen Beckmann

After a long planning period starting in 1965, St. Peter terraced housing estate in Graz was built from 1972 to 1978 as an ensemble of buildings that can be classified as a large housing complex. In addition to a unifying underground garage, characteristic features of this building typology include: pedestrian access to the complex, a high functional mix, structural density, and a clear design and demarcation from the surroundings. Various studies show that the stepped terraced housing estate has a high level of resident satisfaction[1] to this day. It can be assumed that the persistently high satisfaction of the complex's residents is a sign of distinctive architectural and urban development qualities. But what exactly are these qualities? How can these qualities be assessed today and can the terraced housing estate still be regarded as an exemplary new living concept of our time some forty years after its completion? To answer these questions, it is worth taking a closer look at the history of the development, design, and reception of the housing estate.

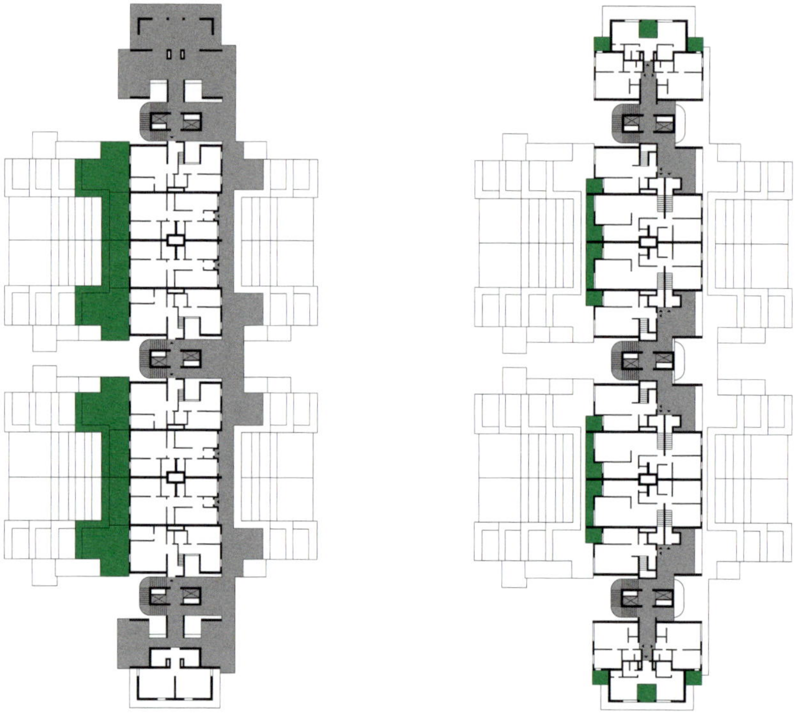

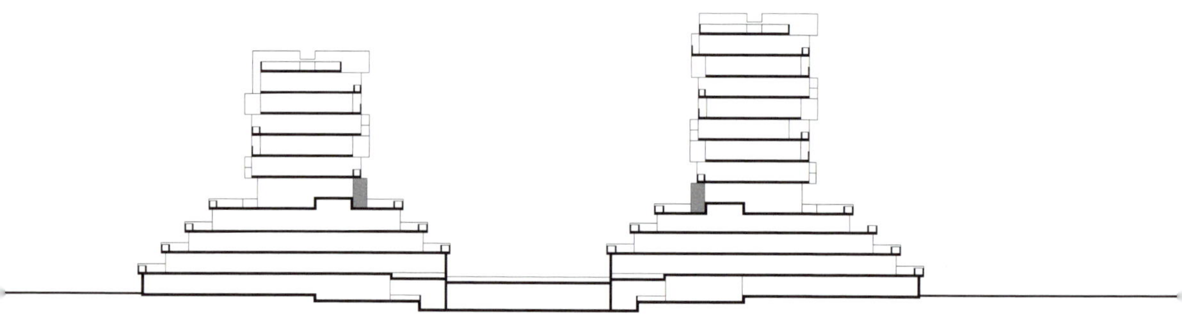

Floor plan 4th and 5th upper floor, Cross-section, 1:1,000

Thinking anew. The development of the stepped terraced housing estate in the context of history.

The building complex was designed by the architects Hermann Pichler, Eugen Gross, Friedrich Gross-Rannsbach, and Werner Hollomey, who joined forces in 1959 under the name Werkgruppe Graz. The international turn away from urban functionalism and the emergence of the architectural theory trend of structuralism that began at that time can be regarded as influencing Werkgruppe Graz's style and its work in the years that followed. For example, in an article titled "How Structuralism Influenced the Graz School of Architecture," Eugen Gross describes the principle of separating primary structures, which functioned as a framework, from secondary structures, which could be exchanged as required. The design is understood as a changeable, expandable, open, and multi-functional system instead of a monofunctional, segregated one.[2] The Graz-St. Peter estate borrows from this structuralist thinking, containing both the approach of having an expandable whole and that of integrating "expansion modules" into the building structure.[3] The concept of the settlement was intended to "encourage actively social living and stimulate public life through communicative facilities."[4]

The international spirit of change, in which ways of thinking such as structuralism were able to establish themselves in architecture and urban planning, could be felt in Austria[5] as well during the estate's planning period in the 1960s. In retrospect, it can be said that the liberal and open, technology and future-minded society of that time, along with a belief in the planning feasibility of large-scale projects, had a decisive influence on the implementation of such projects as the stepped terrace housing estate in Graz.[6]

More than architecture. Design and social life.

A planning process lasting many years preceded the development and realization of the stepped terrace housing estate. In the 1960s, the building site was located on what were the outskirts of Graz. While the surrounding area was characterized by single and multi-family housing, one site remained undeveloped for a considerable

Model in the St. Peter estate's exhibition room

time. It was the site of a former clay pit that had been filled with rubble and waste after the Second World War, making the ground unable to bear any weight.[7] Due to this unstable subsoil, a deep foundation of concrete piles was required, onto which a structural grid of 7 by 7 meters reinforced concrete was laid. This grid formed the basis for the underground car park of the terraced housing estate. Four apartment buildings up to 11 stories high were erected above this. These structures were offset, with terraced bases and apartments on the upper floors. By staggering the buildings in relation to each other and alternating the height of the buildings, not only was optimal lighting and views achieved for all apartments in the development, but pedestrian connections were also created from the surrounding green space into the interior of the development.[8] The car-free open spaces between the buildings above the underground car park were designed as small green spaces that can be accessed, connected, and landscaped in many different ways. A great deal of attention was given to the landscaping of the complex during planning.[9] Not only the open space above the car park was to be designed with planting, but also the facade. The creation of such green spaces was made possible by (roof) terraces and balconies, which were furnished with concrete planters. These were arranged in such a way as to shield the terrace below from view. The design of the approximately 500 apartments comprises one to four-room apartments of different typologies: maisonette, terrace, or studio apartments and spacious outdoor spaces form the overall ensemble. The result is a verdant settlement,

Support structure before mounting the facade elements

in which almost every apartment has its own private outdoor space in the form of a terrace, balcony, or roof terrace.[10] The image of the "stacked single-family house" served as inspiration for the design of the complex.[11]

Above the terraced base of each building is a communicative public level that counterbalances the vertical access of the staircases with a horizontal connection, intended to encourage neighborly relationships through informal contact.[12] The apartments were equipped with individually plannable facade elements, whose appearance still significantly shapes the heterogeneous and varied facade play of the estate today. Future residents of the housing estate were involved in the planning of their apartments and the facade design during the construction phase. A prerequisite for this was the cross wall construction system, which allowed for individualized floor plan designs within the supporting structure. On the communal floor, apartment modules were left open, with neither facades nor interior fittings, so that residents could appropriate the spaces later on.

Today, the functional mix is increasingly achieved by working and living, as well as by the community rooms of the Graz-St. Peter Housing Estate Interest Group. The planning of a center with a hotel, retail spaces, and café was already rejected in the planning phase, when it became clear that the existing infrastructure of the surrounding area was sufficient.[13]

St. Peter housing estate, photos by Walter Kuschel, member of Werkgruppe Graz and resident of the St. Peter estate.

Life in the late 1970s

A celebration in the estate

Space for community. The appropriation of the estate over time.

In a survey of residents conducted between March 2017 and February 2018 as part of the "Stepped Terrace Housing Estate Exploratory Study," the aim of which was to develop modernization guidelines for the next forty years, not only was the high level of resident satisfaction evident, but above all the quality of the inner courtyard areas as communal space was highlighted.[14] Appropriation of and identification with the housing estate are also achieved through the high degree of individuality of the apartments and possibilities for redesign. As a report notes: "The stepped terrace housing estate is not only one of the few utopian projects of this magnitude that has actually been realized, it is also a key project for participation in residential construction."[15] The continuing high level of commitment to the housing estate by the community interest group is also due to the residential structure. The apartments are all freehold apartments and to a large extent also occupied by the owners.

After the "Age of Megastructures" came to an end in the mid-1970s, the estate came under public criticism. Surprisingly, resident satisfaction remained consistently high during this time. Today, a growing interest in 1960s and 1970s brutalist buildings is opening up new perspectives on the building structures of this period.[16] At the same time, it must be stated that the (energetic) refurbishment of the buildings of the 1960s and 1970s is problematic not only for this

estate. In particular, the complexity and scale of the estate makes impending refurbishment measures considerably more difficult.[17] It should also be noted that the appropriation of the public open spaces on the roofs of the buildings has not been sustainably, resulting in these areas now being cordoned off and unused.[18] Nevertheless, for the residents, the positive qualities of the settlement outweigh any shortcomings.

**Urban living.
The qualities of the estate today.**

The qualities of the housing estate, as with many large housing complexes of this era, are founded in the clear form of the complex. The stepped terrace housing estate distinguishes itself clearly from other buildings in the surrounding area while the positioning of the buildings also opens up to the neighborhood. Not only does this create a high degree of resident identification with "our" estate, but also welcomes residents of the surrounding area and visitors to the housing estate. The dense and heterogeneously designed exterior spaces invite residents to linger, while the flowing series of spaces arouses curiosity to discover the complex. Access to the estate is clearly defined by the buildings and is structured by greened, yet clearly defined, edges of the buildings. This creates a variety of spatial experiences, while the clear structure aids orientation. In terms of access, stairwell shafts with only three apartments per floor encourage neighborly interaction. The density found on the ground floor zones is replaced by expanse and views in the upper areas of the building. The different permutations of the apartment floor plans promote a heterogeneous structure and the flexibility enables long-term living. A communal floor on the fourth upper story opens up to a three-dimensional "public" space that makes orientation in the complex easier. A progression from public to private emerges: from public street space, to semi-public outdoor spaces and staircases, and finally to each apartment entrance. This overlapping of public and semi-public and then to private creates individual spaces for appropriation and communication within the community. The walkways within the complex also lead to myriad contacts. Even though the settlement is characterized by a high degree of semi-public space, the spaces between the buildings have an urban feel and are characterized by a complexity and diversity that provides places for encounters, neighborhoods, and places of retreat. Eugen Gross, Werkgruppe Graz architect, highlights two aspects of the stepped terraced housing estate as being decisive for the quality and high level of resident satisfaction: the in-between spaces on different levels, which mediate between community and individual, and the "free center," which he describes as the predominant place of identification.[19]

If these qualities are placed in relation with today's wishes for urban living, many parallels can be found. For some years now, growing urbanization has made topics like densification, the "city of short distances," and functional versatility relevant again. Today, social developments increasingly bring with them the desire for appropriation and identification. A "new urban beginning" can be observed, which requires new ways of living together in cities.[20] Individuality and community, density and open space, and the desire for lived neighborhood, a quality which can arise, for example, through sharing things and spaces and which is supported by proximity to the diverse functions of daily needs, are all key for this kind of development.[21] Residential complexes such as the Graz-St. Peter stepped terrace housing estate offer ideas as to how density, complexity, and diversity, combined with clear building structures, can lead to the creation of identity, appropriation, and community over many years, keeping changing social demands in view and enabling a high level of resident satisfaction.

Notes

1 Cf. N.N. "St. Peter: Schlechtes Image, zufriedene Bewohner." In *Wohnbau,* No. 5, 1981, 3 ff.

2 Gross, Eugen. "Wie beeinflusste der Strukturalismus die Grazer Schule der Architektur?" http://www.gat.st/en/news/wie-beeinflusste-der-strukturalismus-die-grazer-schule-der-architektur? (7 February 2019).

3 Guttmann, Eva, and Gabriele Kaiser. HDA Graz (ed.): *Werkgruppe Graz 1959–1989.* Zurich 2013, 108 f.

4 Messerschmidt, Ingeborg. "'Kontrolliertes Experiment' zur Erprobung geeigneter städtischer Wohnformen." In *Neue Heimat*, Vol. 26, No. 5, 1979, 24.

5 Cf. Eugen Gross in an interview with Eva Guttmann and Gabriele Kaiser in Guttmann, Eva, and Gabriele Kaiser. HDA Graz (ed.): *Werkgruppe Graz 1959–1989.* Zurich 2013, 20.

6 Exemplary for this are also the utopian megastructures of the time, such as Yona Friedmann's Ville Spatial from 1959, Kenzo Tange's Overbuilding of Tokyo Bay from 1961, or Archigram's Plug-in City from 1964.

7 Cf. Guttmann, Eva, and Gabriele Kaiser. HDA Graz (eds.): *Werkgruppe Graz 1959–1989.* Zurich 2013, 107.

8 Cf. ibid., 107.

9 A research project was carried out as part of the prototype building project for the landscaping of the entire complex and especially the higher floors. Cf. Forschungsgesellschaft für Wohnen, Bauen und Planen, Wien: *Demonstrativbauvorhaben Graz-St. Peter.* Part II, Section 2, "Grünraumplanung". Vienna 1980.

10 After initial reticence, the 1979 evaluation of the terraces as a garden replacement was a positive. Cf: Messerschmidt, Ingeborg. "'Kontrolliertes Experiment' zur Erprobung geeigneter städtischer Wohnformen." In *Neue Heimat*, Vol. 26, No. 5, 1979, 28.

11 Cf. Messerschmidt, Ingeborg. "'Kontrolliertes Experiment' zur Erprobung geeigneter städtischer Wohnformen." In *Neue Heimat*, Vol. 26, No. 5, 1979, 24.

12 Cf. ibid., 24.

13 Cf. ibid.

14 Cf. this and the following: http://www.institut-wohnbauforschung.at/wp-content/uploads/2017 /10/Results_20170620.pdf (7 February 2019).

15 http://www.gat.st/news/1965-demonstrativbauvorhaben-terrassenhaussiedlung (31 January 2019).

16 Cf. www.sosbrutalism.org (7 February 2019).

17 Cf. the "SONTE research project" focused on developing a guide for modernization for the next forty years: http://www.institut-wohnbauforschung.at/sonte/#inhalt (7 February 2019).

18 As of 2012.

19 Gross, Eugen. "Wie beeinflusste der Strukturalismus die Grazer Schule der Architektur?" http://www.gat.st/en/news/wie-beeinflusste-der-strukturalismus-die-grazer-schule-der-architektur? (7 February 2019).

20 Cf. Rauterberg, Hanno. *Wir sind die Stadt. Urbanes Leben in der Digitalmoderne*. Berlin 2013, 7.

21 Cf. Zukunftsinstitut GmbH (ed.): *50 Insights. Zukunft des Wohnens.* Frankfurt am Main 2017.

Bibliography

Forschungsgesellschaft für Wohnen, Bauen und Planen, Wien. "Demonstrativbauvorhaben Graz-St. Peter, Teil II, Abschnitt 2, Grünraumplanung." Vienna, 1980.

Jäger-Klein, Carolin. Österreichische Architektur des 19. und 20. Jahrhunderts. Vienna: NWV Verlag, 2010.

Messerschmidt, Ingeborg. "'Kontrolliertes Experiment' zur Erprobung geeigneter städtischer Wohnformen." In *Neue Heimat,* Vol. 26, No. 5, 1979.

N.N.: St. Peter. "Schlechtes Image, zufriedene Bewohner." In *Wohnbau*, No. 5, 1981.

Wagner, Anselm, and Antje Senarclens de Grancy (eds.). *Was bleibt von der "Grazer Schule"? Architektur Utopien seit den 1960ern revisited.* Berlin: Jovis, 2012.

Guttmann, Eva, and Gabriele Kaiser. HDA Graz (eds.). *Werkgruppe Graz 1959–1989.* Zurich: Park Books, 2013.

Beckmann, Karen. *Urbanität durch Dichte? Geschichte und Gegenwart der Großwohnkomplexe der 1970er Jahre.* Bielefeld: Transcript, 2015.

http://www.institut-wohnbauforschung.at/sonte/ ("Sondierungsstudie Terrassenhaussiedlung")

http://www.gat.st/news/1965-demonstrativbauvorhaben-terassenhaussiedlung

http://www.gat.st/en/news/wie-beeinflusste-der-strukturalismus-die-grazer-schule-der-architektur?

ENTRUM

Apartments **ca. 1,548 (34 blocks)**
Floor space index **ca. 1.3**
Built area ratio **32 %**

Site area 119,000 m²
Built area ca. 38,000 m²
Gross floor area ca. 150,000 m²

Collective facilities, infrastructure:
Shops, restaurants, pharmacy, post office, bank, kindergarten

Ljubljana, Slovenia
Ulicar Bratov Ucakar

Architect
Viktor Pust

Clients
SGP Zidar Kočevje, Ingrad Celje

Start of planning 1968 (competition)
Construction 1974–81

Site plan 1:10,000

Koseze Housing Estate, Ljubljana

Viktor Pust

1968–81

The Koseze Settlement in Ljubljana

Nataša Koselj

In the 1960s, public housing became largely available on the post-war market in much of Slovenia, then part of socialist Yugoslavia. Tito's decision to reject rule by the USSR shaped Yugoslavia's political orientation during the Cold War. "Non-aligned" Yugoslavia increasingly opened its borders towards the West, starting to draw away from Communism through a period of self-management, moving towards a market-oriented society, away from a rather totalitarian state via self-managed socialism to democracy. Experimental approaches were at the core of Yugoslavia's move away from its past reliance on agriculture, with craft traditions being replaced by industrial prefabrication. Historic conservation, urban planning, industry, housing, education, healthcare, culture, and tourism made up the majority of architectural tasks in non-aligned Yugoslavia.

In this era, Slovenian urbanism developed, step by step, into its own profession, with Edvard Ravnikar as its pioneer (first in his Dubrovnik paper in 1950 and then together with his students, he introduced the *Stambena zajednica* (communal residence), an experimental neighborhood designed for 5,000 residents and first presented at the *Porodica i domačinstvo* (Home and Family) exhibition in Zagreb in 1958). Marko Šlajmer, a student of Ravnikar's and the first director of the Ljubljana planning office, authored the General Urbanistic Plan (GUP) for Ljubljana together with his team in 1966, dividing

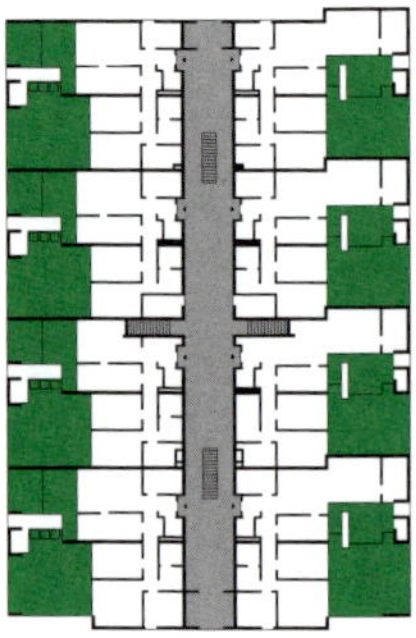

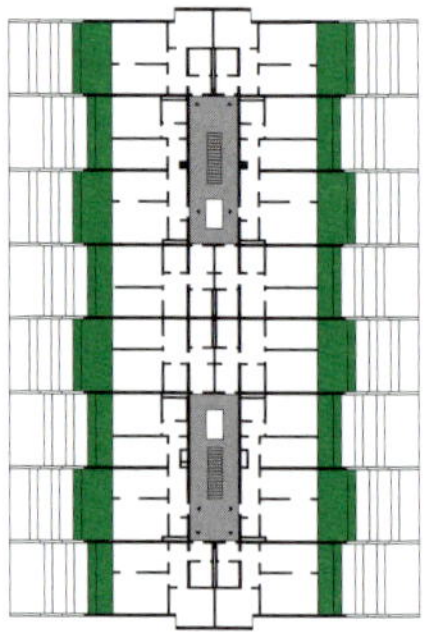

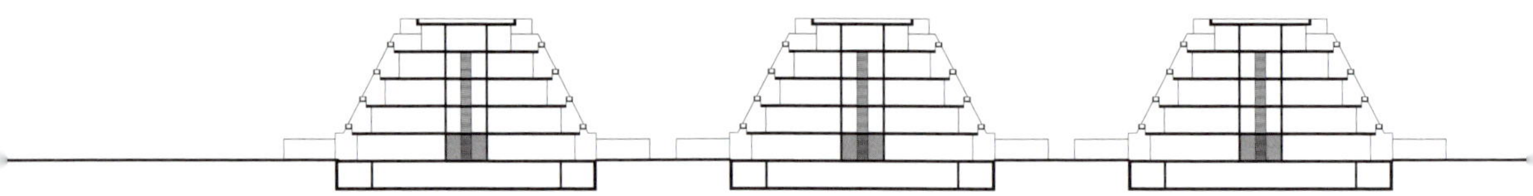

Floor plan 3rd and 4th upper floors, Cross section, 1:1,000

the green areas around the center of Ljubljana into so-called "building islands." This was where the first market-oriented neighborhoods in Slovenia arose in the 1960s, with references to Scandinavian social housing, the ideas of Team X, and Brutalism.

The architect and the concept

The Koseze housing estate represents a positive compromise of high-density, green public housing from the late 1960s that still addresses the social, economic, logistic, and environmental needs of the residents. It attracted significant publicity in local newspapers and public reception was good from the very beginning.

The architect, Viktor Pust (*1937), graduated from the Ljubljana School of Architecture in 1963 under Professor Edo Mihevc. He then went on to study at the École Nationale des Beaux-Arts in Paris in the Candillis-Josić seminar. He was employed by the studio Candilis-Josić-Woods, former Team X members, in 1965. Pust's competition project for the Koseze housing settlement in Ljubljana won in the revolutionary year of 1968, a time in which the city was witnessing student protests similar to those seen in Paris, bringing fresh enthusiasm and appreciation for public housing in Slovenia. The main concept of the project aligned with the ideas of Team X regarding its open structure, mixed functionality, street concept, incorporation of existing natural constants to create dominant views, new green areas, and human scale. High-density, single-family atrium housing was the core of the urban development of the project. Although the competition design was somewhat different from the final realization in terms of planning concept and density, with the first section (east) of the neighborhood being built slightly differently from the second (west), and problems arose (and still remain) regarding leaking, sound protection, and thermal insulation, the public and professional reception of the Koseze housing estate as a whole, was and continues to be, exceptional in Slovenia and abroad.

The original urban concept was designed and advertised as a modern village. Its primary reference was a German project, the 1965 stepped residential complex in Stuttgart by Peter Faller and Hermann Schröder. The location and inspiration of the new Koseze settlement competition project was the existing Koseze village (named after Kosezi, a class of wealthy local nobility), in the northern of Ljubljana

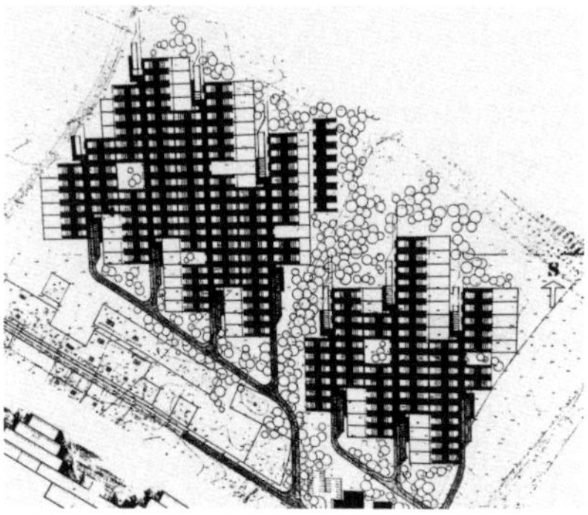

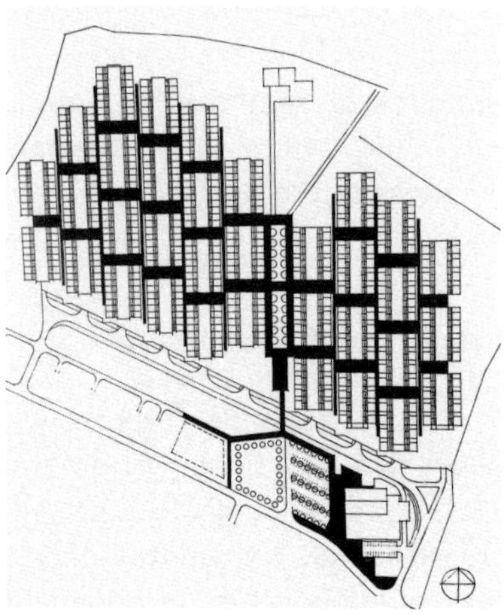

at the time, today inside the Ljubljana Ring and part of Šiška municipality. There is still an active farm in Koseze, where one can buy fresh milk, vegetables, and eggs. At the same time the new structuralist Koseze housing complex was being built, a new Brutalist church was also constructed next to the existing one from 1969 to 1973 by the architect Anton Bitenc. The triangular prismatic blocks of the Koseze settlement are laid out in rows of two, three, and four along a north-south axis, with the main pedestrian avenue looking towards the Karawanks mountain range. In the 1970s these blocks were nicknamed the "hills." Pedestrians and cars are separated by an underground street beneath the block units with garages on either side. A one-way parking corridor beneath the complex also has parking spaces on both sides. A city bus connection is available for the eastern and western parts of the settlement on Vodnikova and Podutiška.

Each block has two main entrances with apartments facing east and west. Each entrance has its own street number and two staircases, one to the upper floors and one to the basement. The apartment floor plans are rational and economic. Ground floor apartments have green atriums surrounded by semi-transparent wooden fences. Apartments on the upper floors have terraces structured by planters made of exposed concrete and iron fencing. The architect's main idea was to give each residence adequate greenery and privacy. The nickname for this part of neighborhood is *"Terasasti bloki."* The size of the apartments ranges from studios to four rooms. Two neighboring apartments each share an installation wall. There is a small cellar for

Koseze housing estate

Competition design 1968,
850 apartments

Site plan of the built design,
1,548 apartments

each apartment and an underground garage. The eastern part of the neighborhood, the first part of which was constructed from 1969 to 1974, has a lower density and sophisticated architectural detailing, more closely following the primary competition concept of the settlement. The western, second part of the neighborhood, built from 1978 to 1981, has a higher density and lower building standard.

Each block shares the entrances, central corridors, and staircases, a room for drying laundry on the top floor, and garbage area in the basement along the underground road. The four blocks have about twenty ground-floor units that face the settlement's central pedestrian zone and have mixed uses such as shops, bars, kindergarten, pharmacy, post office, bank, etc. A kindergarten and a primary school are located in the northern part of the neighborhood. An open market selling fresh local fruit and vegetables, a fitness center with an open-air sports stadium, and a well-known recreation area around Koseze Pond (with excellent cross-country skiing opportunities during the winter) are all nearby. Some residents of the Koseze settlement rent small vegetable garden plots in the field near Koseze Pond. There is also a police station and fire station in the vicinity. The settlement is located four kilometers from Ljubljana's city center and five kilometers from Toško Čelo (part of the Polhov Gradec Dolomites).

The project was originally advertised as a higher standard neighborhood, and the social structure of the residents was, and still is, middle class, including a few popular actors, singers, athletes, academics, and retired ex-Yugoslav army officers. Even though many of

the original residents are no longer there, the Koseze housing estate enjoys a very good reputation in Slovenia in terms of living standard, greenspaces, infrastructure, and social structure. It is also one of the most popular neighborhoods in Ljubljana for the younger generation, with many architects and architecture students living there.

In terms of greenspace and density, the Koseze housing complex lies somewhere between the single-story green Murgle settlement by Marta and France Ivanšek and the tall, dense development of the Ruski Car settlement by Vladimir Braco Mušič, Marjan Bežan, and Nives Starc, both built in Ljubljana in the 1960s. The largest public greenspace is an artificial hill on the northern part of the pedestrian avenue, which offers a good sledding surface in the winter and is located visually in front of the Karawanks. Several different kinds of trees are planted throughout the neighborhood. Along the western side of Koseze, one finds the POT walk, which is part of a more than 30-kilometer-long memorial pathway ring around Ljubljana, marking where barbed wire was put up by Italian fascists during the Second World War. Koseze Pond, a five-minute walk from the settlement, is part of the remains of a former brick factory, the site where clay was once excavated, and is now part of the Gustav Tönnies Park, named after the Swedish man who established the factory in Koseze in the second half of the nineteenth century. While walking the area, it is still possible to see wild deer, hare, or heron moving freely in their natural habitat.

Still from the film *Učna leta izumitelja polža* (*Apprenticeship of the Inventor Polz*) from 1982, filmed in the Koseze estate.

The terrace as living space, drawing by Viktor Pust

Koseze today

Today, approximately 3,000 residents live in the Koseze housing complex. The facades of the Koseze blocks have been refurbished in recent years to meet new EU energy efficiency laws, an issue which is, along with converting open terraces into covered winter gardens, one of the main problems for the settlement, and for Slovenian housing policy overall. As there are no regulations for new facades, the results are bright, acrylic colors that radiate from the sides of the blocks, giving a strongly uneven appearance to the complex.

A functional dilemma is the lack of parking. The social structure of the inhabitants has remained more or less the same, and today more and more young intellectuals and families are coming to live in Koseze. A number of workshops and tours have recently been organized in the community to improve local interaction, including a gardening workshop for adults, and various workshops for children and families. There is an active Koseze Tourist Society and Koseze Elderly Society. The settlement is also often included in the post-war Ljubljana architecture and planning tours that are arranged for specialists. In the 1980s, the teen movie *Učna leta izumitelja polža* (*Apprenticeship of the Inventor Polz*) was filmed inside one of the apartments and in the area outside, making the complex even more recognized and popular.

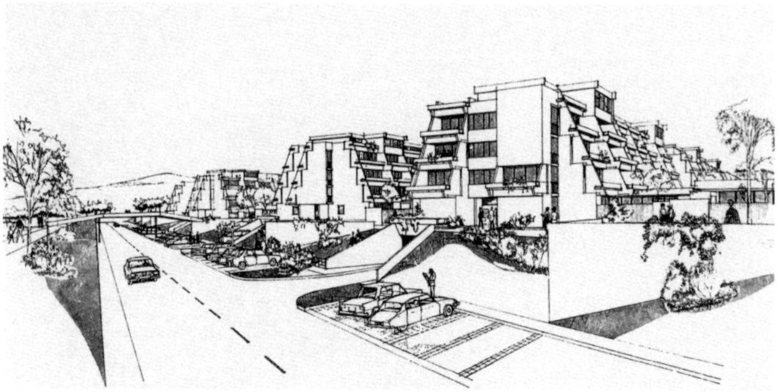

The settlement is regarded more as public housing for the middle class then as social housing for the working class, although the resident population has historically been, and still is, mixed. Thanks to a plentitude of greenspaces with playgrounds, rationally planned apartments, human scale, very good infrastructure, welcoming social structure (there is practically no social segregation), the strategic location within Ljubljana Ring (near Rožnik Hill, Ljubljana Zoo, Koseze Pond, the city center, and the Ljubljana Ring, with the shortest distance from Ljubljana city to Brnik Airport being through the Northern Ring tunnel), the housing complex remains a popular choice compared to the newly built high-density housing in Ljubljana in particular and Slovenia as a whole, mostly due to the high level of greenspace inside and near the neighborhood, good logistics, and strategic position within the Ljubljana Ring.

Diagram of a lower access road with entrances to the underground car parks beneath the ten rows

The Koseze housing estate in the early 1980s, photo by well-known Slovenian cameraman Janez Kališnik

Conclusion

The Koseze housing complex was built around the same time as Edvard Ravnikar's renowned Ferantov Vrt Complex and the Cankar Centre on Republic Square, which together brought Structuralism and Brutalism to the very heart of Ljubljana in the 1960s and 1970s, and were built at the same time as the Alexandra Road Estate by Neave Brown in London. Together with the Murgle and Ruski Car settlements, Koseze is a symbol of the new state policy that was opening the borders of Slovenia to the West step by step, with references to the Scandinavian model of social housing (Murgle settlement) from the 1950s, and tying in a decade later to the ideas of Brutalism and Structuralism in high-density housing (Ferantov Vrt Complex, Ruski Car settlement, Koseze housing complex). The public housing projects mentioned here were built as key models of socially conscious, green, high-density public housing in Slovenia, values for which they continue to stand today.

Bibliography

Bernik, Stane. *Slovenska arhitektura dvajsetega stoletja* (Slovenian Architecture of the Twentieth Century). Ljubljana: Mestna galerija, 2004.

Ivanšek, France. *Enodružinska hiša* (Single family house). Ljubljana: Ambient 1988.

Koselj, Nataša. *Docomomo Slovenia_100.* Ljubljana: AB, Ustanova Ivanšek, 2010.

Mihelič, Breda. *Urbanistični razvoj Ljubljane* (Urban Development of Ljubljana). Ljubljana: Partizanska knjiga, 1983.

Pust, Viktor. *Kako so nastajala moja naselja* (How My Settlements Were Formed). Ajax Studio and Faculty of Architecture, Ljubljana, 2012.

NLB
NLB

CARTE D'OR

Apartments 1,422
Floor space index ca. 1.4
Built area ratio 23 %

Site area 150,000 m²
Built area ca. 34,500 m²
Gross floor area ca. 204,000 m²

Collective facilities
8 rooftop swimming pools, 15 saunas, 42 hobby rooms, 29 playrooms

Infrastructure
2 kindergartens, a school, youth club, church, 2 supermarkets, 6 ball fields, 1,200 parking spaces beneath the building, 62 stairwells of which 17 have elevators

Vienna, Austria
Brünner Strasse 140, Ruthnergasse 89

Architects
Harry Glück & Partner

Client
City of Vienna

Developer
GESIBA — Gemeinnützige Siedlungs- und Bauaktiengesellschaft

Construction
Fertigteilbau Wien

Start of planning 1973
Construction 1979–83

Site plan 1:10,000

Heinz-Nittel-Hof, Vienna

Harry Glück & Partner

1973–83

A Prototype for Viennese Municipal Housing

Gerhard Steixner

These Glück buildings only put nonsense into people's heads.

Housing Councilor Hubert Pfoch[1]

"It is the most revolutionary housing project of the City of Vienna since the construction of the Karl-Marx-Hof," proclaimed the *Profil* in 1976.[2] The news magazine was referring to Marco Polo Terraces, as the project was called at the time, with swimming pools on the roof, high-quality terrace apartments and infrastructure for leisure activities, education, health, and culture embedded in car-free, spacious, park-like greenspaces for recreation, games, and sports.

For the first time, a municipal building was to be constructed by a private housing company. Vienna Municipal Department 24 (MA24), responsible for the management of the municipal housing project, was being increasingly criticized for its poor performance in terms of housing quality, construction, and operating costs. It was, above all, Harry Glück's buildings for private co-operatives that made the difference so starkly visible. One of the busiest architects in Austria at the time, his Vienna-based firm Harry Glück & Partner (Harry Glück, Werner Höfer, Rudolf Neyer, Tadeusz Spychala, and Karl Pethö) had realized almost forty residential complexes by 1976, employing at times around a hundred people. Six of these complexes were completed in that year, including Block A of the Alt-Erlaa Residential Park

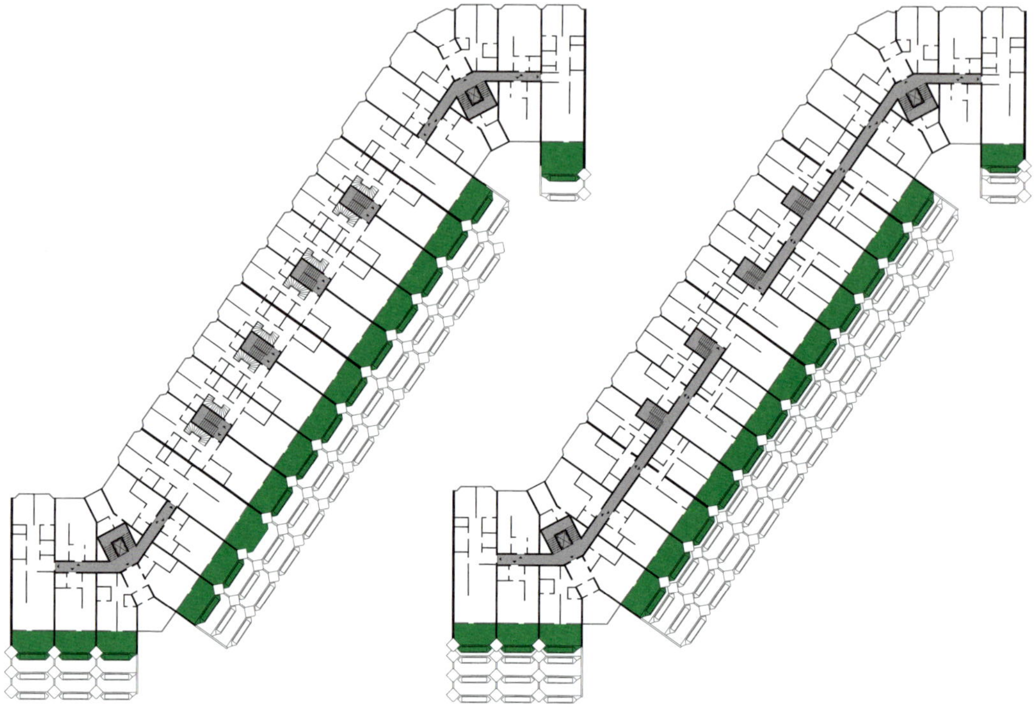

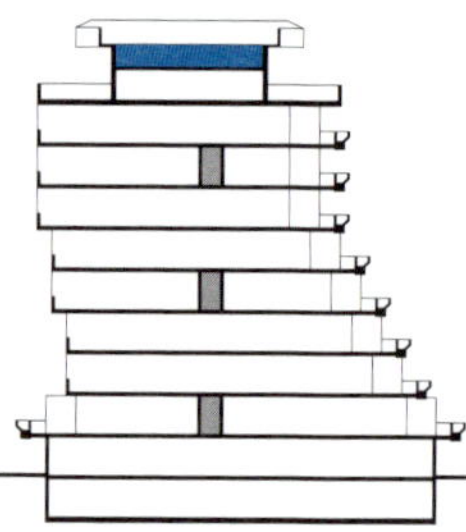

Floor plan 3rd and 4th upper floors, Cross-section, 1:1,000

with 1,000 apartments. 10 residential complexes were under construction, including Block B in Alt-Erlaa with another 1,000 residential units. Marco Polo Terraces, with over 1,400 apartments, was in the planning stage along with many others.

So Glück knew exactly what he was talking about when he personally vouched for adherence to the construction schedule and guaranteed the budget. However, his demand that the City of Vienna permanently transfer MA24's responsibilities to GESIBA, a non-profit housing association likewise owned by the City of Vienna, acquired him powerful opponents in the magistrate's office. For example, the city's building director and "various declared comrades" rejected the project on the grounds that it could cause unrest among the Viennese population and that it could put the party at a disadvantage. The residents of traditional municipal apartments might be outraged if they were not also given swimming pools.

Remarking that the Karl-Marx-Hof had also been revolutionary for its time, Mayor of Vienna Leopold Gratz elegantly took the wind out of the sails of the critics. After months of ideological wrangling, the project was approved by the city council. It was to be a prototype for future Viennese municipal housing.

Red Vienna's 1920s and 1930s buildings owe their international reputation to the radical social program underlying them. In 1924, the mayor of the City of Vienna, Karl Seitz, wrote in the newspaper *Arbeiter Zeitung*: "(...) from the time of the seventies and eighties, we still remember the small houses with their large courtyards, which provided a place of recreation for the youth. Then came the building period of bleak rental barracks, where every last patch of land was made usable. That was a time in which the Viennese were struggling under capitalism, with anyone in a rental apartment dreading the terrible payment deadline. Now, we are entering a new building period, no longer building small, single houses with tiny courtyards, but instead large complexes with communal apartments in which people live together, but where everyone can also live separated according to their individuality. General needs for recreation and activity are fulfilled by beautiful shared parks which benefit everyone."[3]

By more than halving building density compared to the *Gründerzeit* era, this political and humanitarian program was successfully implemented on a large scale within 10 years. The Karl-Marx-Hof was *the* prototype for the buildings of Red Vienna and is known above all

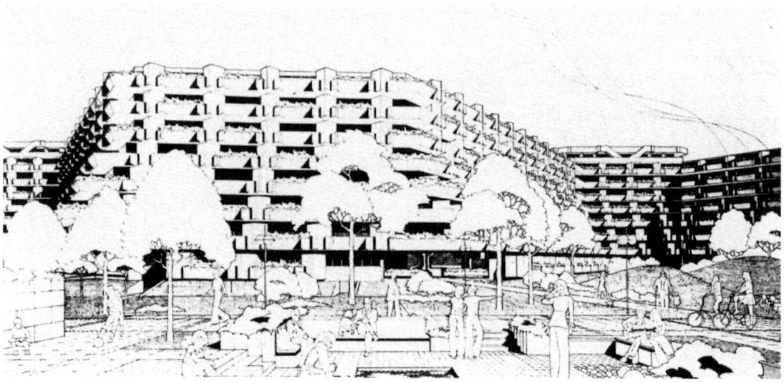

for its striking and dramatic appearance, its name, and its scale. This is "speaking architecture," which tells a tale of division, of us and of others, of inside and outside. Its appearance is defensive and impedes the view of the true qualities of this large housing estate, namely the orientation of all apartments towards large, quiet, pedestrian greenspaces with light, air, and sun and community facilities for education, culture, and leisure.

This is where Marco Polo Terraces come into play again, built 50 years later, with a similar program and number of apartments, but with a leap in quality, in terms of the apartments, open spaces, and the services offered by the communal facilities. Whereas balconies and loggias were once the order of the day, terraces with gardens are now situated in front of the living areas. Whereas there were once wading pools in the courtyard for children, there are now swimming pools and sundecks for everyone on the roof. The housing complex is like a residential machine, a pure, highly efficient structure. It does not try to tell a story; rather it is what it is and what the residents make of it. A 50-year leap had been accomplished.

Sketch of Heinz-Nittel-Hof

Karl-Marx-Hof, Vienna 1927–1930
Architect Karl Ehn
Photo 2019

On the periphery

The building site is located in Floridsdorf, a former working-class district in the suburbs on the northern outskirts of Vienna. The sun-facing strip is approximately one kilometer long, 130 to 150 meters wide, and is bordered to the west by Brünner Strasse, an important arterial road to the north and main access to the city, and to the east by Ruthnergasse. A former field on the northeastern edge, adjacent to Marco Polo Square, gives the project its name. Moving away from the city, there is a huge area of single-family houses which, however, already has dense structures. Glück & Partner were commissioned by GESIBA in 1979, i.e. at the same time the construction of Marco Polo Terraces began, to build a low-rise housing estate of 188 houses on Carabelligasse using the prefabricated construction method.

Towards the city center to the south there is a settlement area with very simple, closely spaced, slightly offset, mostly south-facing, rows of municipal buildings from the 1960s. Here, at this seam of ownership and rent, a prototypical housing estate was to be built, combining the advantages of a detached house with garden, garage, pool, and hobby room with those of communal housing with affordable rents, community, and high density.

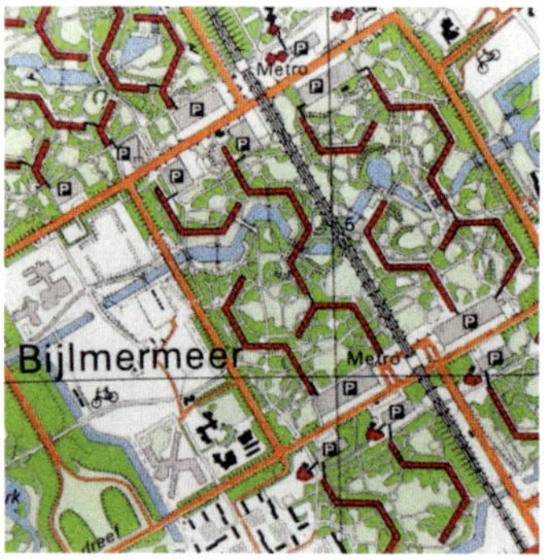

Site plan of the Bijlmermeer urban expansion area, Amsterdam, NL
Architect Siegfried Nassuth,
as of 1960

Heinz-Nittel-Hof, aerial photo taken around 1981–1982

Carabelligasse low-rise estate,
Harry Glück & Partner, Vienna 1979
Photo 2014

Form and scale

The large terraced form is unique and can be recognized from an airplane. The scale and form are comparable with those of other large complexes, like Bijlmermeer in Amsterdam or Le Mirail in Toulouse. It is a modular, four-part, low-lying shape that opens up with terraces from west to east for over a kilometer, meandering to the south. In the plan, its form evokes associations with a wave or a dissected snake. A technician might think of a sheet piling profile. Here, form follows function. Criteria for the development of this particular form were: a low percentage of impervious surfaces, no surface traffic, southern orientation for as many living spaces as possible, connected open greenspaces, solving the corner problem, and cost efficiency. Here, the urban form is the result of an optimization process. Beyond Camillo Sitte or Jane Jacobs, from street or facade, Glück & Partner developed an open structure for over 4,000 residents that is ecological, social, and economical in equal measure.

Only a few elements shape the external appearance of the buildings. On the north side, there are identical, generous, bay-like ribbon windows of cross wall width, and cantilevered projections of the building volumes over several stories. To the south are terraces and loggias, each equipped with a horizontal and a vertical element—a planter and a garden box, the foundation for appropriation. This is where residents are usually out and about, busy at work. Whether tending to flowering shrubs, red currants, roses, hemp, or conifers;

with an awning or a parasol, they transform the abstract, coolly calculated forms into a living structure that is constantly fluctuating through use, weather, and the changing seasons.

Marco-Polo Promenade connects Brünner Strasse with Ruthnergasse like a boulevard and is the main pedestrian connection and interface between two districts. A well frequented, connecting, and communicative space emerges along the hanging gardens, wide green coves, and the simple 1960s municipal buildings. Skraupstrasse runs north-south, crossing the building site approximately in the middle. It once provided a car-friendly connection between the community buildings and the single-family home neighborhood, but was reallocated as a footpath that penetrates the central building axially.

To the north are five underground car park ramps, accessed via two cul-de-sacs and Marco-Polo-Platz, leading to the parking decks beneath the buildings and making it possible to keep the entire surface area free of traffic. The vegetation of the carefully planned and well-maintained greenspaces, together with the greenery of the terraces, noticeably influences the microclimate. These outdoor spaces are planted with trees like in a park, reserved for sports and ball games in the north and the south, and carefully landscaped to encourage contemplation and the observation of nature.

Modules

The building structure consists of eight modules, identical in their fundamental characteristics, that are either arranged in different combinations or freestanding. These are each extended by head modules terraced to the east or west. Each basic module consists of 18 cross walls and a five-story base terraced to the south topped by a three-story extension with cross-wall-wide loggias. Above this is a 25-meter-long swimming pool on the roof with sundecks and sauna as well as around 180 apartments, accessed by two main stairwells with elevators and four secondary staircases. Hobby areas, playrooms, special use rooms, and barrier-free apartments are located on the ground floor. Below this there are storage rooms and approximately 150 parking spots on two levels, only one of which is sunk below the height of the natural terrain. The northern sides have additional external insulation, clad in light beige, vertically mounted, trapezoidal sheet metal panels, while the southern sides are fully glazed. Although Glück would have preferred to use a composite construction method, a concrete slab system was used at the instigation of the City of Vienna.

Pathways and apartments

An essential element of the economic efficiency of many of Glück's complexes is the compactness of the structures, something achieved by high block depths, resulting in a very favorable surface to volume ratio. This is not only relevant for construction and maintenance costs, but also considerably improves the energy performance of the buildings. The central corridor access is highly efficient for those buildings with purely east or west-oriented apartments. In Alt-Erlaa, up to 12 residential units are accessed via a single stairwell. In the case of the Heinz-Nittel-Hof, which essentially has a north-south orientation, the situation is somewhat more complicated. A central corridor on each floor would generate an undesirably high number of north-facing apartments, while a block of flats with interlocking apartments would result in a large number of elevators and reduced range of apartment types. The search was on for an access arrangement as efficient as that of Alt-Erlaa, but allowing for a primarily south orientation of all living spaces. A solution had to be found that combined the advantages of both systems. The answer was based on the notion that it was reasonable to have residents walk up or down *one* story to reach their apartment. This idea made it possible to combine the two systems synergetically. About one third of the apartments are barrier-free. There is a continuous central corridor on the ground floor and only on every third floor above that. On the third and sixth floors, the corridor provides access to two side staircases, via which one can access the apartments inserted one floor higher or lower.

The apartments that are accessed directly from the central corridor either face one side or, at the ends of the corridor, are inserted through to face both sides. In order to increase the proportion of south-facing living spaces and to have a more varied range of apartments available, maisonette apartments with five rooms were designed, with double-story units extending downwards or upwards at the northern end of the central corridor. This made it possible to have a high number of those living spaces with terraces and loggias to face south. This very elaborate, highly efficient system had already been tested in several variants in smaller complexes with about 200 residential units each. According to Glück, 80 percent of the floor space is usable and an average of 83 apartments are served by a single elevator. The money saved through this immense efficiency was used for generous communal facilities, such as rooftop swimming pools, sundecks, saunas, play and hobby rooms, and for landscape design.

Most of the apartments traverse the block, either as single-story flats or, to a lesser extent, as maisonettes. With a block depth of 18 meters and a cross wall axis measuring 5.8 meters, this created relatively generous living spaces of up to 100 square meters for a three-room apartment, a size we can only dream of today. A large living room opens up across the full width of the cross wall grid to the terrace and then the garden and park. The kitchen has a direct entrance from the foyer, but is only partially separated from the living room by a wall panel. Open to the front, it makes space for a dining table near the deck, which is equipped with a planter and a diagonally placed garden box that provides separation between the terraces.

The foyer, sanitary rooms, and lots of storage space with walk-in closets are located in the middle area, which has no natural light. The closets can be equipped with fixtures for hanging and laying to fulfill the function of a wardrobe. The fact that there is a great need for storage space that is not satisfied by the housing sector is shown by the growth of companies that offer such storage space externally. The bedrooms have bay-like ribbon windows facing northeast or northwest so as to also have sunlight.

Reception

The most persistent critic of Glück's concept for social housing protested verbosely in the feature pages of *Die Presse's* weekend edition of 7/8 August 1982, (i.e. even before residents had finished moving in), about the unconditional economic calculation and overriding significance of technology, which was threatening and frightening for him.[4] He notes the complete absence of "architecture" and, with the exception of the apartment floor plans, was utterly scathing of the Heinz-Nittel-Hof, saying that it was "no solution for mass housing." With his polemical and unobjective style, he had clearly set out to discredit the building. Six weeks later, Housing Councilor Johann Hatzl, in office since 1979, and who had inherited his predecessor's project, declared that this building "cannot be a prototype for future municipal housing."[5] Construction had gone considerably over budget due to the prefabricated concrete slab construction method desired by the client and thus also exceeded maximum funding limits.

The Heinz-Nittel-Hof (once again) attracted the attention of the public eye due to its residents' voting behavior in the 2017 election for the Austrian President. 60 percent of the voters in the run-off vote chose the right-wing populist candidate, and in the 2019 parliamentary elections they received over forty percent of the votes from the residents in the electoral district. A possible explanation for this could be the implementation of an EU directive in 2006 opening the municipal building to foreigners, which caused a shift in the resident demographic of the Heinz-Nittel-Hof. This could have been perceived by the established inhabitants as an insult, have caused a feeling of being downgraded, or even the fear of being driven out of paradise. This is truly a dilemma for the Social Democrats, especially as third-country nationals do not have the right to vote.

Despite all this, with the Heinz-Nittel-Hof, Harry Glück created a prototype for the Green City. The meaningful project set new standards in residential construction for large numbers of people and created a benchmark for future public housing.

Notes

1 *Profil, 7 September 1976.*

2 Ibid.

3 Posch, Wilfried. *Die Wiener Gartenstadbewegung*, Edition Tusch 1981, 75.

4 Steiner, Dietmar. "Häuser aus dem Supermarkt." In *Die Presse*, 7/8 August 1982, V.

5 *Kurier*, 29 September 1982.

Bibliography

Freisitzer, Kurt, and Harry Glück. *Sozialer Wohnbau. Entstehung. Zustand. Alternativen*. Vienna: Molden Edition, 1979.

Glück, Harry. "Die Möglichkeit einer grünen Stadt." Unpublished manuscript, 1980.

Glück, Harry. "Höherwertige Alternativen im Massenwohnbau durch wirtschaftliche Planungs- und Konstruktionskonzepte." Dissertation, Innsbruck 1982.Glück, Harry. "Die Möglichkeit einer grünen Stadt." Unpublished manuscript, 1980. Freisitzer, Kurt, and Harry Glück. *Sozialer Wohnbau. Entstehung. Zustand. Alternativen*. Vienna: Molden Edition, 1979.

Machart, Peter. *Wohnbau in Wien*. Vienna: Compress Verlag, 1984, 58.

Seiss, Reinhard. *Harry Glück Wohnbauten*. Salzburg, Vienna: Müry Salzmann, 2014, 188.

Machart, Peter. *Wohnbau in Wien*. Vienna: Compress Verlag, 1984, 58.

Welzig, Maria, and Gerhard Steixner. *Die Architektur und ich – Eine Bilanz der österreichischen Architektur seit 1945 vermittelt durch ihre Protagonisten*. Vienna, Cologne, Weimar: Böhlau Verlag, 2003, 98–116.

nc+

Shaped by Traffic
Arterial road, railway, highway

Hadikgasse Residential Complex, Vienna
Harry Glück & Partner
1970–76

Alexandra Road Estate, London
Neave Brown
1967–79

Autobahnüberbauung Schlangenbader Strasse, Berlin
Georg Heinrichs, Gerhard Krebs, Klaus Krebs
1971–80

Apartments 210
Floor space index ca. 3.2
Built area ratio 54 %

Site area 8,400 m²
Built area 4,500 m²
Gross floor area ca. 26,500 m²

Collective facilities, infrastructure:
Rooftop swimming pool, 2 saunas, gymnastics room, playrooms, workshop, underground garage with 183 parking spaces, petrol station with shop under the Hadikgasse structure, supermarket in the Penzinger Strasse structure, direct subway connection via Hadiksteg

Vienna, Austria
Hadikgasse 128–134,
Penzinger Strasse 129–133

Architects
Harry Glück & Partner,
Alfred Nürnberger, Vienna

Client, developer
GESIBA — Gemeinnützige Siedlungs- und Bauaktiengesellschaft

Construction
PORR

Start of planning 1970
Construction 1975–76

Site plan 1:10,000

Hadikgasse Residential Complex, Vienna

Harry Glück & Partner

1970–76

A Bigger Splash

Gerhard Steixner

In 1976, entering Vienna from the west, I glimpsed a ray of hope on the banks of the Wien River in what was at the time a very grey city. White modernity, like a vacation on the Adriatic. Easy living. A break in the orderly urban structure.

The Hadikgasse residential complex, planned between 1970 and 1972 and completed in 1976, is a remarkable example in a series of experimental, high-quality residential complexes, all of them social housing from the offices of Harry Glück & Partner, one of the busiest architectural firms in Austria at the time. By the late 1990s, largely commissioned by GESIBA, the firm had designed some 14,000 residential units, 6,000 of which were in stepped terraced housing complexes. The structures used cross wall construction and efficient layouts to keep access areas and elevators to a minimum, thereby saving funds that could be reinvested in equipping the apartments with loggias, terraces, and concrete planters, as well as in communal facilities such as rooftop swimming pools and sundecks, and in shared greenspaces.

In the 1970s, Harry Glück & Partner completed an average of five housing estates per year, and no two were alike. This was only possible due to the firm's clear program and motivated staff of up to a hundred employees, partners, and civil engineers and by establishing a planning collective. The employees of the developer and client

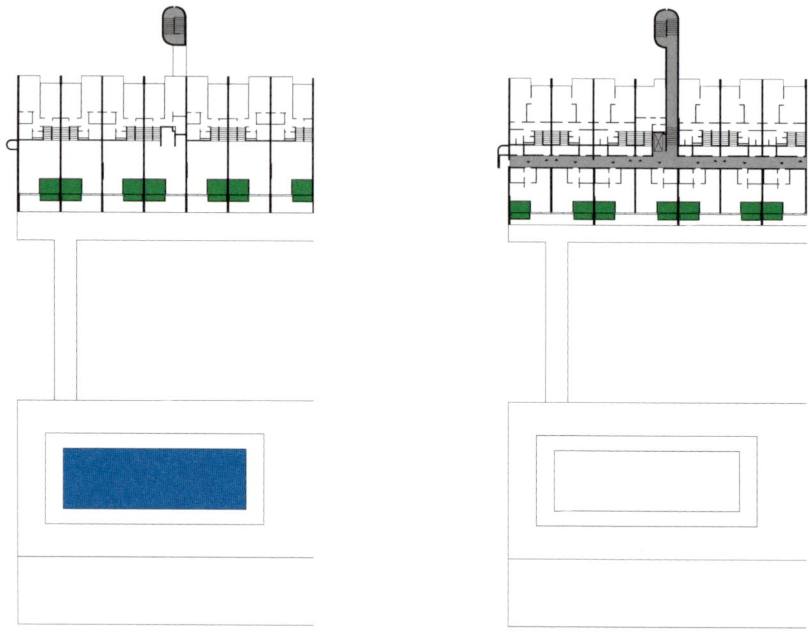

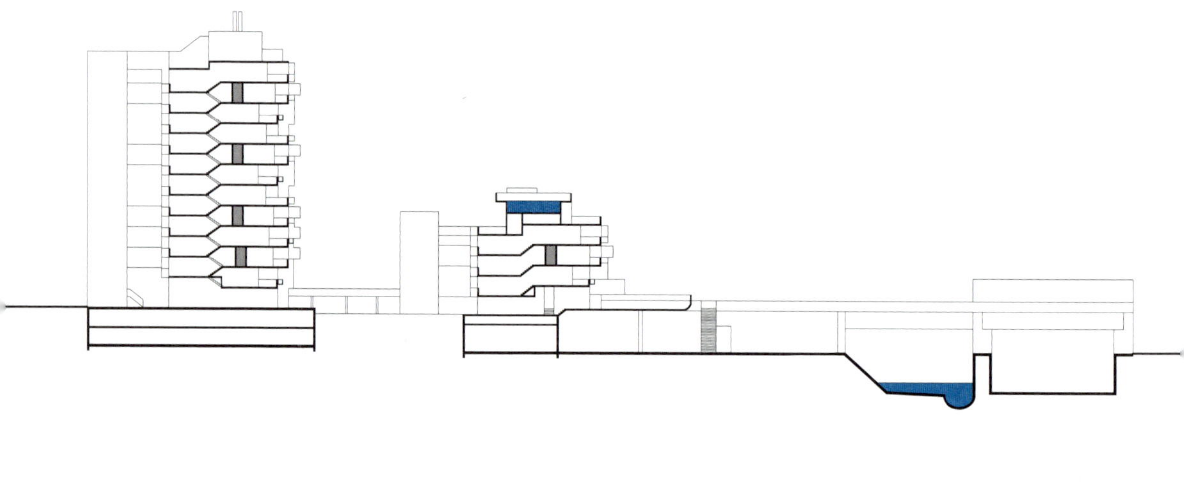

Floor plan 6th and 7th upper floors, Cross-section, 1:1,000

who worked on Glück's buildings were also experienced teams versed in the realization of the often complex, mostly prototypical projects. They took on the technical oversight, business management, and site supervision of the subsidized housing projects, meeting or coming in below the budget. It was often also necessary to collaborate with municipal authorities, for example, to close a road or rezone a street into a pedestrian area. It was even possible that an underground station be relocated or entire building volumes be reallocated, as was the case with the Hadikgasse housing estate.

The building site is located in the west of Vienna, in Penzing, Vienna's 14th district, at the foot of the Wiental (Vienna valley), on the border to the Hietzing district. The site is surrounded on three sides by streets. The one to the south is Hadikgasse, a busy arterial road running parallel to the Wien River, leading to the west. Situated on the river, this was considered a privileged location up into the 1950s, well connected with an urban railway station on the right bank and with good views into the distance. However, this became a liability as traffic steadily increased over the years. The site is on a level southern slope between Hadikgasse and Penzinger Strasse, which is four meters higher in the north, and bordered to the east by Onno-Klopp-Gasse. To the west, a four-story *Gründerzeit*-era perimeter block development encloses a generous greenspace in a U-shape, which once extended into the neighboring tree-covered area of the old Penzinger Baths. By moving the baths, an 8,400-square-meter building site was created for the residential complex, requiring changes to zoning and the land-use plan. It is normal for such changes to be based on local parameters, which in this case were a construction closed off along the street, a block depth of 15 meters, and building heights of up to 18 meters. In any case, it is not suitable as a prototype for anything one could call a standard situation often found in cities. None of these specifications came to fruition. The prerequisite, however, was that the volume resulting from the above rules not be exceeded by that of an alternative structure.

The platform

The project is a strictly orthogonal, a classic block and slab floating on a platform. The front is low, the rear almost three times as high, with little reference to the surrounding building fabric. A foreign body, so to speak, yet well incorporated, open, bright, and friendly. Urban. The result of an optimization process.

It was conceived as an 86-square-meter platform, which extends southwards towards Penzinger Strasse to the front of the building line on Hadikgasse, where it ends. The last 17 meters are slightly raised, with a high, curved sound insulation barrier five meters above the level of Hadikgasse. Under this platform, space was made for a petrol station with shop, two tennis halls, and a double-story, two-lane underground car park.

Above this, indented by 12 meters, a four-story block extends across the entire width. Protected by the rim, this creates a further screen against the already reduced noise of traffic. The second structure is a 12-story slab of equal length, situated in a quieter location, parallel to the first block and 26 meters apart. It towers twice as high as the surrounding buildings. Penzinger Strasse, which has been widened to form a kind of square by shifting back the slab, becomes a tree-filled greenspace, compensating residents for the lack of sunshine. A covered walkway on the ground floor takes one to the shops and connects the external walkways to the courtyard and the block. Submission plans for the project show two, 8-meter-high underground tennis courts between the two buildings. Each tennis court is 800 square meters including infrastructure. These probably were abandoned due to cost. The quality of the courtyard has certainly benefited from this. Today, the greenery and trees between the block and the slab expand into the street, delighting residents and passers-by alike. At the very front of Hadikgasse, a wide, 1.5-meter mass of earth extending across the entire platform makes it possible to plant trees and flowering shrubs. This creates a high quality communal green space shielded from traffic that is lovely to spend time in.

Block and slab

Both wings are 18 meters deep and are offset from each other by half a story at about the center. 16 cross wall partitions determine the length of the wings. The supporting structure is like an open shelf made of reinforced concrete with prominent cross walls measuring out a grid of 5.7 by 2.72 meters—a very tightly dimensioned story height. There are 45 "cubbies" in the three-story block and 165 in the 11 stories of the slab. This corresponds to the respective number of apartments. The finishing elements are largely prefabricated. The ribbon windows, all opening pivot sashes, are made of utile, a plantation wood from West Africa widely in use at the time. The soffits in the foyers and loggias were insulated with visible cork panels and the parapets are prefabricated, insulated panels with integrated shading. While in the case of the stepped terraced residential complex on Inzersdorfer Strasse, completed in 1974, the cross walls penetrate the building envelope without insulation, here they were packed in 4-centimeter-thick insulation paneling. This considerable additional work likely contributed to it no longer being possible to build the two tennis halls. Apparently, they had to fight for every centimeter. The structural floors, for example, are merely given a millimeter-thin leveling layer over which a high-pile carpet is installed, acting as footfall sound insulation.

Access to the apartments

Facade-to-facade apartments accessed via central stairwells would require a great number of stairways and elevators and result in a loss of space, while a central corridor on every floor would generate an undesirably high number of north-facing apartments. What was needed was an efficient access circulation that would combine the advantages of both systems.

One could see the chosen access system as a further development of Le Corbusier's Unités d'Habitation, even more efficient thanks to the split level, which allows a third more apartments to connect to the central corridor. By offsetting the floors of the mezzanine levels at about the center of the building, each corridor provides access to around 45 apartments. The apartments are entered from the central corridor via a landing-wide foyer and a staircase with eight steps,

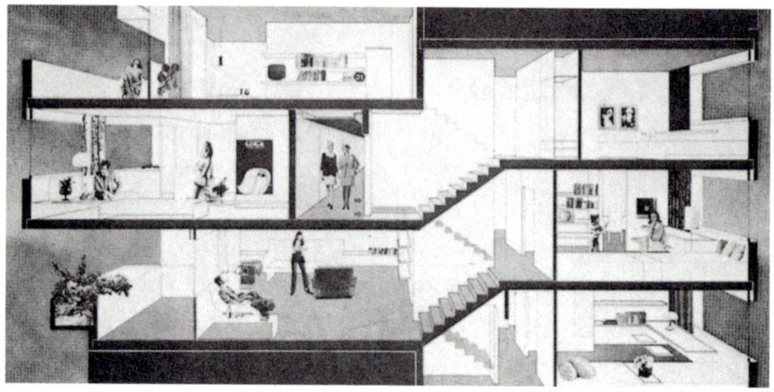

from where the level of the private rooms is reached. These rooms receive either morning or evening sunlight via a corner window and include a bathroom, toilet, and storage space. A further eight steps in the opposite direction lead to the kitchen and living room with loggia and planter to the south. This works both downwards and upwards. Three stories from a unit, accessed by a continuous 86-meter-long corridor. Thirty apartments are inserted in split-level floors, 15 are single-story, south-facing apartments with incoming daylight on one side. There is only one module in the block structure, stacked atop the communal facilities located on the ground floor. The central corridor is accessed via an elevator inside the building and a stair tower on the exterior. Both also provide access to a 25-meter-long swimming pool on the roof with shared terraces. Garbage disposals and exits to the open fire escape stairs are located at both ends of the corridor.

The slab structure is made up of four stacked modules, with the lowest one comprising only thirty apartments, as the ground floor is not used for residential purposes. The four central corridors are not centrally accessed as with the block, but instead by two elevators at the quarter points and freestanding staircase towers. The two building entrances are located in the courtyard and connected by a covered walkway. A staircase and an elevator lead from the foyers to two underground parking levels, with only the elevator leading to the four corridors on the first, fourth, seventh, and 10th floors. 165 apartments are accessed by two elevators, two staircases, and four corridors.

Center corridor: 15 entrances to small apartments on the left, 30 entrances to split-level apartments and maisonettes on the right, photo 2014

Depiction of circulation module and apartment types

Residential complex in Paris, 31–35 rue Saint-Ambroise, 1969 by Roger Anger, Mario Heymann and Pierre Puccinelli, south side, photo 2014

60 of these apartments are 33-square meter (including loggia), barrier-free, mini apartments. The others are three or five-room, split-level apartments or maisonettes ranging from 84 to 122 square meters in size including the loggia. All living spaces open to the south and two thirds of them have a view into the distance. The lack of apartments with two or four rooms is due to the system and the rigid structure.

Exterior appearance

The comparison with a building from one of the most innovative and busy architectural firms of the time in France is striking. Like the residential complex planned by Roger Anger and Mario Heymann in Paris, 31–35 rue Saint-Ambroise, completed in 1969, the south-facing Hadikgasse residential complex focuses on the individual in serial form and the facade as an open space for appropriation. This layer, in several gradations up to three meters deep, can be used for living and planted with greenery. It is a game with rules that only become apparent upon closer study. One might think it is a game of patterns and mirroring, but this is actually only a reflection of the inner structure. In contrast to the Paris example, the cross walls penetrating the building envelope are used here as a design element, although they certainly also take on the functions of privacy, shading, and fire control, as well as increasing the sense of space. Between the walls are loggias and flowering shrubs and bushes growing in concrete planters, along with

bands of bay-like windows between white parapets, shaded by ochre-yellow awnings.

The north side, with continuous ribbon windows regularly folded to create bay windows with white parapets is starkly different. Lack of privacy at the corner windows is prevented by the cross walls, which pierce the ribbon windows to protrude far out from the bay windows. Two massive stair towers, shifted five meters from the building, open up the four corridors with bridges that penetrate the facade on every third floor. The front sides are closed, like firewalls, and all four have a vertical, semi-circular shaft affixed to the exterior, to which a garbage disposal point was created in the corridors with a further projection. There are additional fire escape stairs on both sides of the block, likewise with a soft design. Near the intersection, the Hadiksteg enters at platform level, designed to directly connect the facility with the underground station and the 13th district.

A striking feature is the widely projecting curved edge of the platform, a soundproofing rim adorned with an orange and red stripe on a white background as a symbol for the oil company of the filling station below. This rim is actually an enormous, 86-meter-long plant trough, almost floating, tightly planted with poplar-like trees that tower far above, continuing the facade of the neighboring block as a kind of green wall.

Hadikgasse residential complex, photos 2014

North elevation with ribbon and bay windows

South elevation with loggias and planters

Reception

Buildings from Harry Glück and Partner's office have polarized public opinion again and again. On the one hand were academic colleagues and conservative circles who openly opposed Glück's buildings or simply ignored them when it came to discussing Austrian architecture abroad. His buildings and concepts apparently were also not met with approval in architectural teaching. Glück was neither in demand as a teacher, nor as a lecturer.[1] For specialist critics, the central corridor and apartments lit only from one side were utterly unacceptable features. They severely criticized the "categorical economic calculation" on which these buildings were based. The director of the Architekturzentrum Wien (AzW) and former architecture critic Dietmar Steiner, for example, rejected an exhibition of Harry Glück's works as late as 2015, stating that the AzW was "an architecture center and not a building center."[2] On the other hand, Harry Glück's buildings and his concept for the green city were enthusiastically celebrated in the left-leaning and liberal media, with some editors-in-chief revealing themselves as fervent supporters of this concept of the city and affordable housing.[3] In any case, the extraordinarily high and long-lasting satisfaction of the residents in Glück's buildings, surveyed in several studies, speaks for itself.

The Hadikgasse residential complex continues to be a built criticism of the status quo, then as now. The good condition, the well-kept outdoor facilities, and the abundantly planted residential open

Floating plant troughs above the gas station

spaces indicate a high level of approval by the residents. The apartments are sought-after, the rents are affordable, and the community seems to keep an eye on who they are allocated to. With the rooftop swimming pool, the sundecks, and the sauna facilities, the community has created a kind of stage for otherwise separate white and blue-collar worlds.

Already in use for 44 years, the complex still seems fresh. It is modern, open, and urban. Today, it would no longer fulfill current regulations regarding noise protection, thermal insulation, fire protection, and barrier-free access. This makes the question of the added benefits of these efforts, geared towards steady growth in terms of security, protection, and freedom, an urgent one.

Notes

1 Glück didn't give his first lecture at the TU Wien until he was invited by the author in 2009, when he was already 84 years old.

2 Dietmar Steiner (1951–2020), director of the Architekturzentrum Wien from 1993 to 2016.

3 The *Arbeiterzeitung* newspaper and the *Profil* news magazine. In July 2018, *ARCHITEKTUR* magazine lists Harry Glück as one of the 17 international "planners, thinkers, and visionaries" that have shaped our city since the 20th century.

Bibliography

Submission plans from May 1971

Freisitzer, Kurt, and Harry Glück. *Sozialer Wohnbau. Entstehung. Zustand. Alternativen.* Vienna: Molden Edition, 1979.

Glück, Harry. "Die Möglichkeit einer grünen Stadt." Unpublished manuscript, 1980.

Glück, Harry. "Höherwertige Alternativen im Massenwohnbau durch wirtschaftliche Planungs- und Konstruktionskonzepte." Dissertation, Innsbruck 1982.

Welzig, Maria, and Gerhard Steixner. *Die Architektur und ich – Eine Bilanz der österreichischen Architektur seit 1945 vermittelt durch ihre Protagonisten.* Vienna, Cologne, Weimar: Böhlau Verlag, 2003, 98–116.

AUTOBUS
HALTESTELLE
KONICA MINOLTA

JETZT
REIFEN

SPAR
SPAR
LEDERNARDO

EINGANG

Apartments 522

Site area 66,000 m²

Collective facilities, infrastructure: 1.8 hectares of public park, school, home for disabled children, shops, community center, youth club

London, UK
90B Rowley Way

Architect
Neave Brown

Client
London Borough of Camden

Planning 1967–69
Construction 1972–79

Site plan 1:10,000

Alexandra Road Estate, London

Neave Brown

1967–79

A Street with a Difference: Neave Brown's Alexandra Road

Mark Swenarton

The Alexandra and Ainsworth Estate, or Alexandra Road as it is generally known, is the most ambitious of the housing projects constructed by the London Borough of Camden during its "golden years" of 1965–1973 when Sydney Cook (1910–1979) was in charge of the borough's architectural department. It is also the most celebrated of the housing projects designed by Neave Brown (1929–2017). The project was largely designed in 1967–1969 but there then ensued delays both in tendering and construction, with construction starting in 1972 and completing in 1979.

Brown conceived Alexandra Road as a corrective to the kind of council housing being built at the time. The officially endorsed format, "mixed development," combined high-rise blocks of flats (for childless households) with two-story dwellings (for families with children) with individual gardens where the children could play. But as an influential 1962 report titled *Two to Fives in High Flats* demonstrated, in practice families with young children lived in the towers as well, with detrimental effects on both the children and the parents. To counteract this, Brown wanted to deliver a form of housing based on streets where, as in a traditional city, the street formed both the place of social interaction and the point at which you moved from the public realm to the private—in other words, "front doors on streets."

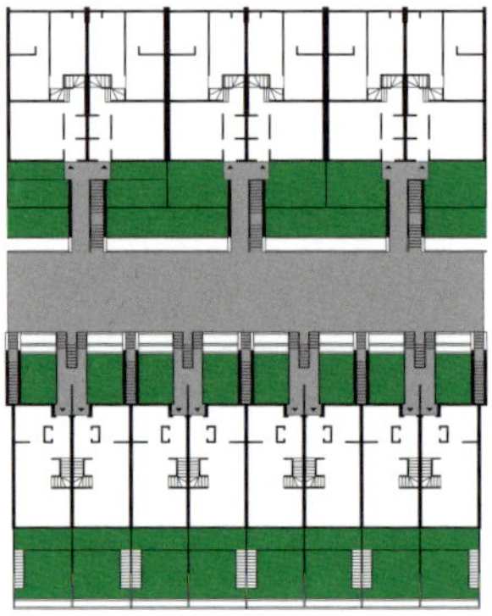

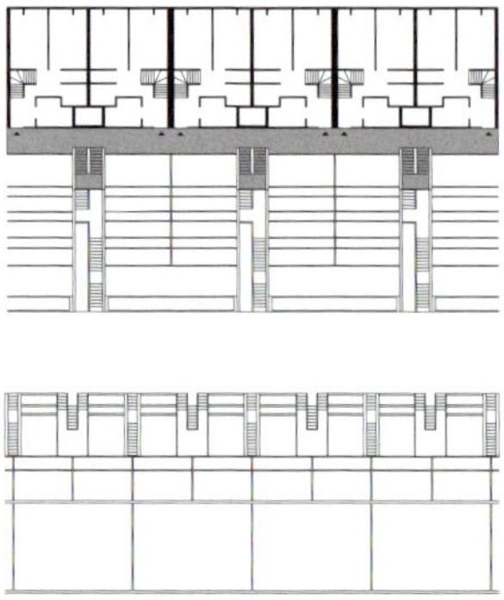

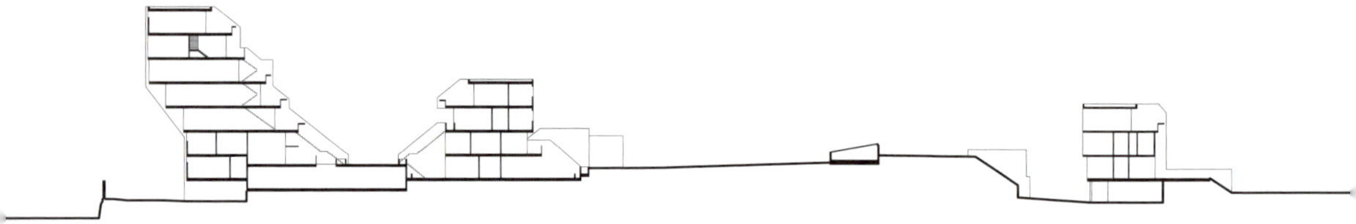

Floor plan ground floor and 4th upper floor, Cross-section, 1:1.000

Brown unveiled his ideas with his first project for Camden, the Fleet Road (Dunboyne Road) estate, designed in 1966–1967. The 72-dwelling scheme was located close to a recently completed "mixed development" council scheme complete with two 15-story towers (Fleet Road Number 1) and the presumption was that Brown would propose something similar. Instead, he showed how, by adopting a "mat" or "carpet" model and building to the extremities of the site, the same density (160 persons per acre/395 persons per hectare) could be provided, but without rising more than 3.5 stories above the ground. Essentially, the figure-ground of a "mixed development" scheme was inverted: instead of the building forming the figure and the site forming the ground, the building formed the ground and figure was formed by the open space excavated from it: communal gardens, individual gardens, and the narrow pedestrian alleys leading to the front doors. A manifesto by Brown, "The Form of Housing," written to accompany the publication of the design in September 1967, explained the general principles.

Immediately after the publication of Fleet Road, Brown was asked by Cook to take on a much larger and more complex project. The 16.3-acre/6.6-hectare Alexandra Road site was bounded between the main London-Birmingham railway running along its northern edge and a 1950s housing estate to the south. As well as housing (522 dwellings) the project included a 4.5-acre/1.8-hectare public park, a school, home for handicapped children, shops, light industry, a community center, a play center, and a youth club. There was also, running along on the southern edge, the existing London County Council (LCC) Ainsworth Estate, comprising a series of six-story gallery-access flats, which was to be incorporated as part of the design.

At Alexandra Road, Brown wanted to create a modern urbanism that did not break with either the existing grain of the city or the way of life of the people who lived there. As in Bloomsbury, Pimlico, and other parts of eighteenth and nineteenth-century London, there would be a continuous public space formed by streets and squares, with the edges of the public space defined by the housing, the houses being entered directly from the street, and every dwelling having its own private open-to-the-sky external space.

In essence, Brown's concept was to treat the entire site as a continuous pedestrian zone comprising streets, squares, and park, with vehicles relegated below ground. Running along the north

Alexandra Road Estate, detail view Block A

was the main pedestrian street, Rowley Way, with on one side the 400-meter-long Block A (6.5 stories), cantilevering over the railway, and on the other the lower Block B (four stories), adjacent to the park. The section of Block A stacked five dwellings one above the other: 1.5-story duplex at the bottom, three levels of flats on the intermediate floors, and a two-story duplex at the top—with a step-back in the section to give each dwelling its own open-to-the-sky external terrace, complete with concrete planter. Block B comprised two double-story duplexes one above the other, the lower with its own garden facing the park and the upper with its own terrace, opening off the living room and overlooking the street. Access to all dwellings was from the pedestrian street, with more than 100 staircases connecting the front doors of the upper dwellings to the street (in addition, five lifts in Block A gave direct access to the walkway connecting the upper duplexes). To the south of the park was another pedestrian street, much smaller in scale, which similarly provided access to a third row of housing, Block C (three-story houses), and the pre-existing LCC flats. At the eastern end of Rowley Way was the main sequence of public spaces, including the central plaza and the vehicle court, forming part of a complex multi-level block (the D-grid) containing the community center, shops, school, youth club, etc.

At the heart of the scheme was the 1.8-hectare public park. For Brown, the park formed "the centre of a continuous pedestrian urban architecture" and, as in eighteenth-century London, it was "'the picture in the frame" formed by the adjacent buildings. Brown

Northeast end of the facility, Block A (right), Block B (left)

designed the park as a series of distinct spaces, each with a different use and character (open play space, play area for younger children/older children, open-air amphitheater, etc.), with each space configured diagonally to make it feel bigger. To undertake the planting design, Brown secured the appointment of his friend, the landscape architect Janet Jack, who had originally trained with him at the Architectural Association in the 1950s. Following its £1.5 million restoration in 2013–2015, funded by the Heritage Lottery Fund, the park today looks as verdant as its creators intended.

Despite the programmatic complexity of the project, encompassing infrastructure as well as residential and public buildings, a consistent palette of materials was used throughout: concrete (both precast and in situ) for the walls, roof, and structure and dark-stained timber for doors and windows. The external walls were finished in board-marked white unpainted concrete, while to counter the effects of the passing trains, the cross walls of the block next to the railway were mounted on 18-meter-deep, 1-meter-diameter piles with steel/rubber anti-vibration pads. Cast into the 178-mm-thick cross walls were the pipe coils of an innovative heating system designed by services engineer Max Fordham, which converted the cross walls into low-output radiators, heated by a central boiler located in the D-grid block.

The main principles of the housing types were as established at Fleet Road and in "the form of housing." The dwellings were in continuous terraces (rows) fronting onto pedestrian streets, with front doors accessed from the street. Every dwelling had its own open-to-the-sky external space of at least 100 square feet (9.3 square meters) opening from the living room. The two-story dwellings followed the "upside down" principle of Fleet Road, with the living room and kitchen on the upper floor and bedrooms below (so that nobody would have the living room or kitchen of their upstairs neighbors immediately above their bedroom). Extensive use was made of sliding partitions to facilitate family living—for example between the kitchen/dining area and living areas, so that some family members could watch television while others did their homework. Block A comprised two-bedroom four-person (2B/4P) duplexes on the top floors, 1B/2P flats on the intermediate floors, and 3B/5P duplexes on the bottom floors. Block B comprised 2B/3P duplexes above and 3B/4P duplexes below. Block C comprised 4B/6P houses. Internal floor sizes ranged from 50 square meters for the 1B/2P flats to 115 square meters for the 4B/6P houses. Overall, the built density was 214 persons per acre (528 persons per hectare).

Construction of the project was fraught with difficulty, not just because of its scale and complexity, but also because of the severe problems facing the building industry during the 1970s. With inflation soaring, peaking at an annual 35 percent, contractors could no longer deliver large projects at the original tendered price. The choice was either to go into liquidation (as happened with the contractor for Chelsea and Kensington's World End estate in 1973 and for Camden's Highgate New Town estate in 1976) or to go back to the council and seek a new contract.

At Alexandra Road, faced with this choice, Camden decided on the latter, and in 1976 agreed a "prime costs" contract in which payments to the contractor were based not on an overall price, but on incurred and verified expenditure. As the council's cost consultants repeatedly made clear, this meant that the council would not know the overall cost of the project until the work was complete. But as the project was nearing completion and the enormous cost (almost £20 million, as compared to £5 million in the original contract) was becoming clear, the councilors took fright and set up a public enquiry in the hope of finding someone else to blame. The enquiry lasted for more than two years, but to the councilors' chagrin ended up exonerating Neave Brown (who by this stage had left the council's employ), pointing the finger instead at the councilors themselves. But the damage had been done. While in the architectural media, Alexandra Road was applauded worldwide—in the UK, in mainland Europe, in America, and in Japan—at home, the reputational damage was irrecoverable: Brown would never work as an architect in Britain again.

One of the reasons for setting up the public enquiry was that the councilors feared that Alexandra Road would prove unpopular and therefore that the dwellings would be hard to let. In the event, the opposite was the case and, as the housing manager reported, tenancies on the estate were taken up faster than on any other housing development that Camden had built. Features like the large private terraces for every flat proved as attractive to prospective tenants—nurses, teachers, postmen, railway workers—as Brown had anticipated.

Originally all the dwellings were rented to tenants of Camden council. But under the "right to buy" policy introduced by Margaret Thatcher in 1980, all council tenants were permitted to purchase their homes at a discount of up to 50 percent, with the right to sell them on the open market after a few years. Today at Alexandra Road about one in five have transferred out of council ownership, with many being sold on to "young creatives"—architects, designers, and journalists—attracted by the outstanding design of the homes and (for London) the relatively reasonable prices.

While externally there have been some unsympathetic interventions (lighting, surface-mounted cabling etc.), overall, the fabric today is in reasonable condition, thanks largely to the vigilance of residents who care deeply about their estate. In the first decade or so the estate suffered from a number of problems, many stemming from inadequate maintenance by a council which was itself being squeezed of funds by central government. The physical fabric of the estate deteriorated, particularly the landscaped and planted areas, the lighting of the public areas was not maintained, and community facilities ceased to function effectively. In 1989, the residents voted to form a tenants' management co-operative and appointed consultants to undertake a program of repairs, but the council insisted on taking over the program with its own consultant architects in charge.

To forestall the damage to the fabric that this would undoubtedly have entailed, the heritage authorities intervened, and in August 1993

Alexandra Road Estate,
top floor living rooms,
Block B (left), Block A (right)

the estate was "spot-listed." On the advice of English Heritage, the secretary of state, Peter Brooke set aside the rule that a building had to be at least 30 years old to be considered for listing and announced that the Alexandra and Ainsworth Estate, as "one of the most distinguished groups of buildings in England (constructed) since the Second World War" was now listed at Grade II*. As such, it was not only the first post-war housing estate to be listed, but also the youngest building ever listed. The main non-residential elements followed, at the slightly lower Grade II listing, in 2013.

The completion of Alexandra Road in 1979 coincided with Margaret Thatcher's accession to power and her drive to cut back on council housing. By 1981, new starts were little more than a fifth of what they had been in the mid-1970s and soon councils, with no housing to build, were closing down their architects' departments (Camden's closed in 1984). As a result, Alexandra Road never had the impact in the UK that it merited. Its most direct legacy was in the Netherlands. Here, in the 1980s, Brown worked with David Porter on Zwolsestraat, a major residential/infrastructural scheme at Scheveningen in The Hague, from which they eventually withdrew due to differences with the developer.

And then in the 1990s came Eindhoven where, at the invitation of master city planner Jo Coenen, Brown delivered his final masterwork, the Medina. Here, a pedestrian street is combined with a block containing four strips of stepped housing, each with a terrace on the roof of the one in front.

Today, the reputation of Neave Brown and Alexandra Road has never been higher. Architects in the UK, such as Peter Barber and Feilden Clegg Bradley, who are at the leading edge of innovative housing design, regard Brown as Britain's finest housing architect. In keeping with this perception in 2017, shortly before he died, Brown was awarded the RIBA Royal Gold Medal for architecture and in 2019 the RIBA announced the establishment of an annual Neave Brown Award for Housing. In this way, the legacy of Alexandra Road lives on today.

Bibliography

"Alexandra Road." In *Architectural Review 166*, No. 990, 76–92, 1979.

Brown, Neave. "The Form of Housing." In *Architectural Design 37*, No. 9, 1967, 432–33.

Brown, Neave. "Alexandra Road, London; Fleet Road, London; Winscombe Street, London." In *A+U 122*, 1980, 4–54.

Freear, Andrew. "Alexandra Road: The Last Great Social Housing Project." In *AA Files*, No. 30, 1995, 35–46.

Johnston, Pamela (ed.). "Neave Brown." *Project Interrupted: Lectures by British Housing Architects.* London: The Architecture Foundation, 2018, 11–45.

Swenarton, Mark and Thomas Weaver. "Neave Brown in conversation with Mark Swenarton & Thomas Weaver." In *AA Files*, No. 67, 2013, 75–91.

Swenarton, Mark. *Cook's Camden: The Making of Modern Housing.* London: Lund Humphries, 2017.

HEIGHT
AHEAD

102

Tenants Hall
Ainsworth Way
South Hampstead Education & Lifelong Learning Centre

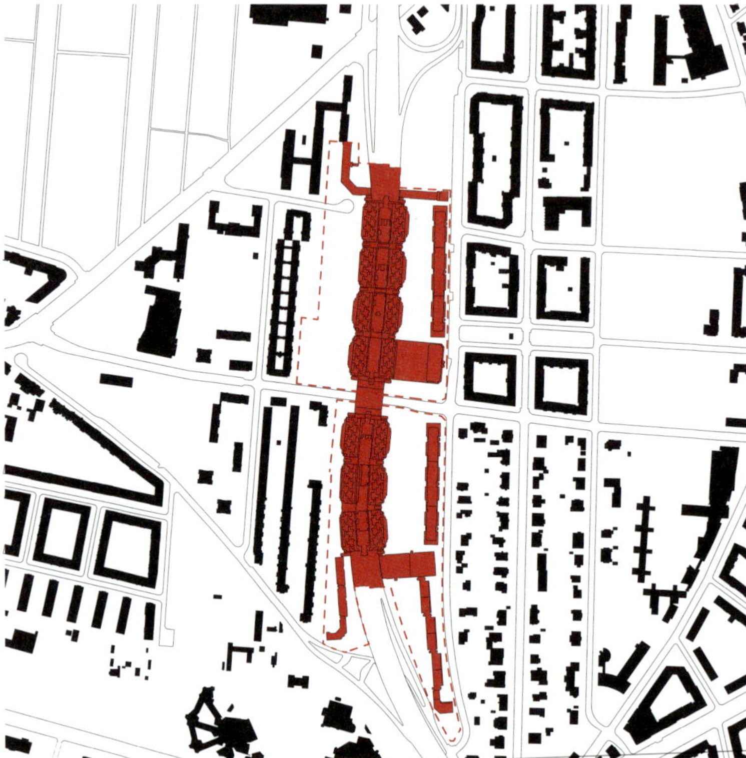

Apartments 1,758
Built area ratio 47 %

Site area ca. 103,100 m²
Built area 48,100 m²
Terrace apartments 1,064

Collective facilities: 118 hobby rooms, 4 guest apartments, 12 community rooms
Infrastructure: School, kindergarten, shops and restaurants in the ground floor zone on Schlangenbader Strasse, shopping center on Wiesbadener Strasse, 2 garage decks with 760 parking spaces

Special equipment
Pneumatic waste disposal system

Walkable art installations
Haus-Rucker-Co, Georg Seibert

Berlin-Wilmersdorf, Germany
Schlangenbader Strasse, Wiesbadener Strasse and others

Architects
Georg Heinrichs, Gerhard Krebs, Klaus Krebs
Landscape planning
Paul-Heinz Gischow, Walter Rossow

Clients
Heinz Mosch KG (1971–1974); degewo – Deutsche Gesellschaft zur Förderung des Wohnungsbaues (from 1974)

Planning and construction
1971–80

Site plan 1:10,000

Autobahnüberbauung Schlangenbader Strasse, Berlin

Georg Heinrichs, Gerhard Krebs, Klaus Krebs

1971–80

Stepped Terrace Housing as a Motorway Enclosure. Berlin's Schlangenbader Strasse Gamble

Maria Welzig

The Autobahnüberbauung Schlangenbader Strasse, a housing project spanning a busy freeway, is the first implementation of an architectural vision that had been developing in response to the explosive growth of cities and motorized traffic since the early twentieth century, with urban planners and architects such as Edgar Chambless, Hugh Ferris, Hans Schierloh, Le Corbusier, Paul Rudolph, and Kenzo Tange exploring new approaches to urban planning in which traffic axes and superstructures were fused into multifunctional structures.[1] The ideal structural form for this was the likewise newly developed typology of the stepped terrace house, the dark "belly" of which could accommodate traffic routes.

Progress towards rapid automobile transport seemed unavoidable, even desirable, in those decades of technological optimism. In the 1950s, zoning plans for West Berlin included a motorway ring around the city center. The particular situation in West Berlin—the limited land and competition for modernity between East and West Berlin during the Cold War—provided the necessary impetus to take the risk of building a superstructure development for the first time in the 1970s. The Steglitz feeder in Wilmersdorf was chosen as the site, as the north-south route of this autobahn section offered the favorable possibility of building east/west-facing housing.

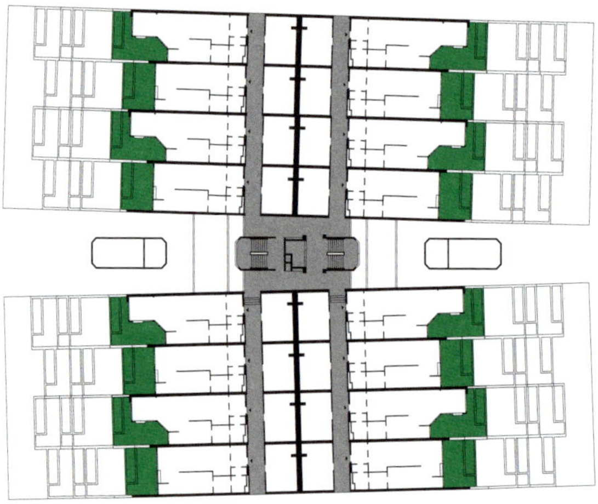

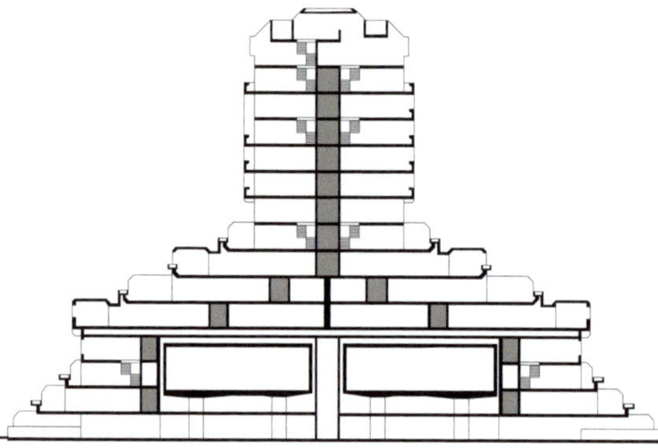

Floor plan 5th upper floor, Cross-section 1:1,000

The technically complex and costly experiment was initially carried out by a private client. Heinz Mosch AG developed the pioneering project in collaboration with the architects Georg Heinrichs and Gerhard Krebs as well as with experts in traffic, noise protection, aerodynamics, etc., and supported by political decision-makers. Georg Heinrichs was the project manager of the scheme, with a stance decidedly reminiscent of 1920s modernism. For his part, Gerhard Krebs had been researching the fundamental possibilities of building over inner-city transport arteries together with other experts in a citizens' initiative titled Arbeitskreis 6 since 1970.[2]

When the oil crisis hit in 1973, the edge building along Schlangenbader Strasse was already under construction, and the property developer ran into financial difficulties. The public sector stepped in and the German Society for the Promotion of Housing Construction (degewo) in Berlin, founded in 1924, continued the building as an exemplary project of the federal government within the framework of subsidized social housing.

The transfer of the project to the public sector led to a stronger social orientation of the company in terms of rents, infrastructure, and the remarkable green and open space design.

Despite the enormous technical challenges and growing public resistance—there was even a citizens' initiative actively opposing the project—and in spite of the fact that the budget was significantly exceeded, the Autobahnüberbauung Schlangenbader Strasse project was completed at the end of 1979.

The complex and its position in the city district

The notion of a motorway in the "belly" of a residential building was an undertaking without precedent, with the possibility of technical solutions for sound insulation and exhaust fumes doubted by many. The prerequisite for success was the construction of two tunnels completely separates from the residential buildings themselves. The superstructure runs a length of almost 600 meters and reaches a height of up to 46 meters. The motorway tunnel bridges Wiesbadener Strasse, which crosses in the middle. Seven access towers, set 60 meters apart, give the large structure a rhythm. They also articulate the inflection points in the complex, which follows the curve of the motorway. The lower seven floors of the superstructure are set back and fronted by terraces. Above them are up to six stories with loggias and a terraced rooftop level. Parking spaces for about 760 cars are located on two levels below the tunnels. The supporting structure is a reinforced concrete, cross-wall construction.

A lower, five-story block runs parallel to the superstructure on Schlangenbader Strasse. At the northern and southern ends of the complex, where the tunnel sheath ends, additional five-story buildings, including a multi-story car park, provide additional screening and noise protection. Generous and diversely planted greenspaces are situated along both sides of the superstructure. On the eastern side, the edge buildings on Schlangenbader Strasse turn these into sheltered courtyard-like areas.

One of the special features of the complex is its excellent inner-city location. Wilmersdorf, Schmargendorf, Steglitz—this is a "good neighborhood" with avenues, allotment gardens, spacious squares, and residential buildings from the 1920s. Although the large structures of the development introduce a completely new typology, towering above the surrounding buildings with over 40 meters of height, it is at the same time integrated into the surrounding city. The height, shape, and color of the edge buildings link into to the neighboring residential buildings. Above all, however, it is thanks to the superstructure that the neighborhood has been preserved as a coherent urban space despite the motorway. Neither in the complex nor in the apartments does one hear any noise from the up to 80,000 cars that drive through daily.

The ground floor zone on Schlangenbader Strasse is generous and open, filled with restaurants and shops, thus enriching the neighborhood with a new semi-public layer. There is a service and shopping center for the neighborhood at the point where Wiesbadener Strasse crosses the complex. The residential complex shares its rich green space with the neighborhood.

Diversity of dwellings and residents

A guiding principle of the Schlangenbader Strasse development was the creation of a mixed city, particularly in social terms. On the one hand, by implementing social housing in the advantaged inner-city area and, on the other hand, within the complex. The residents—a group of almost 4,000 people—were to be as diverse as possible. To achieve this, a wide range of housing typologies was developed. Thirty percent of the apartments in the complex were intended for single people, thirty percent for couples, and forty percent for families.[3] 80 apartments were specially designed for elderly occupants.

At a distance of 6.4 meters, the cross walls define apartments width. The apartments in the superstructure are accessed above the tunnel via central corridors. Storage rooms assigned to the apartments on the fifth floor are located at the center of the building. Half of the apartments have terraces with an average size of 15 square meters. The apartments on the upper, non-terraced floors are equipped with loggias. The two upper floors hold maisonettes with terraces facing west and east. Thirty percent of all apartments are maisonettes.

Corner glazing to the terraces, horizontal windows, and in some cases skylights provide good lighting. There are open plan kitchens or bar kitchens. Folding doors ensure flexibility. Baths and toilets are separate and many bedrooms have en suite bathrooms. The hallways of the larger apartments go full circle and the bedrooms have walk-in wardrobes. Foyers and stairwells are carefully designed in terms of color, feel, and form and have direct incoming light.

Communal rooms

A generous variety of communal spaces creates additional possibilities for the residents, promoting interaction and a sense of community. The entire fourth story, above the tunnel, is designed as a shared floor. Here, one can traverse the entire length of the superstructure on an internal street. “Connected to this indoor street are four common rooms near the center, each 80 m^2 in size with a terrace, and equipped with a kitchenette and toilet facilities. These rooms can be used for parent-child groups, homework groups, lectures, or for festivities. On the other side of the corridor there are twelve playrooms measuring 6 by 12 m, where table tennis tables and similar equipment is set up. 80 rentable hobby rooms with an average size of 8 m^2 also line this indoor street, intended as an extension of the apartment to be used for various activities and to stimulate interaction between the tenants.”[4] Shared terraces are located at the southern and northern ends of the indoor street. A south-facing viewing

Aerial view of the Schlangenbader Strasse development, photo 2012

Open space and greenspace between the superstructure on the right and the perimeter development on Schlangenbader Strasse, photo taken in 2018

deck on the thirteenth floor was once open to tenants, but was closed in 1990 "due to climbing."[5] The provision of guest apartments was also innovative. The guest apartments were popular from the very beginning and remain so today. The same is true of the hobby rooms.[6] In recent years, tenants have been increasingly worried about the commercialization of these shared rooms by the owner.[7]

However, in recent years the Schlangenbader Strasse development has also shown how sustainable the original spatial layout and the spark to create community really is. Tenants come together to found the Neighbors for Neighbors group, which organizes numerous community activities.[8] In 2014, a confrontational tenants' initiative was created, committed to the historic preservation listing of the complex among other things.

Green and open spaces as (play) landscapes

Great significance was given to the planning of the green and open spaces extending on both sides of the development (designed by landscape planners Paul-Heinz Gischow and Walter Rossow, 1979–1981). Years before construction completion, the developer, with foresight, purchased the trees. The varied planting of groups of trees, flowering shrubs, and evergreens, as well as the landscaping of the terrain divide the extensive open space into various protected play and relaxation areas. Children and youths, adults, and the elderly are all provided with areas adapted to their needs. The playgrounds and

sports fields stimulate a sense of adventure and the playful desire for movement. Four art installations (by Haus-Rucker-Co and Georg Seibert) demarcate the main intersections of the transverse, longitudinal, and diagonal paths and personalize the large facility.

A vertical green space has been created by the intensive planting of the private terraces, enabled by concrete planters—installed already planted—suspended in front of the facade. The residents used the opportunity to design their own private green space extensively, and distinctive individual gardens were created. The planters also act as an efficient privacy screen.

Reception: media, criticism, residents

The Schlangenbader Strasse development was intensely criticized by the media, who rejected the project after completion. Protest against the development was often combined with protest against the construction of the motorway itself. The citizens' initiative that became active against the project in the 1970s also often equated the construction of the superstructure with the building of the motorway. In fact, building over the motorway is more of an urban restoration than anything else. Another aspect that aroused opposition and stirred up fear was the sheer size of the complex. Other large housing estates—although far larger and located on the outskirts—which had been built in West Berlin since the 1960s were seen as a deterrent.

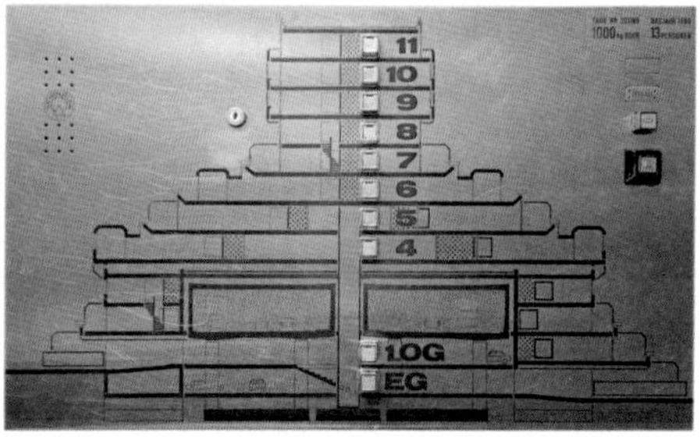

Elevator panel in the Schlangenbader Strasse development

Mr. and Mrs. Schnock in their apartment in the Schlangenbader Strasse development, 2017

Hans Stimmann, who later became the city's director of urban development, created a massive public outcry against the housing estate in the 1980s. As an employee of the city, editor of the magazine *Bauwelt,* and a very active media personality, he contributed greatly to the overwhelmingly negative image.[9]

Although inner-city living was the theme of the 1987 International Building Exhibition (IBA), which was dominated by post-modernism—the Schlangenbader Strasse development was not even mentioned, prompting its principal planners to publish a comprehensive volume on the complex, stating: "If it is true that experiment and risk are and should remain an indispensable part of architecture and urban development, then it is utterly incomprehensible that the unique prototypical project of an urban motorway superstructure is not shown or even mentioned at the 1987 International Building Exhibition Berlin (IBA) '750 Years of Architecture and Urban Development in Berlin.' Not only did the motorway superstructure correspond to the original objective of the IBA—'Living in the City Center'—due to its urban location, but its urban development approach also fulfills many fundamental requirements of ecological urban planning."[10]

From the very beginning, the residents were highly satisfied. A 1990 résumé reads as follows: "The community has no vacancies, but rather a highly satisfied tenant base characterized by low fluctuation."[11] A tenant satisfaction analysis conducted by degewo in 2018 once again showed above-average satisfaction.[12] In 2014, tenants founded an initiative "with the aim (...) of contributing to the protec-

tion, preservation, and care of their environment." This was triggered by the announcement—then implemented in 2015—of the closure of the automatic waste extraction system.[13] Subsequently, the tenants campaigned for the protection of the greenspaces and applied for the protection of "their" facility as a listed building.

The architectural and historical uniqueness and high quality of the residential complex, which has proven itself in the almost forty years of its existence, was finally acknowledged in December 2017 in a trendsetting decision by the Berlin Monument Authority. The preservation of the Schlangenbader Strasse development has not only been interpreted as a historical appreciation, but also as a stimulus for future residential construction. Architectural historian Nikolaus Bernau wrote: "Here you can see the individuality that large-scale industrial housing is capable of."[14] The Schlangenbader Strasse development stands "for the optimism of social architecture that has been cultivated in Berlin since the imperial era. In other words, it is what we should study more closely, especially in light of the fashionable enthusiasm for re-building historic old towns."[15]

The *Welt* states: "Listing the development as a monument is a good decision from the point of view of architectural history. It would also be important to derive solutions for future housing construction from it."[16] In 2018, the SPD submitted a motion to the Berlin House of Representatives in which the construction of superstructures over other sections of the motorway is proposed, using the Schlangenbader Strasse development as a model.[17]

Notes

1 Thorsten Dame first dealt with the history of ideas for building over transportation infrastructure in his comprehensive architectural report on the Schlangenbader Strasse development commissioned by the Berlin Monument Authority. Cf. Dame 2015. We would like to thank the Berlin Monument Authority, in particular Dr. Bernhard Kohlenbach, for the generous provision of the report.

2 Arbeitskreis 6 initially addressed the construction of railroad superstructures in West Berlin, but these were under Soviet administration.

3 The sizes for the three different target groups mentioned above are: a) 1–1.5 rooms of 42–52 square meters, b) 2 rooms of around 67 square meters, some with an additional work room, and c) 2.5–3.5 rooms of 80–120 square meters.

4 Bertelsmann, Wolf. "Projektentwicklung, Konzeption, Erfahrungen." In Seidel/Bertelsmann, 1990, 30.

5 Cf. Note 4.

6 Cf. "Der Eigentümer: Autobahnüberbauung Schlangenbader Straße–Acht Jahre Erfahrung der DEGEWO bei der Verwaltung und Bewirtschaftung des Objektes." In Seidel/Bertelsmann 1990, 47–50, as well as helpful information via email from degewo to the author on 25 April 2019.

7 Cf. Leiß, 2017 and helpful information from Christine Wußmann-Nergiz, resident and founder of the Tenants' Initiative 2014 in an email to the author on 24 May 2019.

8 I would like to thank Doris Lochau, resident of the Schlangenbader Strasse development since 2004, co-founder of the Tenants' Initiative and key figure behind the tenants' application for monument protection, for this information. Telephone call on 19 June 2019.

9 Stimmann judged the Schlangenbader Strasse development in 1980–1981 to be a "disfigurement of a residential quarter," an "urban planning mistake," and a "failed attempt by a private property developer," quoted in Seidel/Bertelsmann 1990, 95.

10 Seidel, Ernst. Foreword. In Seidel/Bertelsmann 1990, 5.

11 Seidel/Bertelsmann 1990

12 Information from degewo in an email to the author on 24 April 2019.

13 See http://www.mi-schlange.de (12 September 2019).

14 Bernau, Nikolaus. "Denkmalschutz für Schlange: Gelungener sozialer Wohnungsbau aus den 1970ern." In *Berliner Zeitung*, 10 December 2017, https://www.berliner-zeitung.de/kultur/denkmalschutz-fuer-schlange-gelungener-sozialer-wohnungsbau-aus-den-1970ern-29271332 (10 May 2019).

15 Bernau, Nikolaus. "Berliner Star-Architekt Georg Heinrichs wird 90." In *Berliner Zeitung*, 10 June 2016, https://www.berliner-zeitung.de/kultur/geburtstag-berliner-star-architekt-georg-heinrichs-wird-90-24199656 (10 June 2019).

16 Woeller, Marcus. "Warum die Berliner ‚Schlange' jetzt Denkmalschutz genießt." In *Die Welt,* 12 December 2017, https://www.welt.de/ kultur/article171499739/Warum-die-Berliner-Schlange-jetzt-Denkmalschutz-geniesst.html (3 March 2019).

17 Abel, Andreas. "Neue Wohnhäuser über der Stadtautobahn A 100." In *Berliner Morgenpost*, 3 July 2018, https://www.morgenpost.de/berlin/article214748501/Neue-Wohnhaeuser-ueber-der-Autobahn-A-100.html (28 November 2019).

Bibliography

Dame, Thorsten. "Autobahnüberbauung Schlangenbader Straße." Unpublished report. Landesdenkmalamt Berlin. Berlin, 2015.

DEGEWO (ed.). *Autobahnüberbauung Berlin Schlangenbader Straße. Ein Bauvorhaben der DEGEWO*. Berlin, 1980.

G+P Landschaftsarchitekten. Website: Stadtautobahnüberbauung Schlangenbader Straße Berlin-Wilmersdorf, http://www.gp-landschaft.net/dl_2016/Wohnungsbau_Dachgruen_k.pdf (accessed on 28 April 2019).

Leiß, Birgit. "Wohnen in außergewöhnlichen Häusern–Die Autobahn im Haus." Edited by Berliner Mieterverein. *Mieter Magazin* 11/2017. https://www.berliner-mieterverein.de/magazin/online/mm1117/wohnkomplex-schlangenbader-strasse-die-autobahn-im-haus-111724.htm (accessed on 20 September 2019).

Mosch KG. "Stadtautobahnbebauung Berlin 31-Wilmersdorf." Planning status May 1972, Berlin, 1972.

Petty, James. "Life Above the Autobahn." 2012. http://www.pettydesign.com/2012/03/11/life-above-the-autobahn/

Seidel, Ernst and Wolf Bertelsmann (eds.). *Autobahnüberbauung Schlangenbader Straße. Vom Abenteuer, das Unmögliche zu wagen ...*, Berlin: Konopka Verlag, 1990.

Senator für Bau- und Wohnungswesen (ed.). *Autobahnüberbauung Schlangenbader Straße*. Berlin, 1980.

Stimmann, Hans. "Verkehrsflächenüberbauung." Dissertation TU Berlin, workbooks 15/16 of the Institut für Stadt- und Regionalplanung. Berlin, 1980.

Stimmann, Hans. "Autobahnüberbauung Schlangenbader Straße in Berlin." In *Bauwelt 72*, No. 18, 1981, 727–732.

60

degewo
60

24
23

Schritt
fahren!
SCHLANGENBADER STRASSE
12 A-E

DURCHGANG
19, 19A - 19E

SCHLANGENBADER STRASSE
20 A-E
Müllraum

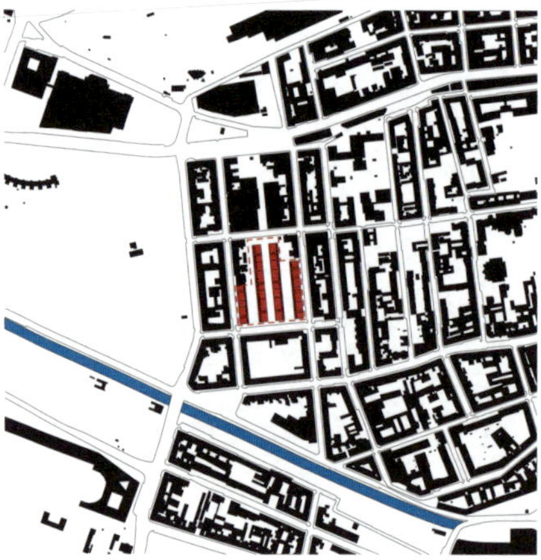

Density in Block Grids

Inzersdorfer Strasse
Residential Complex, Vienna
Harry Glück & Partner
1969–74

Wohnen Morgen Wien
Wilhelm Holzbauer
1973–80

Apartments 222
Floor space index 4.1
Built area ratio 75 %

Site area 6,060 m²
Built area 4,550 m²
Gross floor area 25,000 m²

Collective facilities, infrastructure:
Rooftop swimming pool, 2 saunas, kindergarten, recreation rooms

Vienna, Austria
Inzersdorfer Strasse 113

Architects
Harry Glück & Partner

Client
GESIBA — Gemeinnützige Siedlungs- und Bauaktiengesellschaft

Construction
PORR

Planning and construction
1969–74

Site plan 1:10,000

Inzersdorfer Strasse Residential Complex, Vienna

Harry Glück & Partner

1969–74

The Birth of a Prototype—Inzersdorfer Strasse Residential Complex

San-Hwan Lu

When one speaks of stepped terrace housing, Harry Glück's large-scale projects on the periphery spring to mind. The history of his stepped terrace projects, though, begins with a comparatively small, inner-city project.

This was in the late 1960s, when the architectural scene was in a state of change and a more humane response to car-centric cities was being sought. Stepped terrace buildings seemed to offer a possible solution. Some ideas remained utopian, contributing to the debate—such as the Wiener Flur projects—while others were already being realized internationally. These included residential complexes for major events such as the Olympic Games in Munich, the Montreal World Expo, or social housing on the outskirts of London and Paris. In terms of the concrete formulation of ideas, the buildings sometimes differ greatly. What the projects have in common, though, is that they are all larger housing estates and part of an urban utopia: the Green City.

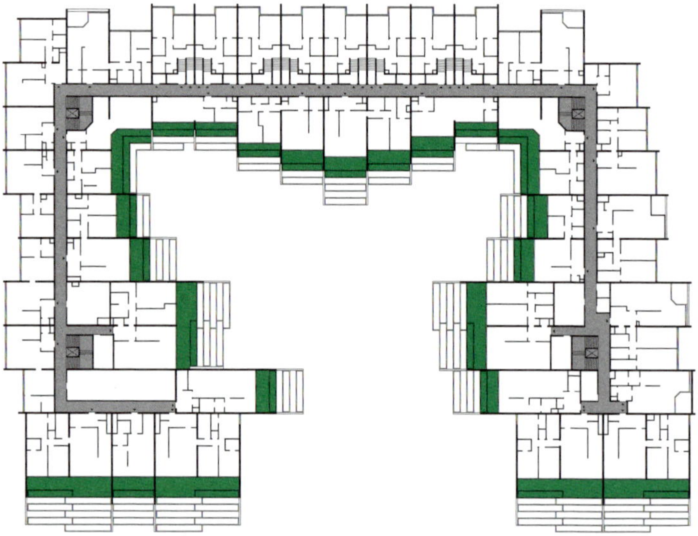

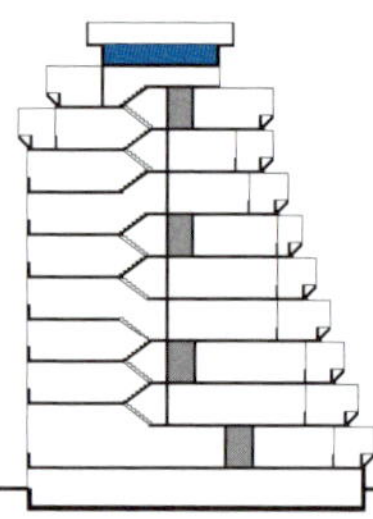

Floor plan 2nd and 3rd upper floors, Cross-section, 1:1,000

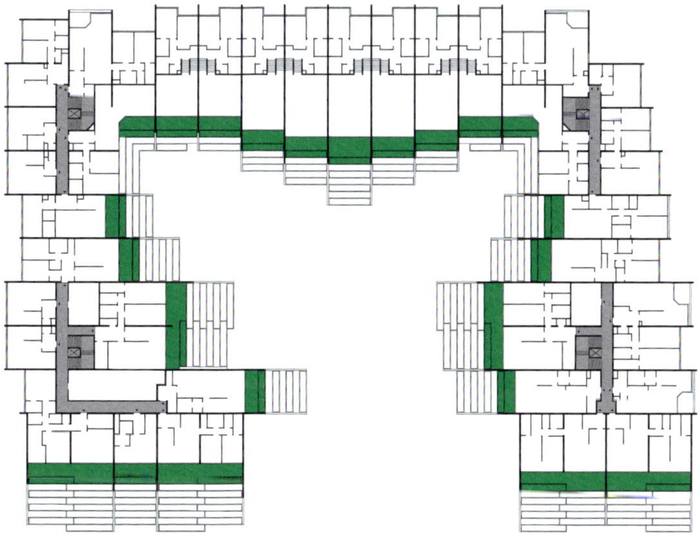

The background

At the time, Harry Glück was a young Viennese architect who had just completed his first residential buildings. These were mainly inner-city projects, often embedded in a traditional perimeter block structure, one of which is the Angeligasse project for GESIBA in Vienna's 10th district. The complex is located on a north-facing slope in a U-shape, open to the south. The two side wings house apartments facing east and west, separated by a central corridor, each half with sunlight exposure for half the day. The connecting section of the building, to the north, is also accessed by a central corridor. This provides a higher density than with a south-facing balcony walkway, and the few north-facing apartments that result are tolerated. Structurally, the complex is still a conventional multi-story apartment building, although Glück was already testing and refining the basic logic which was later to be implemented at Inzersdorfer Strasse. The property developer was highly satisfied with this first collaboration and, in 1971, commissioned Glück with a follow-up project on a somewhat larger site directly to the north, on Inzersdorfer Strasse.

Glück's firm had been working on the Alt-Erlaa residential park project since 1968, with early models featured in a 1970 edition of *Architektur.aktuell*, although the designs were still in a conceptual phase at that time. Thus the project in Inzersdorfer Strasse became a test case for the stepped terrace concept Glück had been working on during the previous years. The prototypical character and inner-city location make the complex highly unusual and interesting, with many elements that anticipate those used in many of his later residential buildings.

Specific solutions for specific challenges—the basic form

In order to realize a stepped terrace building in the specific confined context of the inner city, Glück had to develop a series of creative solutions for specific problems. To date, there are hardly any other stepped terrace complexes with a similar concentration of unique solutions to be found worldwide. The Inzersdorfer Strasse complex follows the surrounding block structure in a U-shape on three sides, with the communal greenspace opening up to the south to Angeligasse, a pedestrian zone at this point.

The logic of the complex initially followed that of a conventional apartment building, but the terracing inevitably led to several essential structural changes. Due to the stepped gradation, the depth of the floors decreases as the height increases, resulting in larger floor plans on the ground floor with potentially difficult-to-use depths. In corner situations, geometrically speaking, the protrusion of the lower floors leads to intersecting areas facing the courtyard. Glück would later solve this problem at Arndtstrasse and Heinz-Nittel-Hof with a bridge section, mitigating the problem by implementing obtuse angles. For other, narrower sites, such as at Magdeburger Strasse, Glück resorted to a simple row development. At Inzersdorfer Strasse he changed the terrace dimensions. At the corner and in the adjacent partitions, the terraces recede only every other story, while each alternate story is terraced. This provides greater depth in these areas, thus reducing the corner problem significantly.

At the two south-facing ends of the U-shape, Glück placed two short blocks that provide a logical conclusion to the east-west oriented tracts and create a row of additional high-quality dwellings and—typical of Glück—at the same time further increase the site utilization and thus the economic efficiency of the project.

These short blocks alone encompass a microcosm of stepped terrace housing: one east and one west-facing apartment are inserted into each of the five lower floors, also terraced. The dark interior areas hold storage rooms for the tenants and additional communal use rooms are located on the ground floor. The situation changes on the upper three floors. Due to the receding terraces, the depths are particularly shallow here. There are smaller dwellings here and apartments extend across numerous cross-wall partitions. The problem is particularly pronounced in the units facing Braunspergengasse,

Inzersdorfer Strasse residential complex, south side, 1973

Depiction of circulation and apartment types

where the street side must also be stepped back to the maintain the angle of light incidence in relation to the neighboring buildings. This means that there are no standard apartments on the upper floors here; each apartment unit is unique and adapted to the specific situation.

Circulation

The complex is accessed via four staircases. The two staircases on Inzersdorfer Strasse have a dual function, each serving two different areas of the building. On the one hand, they provide access to the apartments in the main wing via three central corridors that, highly economical, are only situated on every third floor. This is made possible by the split-level arrangement of maisonette apartments, which represent the majority of apartments in this part of the building.

Entering an apartment from the corridor, one first goes up or down half a level to the north-facing bedrooms and from there another half floor level further on to the courtyard-facing living areas, which are located either above or below the corridor level. Two of the three corridor floors also access apartments on the same level that are oriented southwards. From the middle wing, the same staircases also serve as a multi-level access to the side wings. Each floor has an additional short corridor to the side wings from which four to five east-west oriented apartments, including the corner apartments, can be accessed. The final two staircases, located at the ends of the U-shape, connect to seven apartments per floor in a similar manner. There is

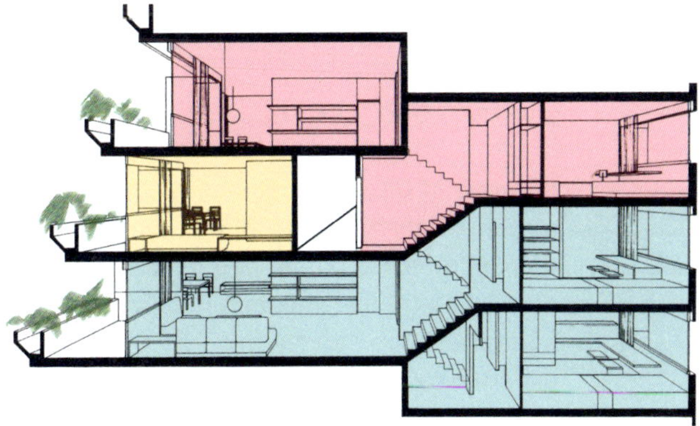

always a dwelling at the ends of the corridors, further optimizing the use of space. Only on the second floor does the corridor intersect with all the staircases, making it possible to pass through the entire complex internally.

Apartment typology

In general, the high variability of access situations and block depths results in a wide range of housing types, in terms of size, orientation, and layout. The dwellings themselves—currently 222 in number—follow a similar organizational logic despite all their differences. The distance of 5.6 meters between the partitions makes either one larger room, such as a living room, or two smaller rooms each 2.76 meters wide possible. This means that apartment size varies more in terms of unit depth than by width. Double partition apartments have an area ranging between 70 and 90 square meters. The largest apartments are maisonettes in the central area, with about 139 square meters of floor area. There are, however, also far smaller units with a total area of about 32 square meters. The living room, kitchen, and private areas can be accessed separately from the central entrance area of the apartments. Kitchens have a width of 190 centimeters and are generally located in the same cross-wall partition as the living room, connected to the living room via the dining area. Servant spaces such as sanitary and storage rooms are accommodated in the interior, less well-lit zones.

Construction method

In terms of design, Glück uses the proven cross-wall construction method, which—resembling an open shelf—allows him to dispense with a conventional facade on the terraced side. Floor-to-ceiling glazing elements are used here instead, which visually completely open the living spaces towards the terrace and thus creating a full experience of the greenery outside from the interior and truly making the terrace an extended living room.

This consistent opening of the rooms not only shapes the spatial experience, it also maximizes the incidence of light into the depths of the rooms, and reduces construction costs and time. Instead of "cheese with holes," as perforated facades were called in those days, an economically, human-ecologically, basically in every respect better, transition between inside and outside is created. These guiding design ideas are carried out consistently down to the smallest detail. For example, the window profiles were developed in-house by Glück's office using frameless all-glass panes in a mahogany frame. The planters were formative elements of Glück's buildings and the subject of constant development. In this case, they are 62-centimeter-high precast concrete elements placed directly onto the floor slab. From the inside, they act as a simple parapet wall that reaches to the ground yet, due to its low height, allows more greenery and light to enter. A steel handrail fulfills the regulation height.

In later projects, such as the Alt-Erlaa residential park, Glück elevates fiberglass planters from the ground. The depth of the planters, filled with greenery, makes it difficult to see the terraces below, while clever projections, recesses, and wall panels between dwellings prevent views between neighbors. The consistent design principles of his terraces, namely a usable depth, a high degree of visual privacy, and the persistent inclusion of greenery are otherwise found in only a few examples at the time: Alexandra Road in London has only narrow concrete slabs, the Brunswick Centre provides no options for planting at all—only the Olympic Village in Munich shows similar considerations regarding planting.

Some differences in the choice of materials and fixtures can be observed in relation to current practices. Sound insulation was provided by fitted carpets in the apartments and needle-felt in the hallways. This would no longer be possible today, as building regulations assume that the building structure alone should suffice as the sound insulation. Eight-centimeter-thick partition walls were made of autoclaved aerated concrete. Kitchens, bathrooms, and toilets were equipped with a mechanical forced-air ventilation system above the roof. Thermal insulation was provided on the roof with five centimeters of expanded polystyrene, and the soffits of the cantilevered building components are insulated with cork panels, terraces as well as some bay windows. Today, these insulation thicknesses would certainly be higher, but by themselves do not cause any essential structural differences. It is only today's barrier-free access requirements that could no longer be achieved without split-level ceilings.

Outdoor facilities

The entire complex has a number of features in the outdoor areas that became characteristic in later buildings. The first stepped terrace building already has not only a swimming pool on the roof, but also a large sundeck and two sauna areas. On the northeast corner of the ground floor there is now a kindergarten, which was formerly a supermarket. Parking is in the basement.

One can see how Glück places the various elements of the stepped terrace building at the Inzersdorfer Strasse residential complex like a chess player positions his pieces. Many of these elements are later found in various future projects. This specific combined vertical and horizontal shared access typology will be seen again at the Heinz-Nittel-Hof, while the maisonettes are found again at the Hadikgasse housing estate. Other elements, such as the floor plan solutions and the continuous glazing on the terrace side, will become integral parts of all future stepped terrace structures.

The swimming pool on the roof will become the new social meeting place, replacing involuntary meetings at the *Bassena*, the water basin once located in the corridors of historic buildings. As in later projects, Glück succeeds in implementing a very high standard of furnishings, high not only for social housing, and only possible thanks to the great inherent economy of the design principles. Precisely this point—being able to create the highest quality for the greatest possible number, something in which others obviously did not succeed to the same extent—was and still is perceived as being paradoxical and impossible. Glück was confronted with this skepticism despite the number of apartments actually built. In his dissertation, Glück therefore provides detailed calculations to dispel the widespread misconception that stepped terrace housing must be more expensive to build than conventional structures. Today, the cycle that began with Inzersdorfer Strasse is closing once again—questions of economy, ecology, and humane building for the greatest possible number is more important now than ever.

Reception

Glück's buildings were already strongly polarizing during construction. Time has refuted many of the arguments of his contemporary challengers—none of the buildings today can be described as desolate concrete deserts—while the architect's declared goals can be judged as having been accomplished based upon many years of resident surveys. Just how unobjective, sometimes even absurd, the discussion at the time was is shown by the question of economy of means. For contemporary critics, this was not even up for debate. On the contrary, economic efficiency, i.e. the best possible use of available resources, was repeatedly emphasized as a point particularly worthy of criticism.

In order to better understand the vehemence of the debate, it is necessary to take a step back and look at the overall context. In fact, the debate is less about the actual building, with the reception reflecting instead a fundamental Austrian and international discourse within the architectural community about the nature of architecture. Thus architecture is understood as an expression of traditional, formal values, a distinctive interpretation of architectural concepts, of architecture and building culture as a primarily artistic activity, and sees few points of identification in the functional maximization of stepped terrace housing.

The Austrian architecture critic Friedrich Achleitner has repeatedly addressed this critique of functional modernism—representative of many others—in interviews and articles. In an article in *Falter* newspaper (25/83), for example, he explains that Glück's buildings had little to do with architecture. Of course, this line of argumentation is daring in terms of architectural theory, because it de facto denies the entire functional modernism's role in architecture. Many others, however, did not share this criticism. On the contrary, journalists have written books and users completed surveys giving glowing, enthusiastic testimonials about Glück's buildings. Not surprisingly, considering that the goal of functionalist modernism, to serve the needs of the people, was indeed impressively achieved. However, the project on Inzersdorfer Strasse was only the beginning of a debate that was to intensify considerably over the years, and still continues today.

Bibliography

Glück, Harry. "Einreichplan für die Errichtung eines Wohnhauses." In *Wien 10*, MA37, Vienna, 1971.

Glück, Harry. "Bestandsplan für eine Wohnhausanlage." In *Wien 10*, Vienna, 1973.

Glück, Harry. "Höherwertige Alternativen im Massenwohnbau durch wirtschaftliche Planungs- und Konstruktionskonzepte." Dissertation, 1982.

ERVICE
LV464DN

Apartments 291
Floor space index 2.3
Built area ratio 44 %

Site area ca. 17,300 m²
Built area 7,600 m²
Gross floor area ca. 40,000 m²

Collective facilities, infrastructure:
Community rooms, shops and bars

Vienna, Austria
Weiglgasse 6–10—Anschützgasse—Siebeneichengasse—Jheringgasse

Architect
Wilhelm Holzbauer

Client
City of Vienna, part of the Wohnen Morgen initiative of the Austrian Federal Ministry of Buildings and Technology in 1968

Start of planning 1973 (competition)
Construction 1976–80

Site plan 1:10,000

Wohnen Morgen Wien

Wilhelm Holzbauer

1973–80

Between Street and Garden[1]

Maria Welzig

In 1968, a revolutionary year, the Austrian federal government—governed solely by the People's Party at the time—founded a housing research department. Its first initiative was the *Wohnen Morgen* (Living Tomorrow) campaign—a series of architectural competitions held Austria's nine states[2] aiming to "show new paths in housing—technically, economically, and socially."[3] Although the objectives were not taken very seriously, and were only implemented in two of the nine competitions, namely in Vienna and Lower Austria, the initiative remains exemplary today—and unique. Wohnen Morgen was a government initiative, however, the selection of the site, the organization of the competition, and its realization—with federal funding—was the responsibility of the individual states.

Stepped terrace housing in a Gründerzeit neighborhood

The competition for Wohnen Morgen Wien took place 1973, a time when the debate on housing and urban development was increasingly focusing on inner-city regeneration. The City of Vienna chose its planning area accordingly: a *Gründerzeit* district erected in the late nineteenth century as a purely financial venture. The fifteenth district on Weiglgasse was clearly below the Vienna average in all social parameters. The new housing project was planned at the site of a

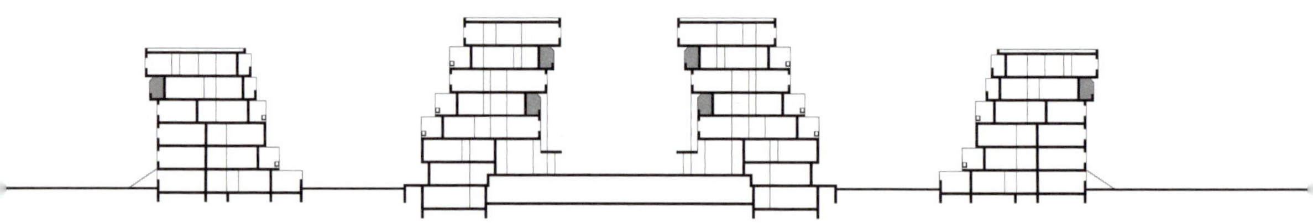

Floor plan 1st and 3rd upper floors, Cross-section 1:1,000

turn-of-the-century tram depot, with the southern part of the depot being replaced by the realized project.[4] The northern part, beyond Siebeneichengasse (today Rudolfsheim Service Depot), was also designated by the competition as a planning area for a second phase of realization and formed part of the call for proposals. However, the second phase was never implemented.[5] The remaining part of the depot, with its innovative construction dating back to the early twentieth century, is now listed as a historical monument.

In February 1974, the competition jury selected a project by Wilhelm Holzbauer as the winner from sixty-five submitted projects.[6] Holzbauer (1930–2019) started out as a member of Arbeitsgruppe 4, had spent a decade in the USA and Canada, and was already a successful architect with offices in Vienna and Amsterdam at the time. He knew how to integrate the stepped terrace structure, a central residential and urban planning theme of the 1968 era, into the inner city area and how to tie it into the topic of public space.

The project breaks away from the existing perimeter block scheme to propose a new structural concept for urban regeneration: an alternating sequence of green zones, streets, and pedestrian areas with parallel linear buildings between them.

In this specific case, there are four north-south running rows. The two outer rows are six stories high, while the two inner ones are seven stories high. The buildings have stepped terraces on one side, overlooking the greenspaces. Contrasting this on the other side, the buildings project towards the central pedestrian street and the adjoining avenues. Structurally, the building is a cross-wall construction with load-bearing walls set 5.5 meters apart. To accommodate the cantilevers, every third supporting wall is drawn forward to the cantilever and then extended to the ground like a column, thus creating a formal defining element.

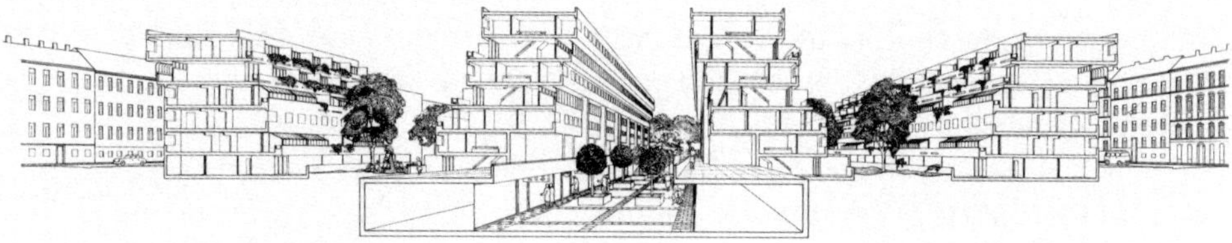

The pedestrian street as a place of communication

In his project statement, the architect describes the pedestrian street, a traffic calmed avenue, as the guiding theme of his design: "The pedestrian avenue includes all the functions that the 'street' has always had: shopping, playground, market lane, etc."[7] The street, he says, acts as a "communicative urban planning element."[8] The prerequisite for this is freeing the space from the dominance of cars. In the Wohnen Morgen complex, cars drive from Weiglgasse into a double-story underground car park below the two central apartment blocks. Having an urban shop zone is also a central concept of the Brunswick Centre in London, which had already been extensively published in 1972.[9]

The pedestrian street has a big city feel. The cantilevers of the linear buildings look like the edges of a roof canopy, contributing to the urban character. The large scale and compact form of the buildings creates a new kind of city space. Holzbauer has sunk the southern section of the pedestrian street to form a square situated at a lower level. For a quarter of a century, this square functioned as a site of communication and shopping center that included a restaurant, grocery store, butcher, and fruit and vegetable shop.[10] The cafés, restaurants, and shops were also frequented by people from outside of the neighborhood. The sunken square functioned as a local supply center until 2006, When the City of Vienna built an additional underground parking garage in its place—a questionable

Wilhelm Holzbauer, Wohnen Morgen Wien, sectional, 1975, view from the south

Glazed staircase, garden elevation, photo 2019

decision at best. As of 2019, an office supplies store, a nail studio, and a dog salon were still operating in the pedestrian street. The common rooms are still available to residents. The demand for use—now primarily for individual purposes, and less for the tenant community—is high.

Stacked single-family homes

The competition project had envisaged having only maisonette apartments, all with larger floor plans (65 and 117 square meters) and accessed via balcony walkways. For the realization, however, the City of Vienna stipulated a greater variety of apartment types and sizes.[11] The 291 finished apartments vary in size from 45 to 130 square meters (including terraces and loggias) and are of several different types. The apartments are mainly split-level (1st and 2nd levels) and maisonette (4th, 5th, 6th, and 7th levels), and single-story apartments (3rd level) were also added. The complex also offers nine apartments specifically designed for the elderly and disabled on the ground floor.

Balcony walkways—at the time rather frowned upon—access the maisonette apartments on the upper floors. The curving glazed walkways are a recognizable feature of the complex. The staircases give the facades rhythm and form monumental niches facing the streets. The facades towards the greenspaces are generously glazed and highlighted by distinctive circular windows. Another form of access—and a distinctive trait of the complex—is the direct entry

Living street with play niche, ca, 1980

Living street with a sunken square removed in 2006 for an expansion of the underground garage. Ca. 1980

to the apartments from outside. On the ground floor, one can enter the split-level apartments directly from the pedestrian street, while outside stairs lead to the apartments on the third level. This kind of direct access to the apartments of a multi-story building is atypical for Vienna. In Anglo-Saxon countries, however, it is widespread and this type of access is also found in the Alexandra Road Estate (see p. 289ff). This type of circulation conveys a feeling of living in one's own house, as do maisonette and split-level apartments. The principle of stacked single-family homes is thus clearly visible in the Wohnen Morgen Wien project.

The living rooms and some of the bedrooms are oriented towards the greenspace. The entrance, kitchen, adjoining rooms, and the remaining bedrooms face either the pedestrian street or an adjacent avenue. Although the structure of Wohnen Morgen Wien would have allowed generous fenestration, the apartments often have punch windows. Each apartment has a 12-square meter terrace or a garden courtyard and terraces are equipped with large polyester planters.

Form versus open-use structure

With the Monte Amiata residential complex in Gallaratese near Milan, built from 1967 to 1972 and widely published, Carlo Aymonino and Aldo Rossi introduced classical tendencies into architecture. The Wohnen Morgen Wien complex bears a number of references to it, including an emphasis on formal aspects, the row of partitions

that appear as monumental pillars facing the pedestrian street, the strong plasticity of the niches, the rhythmically aligned punch windows, the use of color as a design element,[12] and the street/square theme.

Although Wohnen Morgen uses a cross-wall structural system, load-bearing exterior walls are suggested—a formal gesture that refers back to the "facade."

In contrast to Aymonino and Rossi, about whose scheme it was said "that neither nature nor man has a place in this architecture,"[13] Holzbauer combines the street with greenspaces and gives residents private outdoor spaces oriented towards the greenspace. However, the stepped terrace housing principle of providing a "raw structure" within which each terrace can become a small, personal realm of greenery becomes secondary to his desire for form in the project.[14]

Social climate

A total of 450 square meters were allocated for all communal areas: four shared recreation rooms and a youth club, as well as laundry rooms and other infrastructural spaces. The recreation rooms are located right on the pedestrian street with large glazed areas allowing views both in and out. In addition, six spacious alcoves on the ground floor create an inviting space for undercover outdoor play.

Wohnen Morgen Wien demonstrates what a powerful effect architecture can have. The innovative architectural statement was a catalyst for the residents of the municipal building to empower themselves, to establish the *Wohnen heute* tenants' association, and to publish an informational leaflet with the same title.[15] The residents successfully fought to get the keys to the communal rooms from the City of Vienna, who had denied them the use of the spaces for a year and a half.

The majority of residents had voted to use the four shared spaces for the following purposes: Room 1: General events area for discussions, film screenings, lectures, etc.; Room 2: Exhibition space; Room 3: Arts and crafts room; Room 4: "Family room," possibly a kindergarten for some hours.[16]

The *Wohnen heute* association subsequently organized numerous events, from children's parties, to discussions and film screenings. It also dealt with legal issues and tenant concerns. Its aim was "to support a way for residents to live together in this exemplary housing estate that, along with its unique architectural design, could make this housing estate a model for contemporary living."[17] Residents also founded the Wohnen Morgen Sports and Leisure Club shortly after the complex was moved into.

Automobile access on the sunken square turned out to be problematic. It was actually only intended for deliveries, but soon mutated into a parking area. The green zones between the residential rows were initially based on a shared space approach, as was the pedestrian street. However, this public accessibility led to problems and the green areas were fenced off along the streets and reserved for residents only, as had initially been planned.[18]

In a 1983 study on social housing satisfaction in Austria, *Wohnen morgen Wien* achieved an above-average rating—partly due to the social aspect.[19] On an evening in June 2019: The linden trees, planted as part of the residential complex, are fragrant. On the street, two little boys are driving around in electric sports cars, women are sitting and chatting on the benches along Siebeneichengasse, and young men are playing football with a can. A man open his apartment door, entering directly from the street. Teenagers now hang out in the sunken area in front of the garage, a remnant of the original sunken square. A group of young girls are playing in one of the alcoves with their dolls and a toy buggy.

Alternatives to the perimeter block grid

The complex ties into the surrounding development structure by positioning the buildings along the perimeter of the north-south axial road. The new scheme also connects to the existing *Gründerzeit* buildings along these two roads, mirroring their height. Wohnen Morgen, however, does not form a perimeter block closed on all sides, instead, the open square and greenspaces of the complex are shared with the surroundings.

New typologies are introduced by the pedestrian street, greenspaces, front gardens, and stepped terraces. The residential complex shows that alternatives to the stringent perimeter block grids of the *Gründerzeit* era are indeed possible. The fact that an alternative, an upgrade, was deliberately sought is shown by the departure from the *Gründerzeit* building line along all four adjoining streets. The Wohnen Morgen development is shifted back to enable tree-filled front gardens in a grey neighborhood, an effective method of attaining a more ecological city.

Notes

1 Echoing the title of a report on Wohnen Morgen Wien "Entre rue et jardin. Opération Wohnen-Morgen, Vienne, Autriche." In *L'architecture d'aujourdhui*, 215 (1981), 10–15.

2 At the same time as the Department of Housing Research was established in 1968, the new Housing Subsidies Act made housing promotion the responsibility of each state.

3 Heiduk, Kurt (ed.). *Wohnen morgen—Baukünstlerischer Wettbewerb Kärnten.* Federal Ministry for Buildings and Technology, Vienna 1970.

4 This was the location of the main Wiener Linien service station, now relocated.

5 The constructed building is located between Weiglgasse, Anschützgasse, Siebeneichengasse, and Jheringgasse.

6 Jury head was the architect Hans Aigner. The jury included Gustav Peichl, also a member of the Housing Advisory Board.

7 Holzbauer, Wilhelm. "Baubeschreibung Wettbewerb, 1974." In *Wohnen Morgen Wien*, report 1982, 5.

8 Ibid., 4.

9 Cf. in this book, the chapter by Clare Melhuish on the Brunswick Centre.

10 See photos from the time of completion as well as information from Erika Klabouch, a tenant in the complex since 1980. She has organized numerous activities for children in the residential complex since the 1990s and has established a women's group. Together with another resident, she also manages the use of the common rooms.

11 In addition, the center-to-center distance of the cross walls was increased from 5.2 meters to 5.5 meters and the height of the inner rows was reduced from eight to seven stories. The long elevations to the streets were constructed without the pronounced staggered projections.

12 Holzbauer had originally had proposed a red mosaic cladding for the cantilevered sections of the building. Cf. Sterk, Harald. "Wohnen morgen—nur in Wien und Neumarkt?" In *Wien Aktuell,* 1976, 15.

13 A statement by Margrit Kennedy after a lecture by Carlo Aymoninos at the Berlin Summer Academy 1978 on Gallaratese, published in: *bauwelt 31/1978*, quoted from genova, Architektur und Dogma 3's blog - Gallaratese: "Beklemmende Atmosphäre," 3 July 2014. https://exportabel.wordpress.com/2014/07/03/gallaratese-beklemmende-atmosphare/ (28.09.2019). In this lecture, Aymonino reported that he had successfully prevented the planting of a row of trees.

14 Lorenzo de Chiffre refers to the possible prototypical effect of James Sterling's Southgate Estate in Runcorn New Town (built from 1968 to 1977) for timber builders, see De Chiffre 2016, p. 177.

15 Josef Michlmayr, resident and co-founder of the *Wohnen heute* association, wrote in 1982: "Inspired by the architecture of Wohnen Morgen Wien, it was only natural that residents established contact with each other, and they soon formed a community of interest. This community has evolved into an association to which a substantial part of the residents of our housing estate belong today." In: Information sheet "Wohnen heute," No. 7–8, 1981/1982, 12, In *Wohnen Morgen Wien,* Report, 1982, Appendix.

16 "Gemeinschaftsraum-Story 3. Teil. Geschichte mit 'Happy End?'" In: Information sheet *Wohnen heute*, 4, 1981, 2 In *Wohnen Morgen Wien*, Report, 1982, Appendix.

17 Steinböck, Hans. "Ein Jahr 'Wohnen heute.'" In: Informationsblatt *Wohnen heute*, Nr. 7–8, 1981/1982, 9. In *Wohnen Morgen Wien*, Report, 1982, Appendix.

18 Cf. Fröschl, Johann. "2 Jahre 'wohnen morgen wien,' information sheet *Wohnen heute* 11 (1982, In *Wohnen Morgen Wien*, Report, 1982, Appendix, 3.

19 "Wohnwertuntersuchung für den sozialen Wohnbau in Österreich." Federal Ministry for Buildings and Technology, Vienna 1983.

Bibliography

De Chiffre, Lorenzo. "Das Wiener Terrassenhaus. Entwicklungsphasen und Aktualität eines historischen Wohntypus mit Fokus auf den lokalspezifischen architektonischen Diskurs." Dissertation at the Faculty of Architecture and Spatial Planning of the TU Wien, Vienna, 2016, 163–178.

"Entre rue et jardin. Opération Wohnen-Morgen, Vienne, Autriche." In *L'architecture d'aujourdhui*, 215, 1981, 10–15.

Heiduk, Kurt (ed.). "Wohnen morgen—Baukünstlerischer Wettbewerb Wien." Federal Ministry for Buildings and Technology. Vienna, 1974.

Holzbauer, Wilhelm. "Wohnquartier in Wien, 15. Bezirk." In *Baumeister*, 5, 480–482, 1980.

Holzbauer, Wilhelm. "Social Housing 'Wohnen Morgen', Vienna." In *GA Document 2*, 1980, 108–115.

Holzbauer, Wilhelm. *Wilhelm Holzbauer: Bauten und Projekte 1953–1985*. Salzberg: Residenzverlag, 1985, 92–101.

Holzbauer, Wilhelm. *Wilhelm Holzbauer: Buildings and Projects. Bauten und Projekte*. Stuttgart: Menges, 1995, 68–73.

"Housing Project 'Wohnen Morgen.'" In *AD-Toshi-Jutaicu*, 7, 1981, 6–13.

Johann, W. "Experimentele Woningbouw in Wenen: Een invuloefening van Holzbauer." In *De Architect*, 10, 1981, 55–99.

Kneissl, Franz E., Elsa Prochazka, and Rudolf Wessely. "Wohnen Morgen." In *Architektur.aktuell*, No. 50, 1975, 21–32.

"La Memoria della città/A city's memory." In *Domus*, 615, 1981, 17–19.

Sterk, Harald. "Wohnen morgen–nur in Wien und Neumarkt?" In *Wien Aktuell*, Official publication of the Federal Capital, City of Vienna Press and Information Service, 12, 1976, 13–15.

"Urbanes Leben: Demonstrativbau des Wettbewerbes 'Wohnen Morgen.'" In *Wien 15, Wohnen Morgen Wien*, report, compiled by Wilhelm Holzbauer, edited by the Federal Ministry for Buildings and Technology, Vienna, 1982.

Waechter-Böhm, Liesbeth (ed.). *Wilhelm Holzbauer: Holzbauer und Partner, Holzbauer und Irresberger*. Vienna: Springer, 2006, 156–161.

13

EINBAHN
15., Weiglgasse
ARMUT

B8

Inner-City Hybrids

Brunswick Centre, London
Patrick Hodgkinson
1967–72

La Serra, Ivrea
Iginio Cappai, Pietro Mainardis
1967–75

Apartments 560
Built area ratio 67 %

Site area ca. 27,600 m²
Built area 18,500 m²

Collective facilities, infrastructure:
Shops, supermarket, cinema, underground parking

London, UK
Brunswick Square, Bloomsbury

Architect
Patrick Hodgkinson

Client
London Borough of Camden

Planning 1967–69
Construction 1969–72

Site plan 1:10,000

Brunswick Centre, London

Patrick Hodgkinson

1967–72

The Brunswick, Revisited as a Model for Housing in a Green and Equitable City

Clare Melhuish

Architect Patrick Hodgkinson described his design for the Brunswick, formerly known as the Brunswick Centre, as being "about making a new village for central London, rich with the panoply of life of the West End's villages of old, yet possessing a new, life-giving spirit."[1] He argued that, in contrast to the radial slab block model presented by Le Corbusier in his Unité d'Habitation, Britain's linear Georgian terraced housing—exemplified in the Bloomsbury/Holborn area of central London—could support high densities of occupation in conjunction with open spaces, in a form suitable to the temperate native climate and customs. However, one aspect of that historical model which he did not favor was the clear social hierarchy it embodied in houses visually ordered into recognizable classes of dwelling. His vision for the Brunswick was infused by a dream of social equality and was intended to provide a mix of housing types where people of all social classes and identities could live alongside each other without distinction. In that sense, it continues to represent a relevant model for mixed-use housing development in central urban areas today, even though the architect's social vision has never been fully realized due to changes to the design and ownership of the building that were implemented just prior to construction.

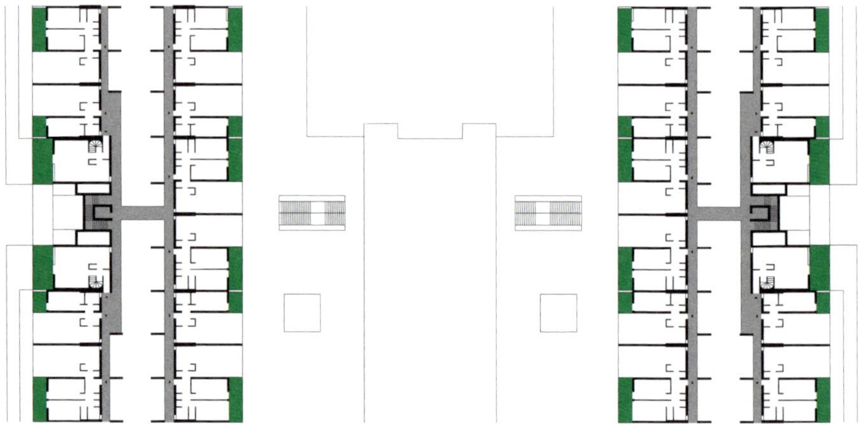

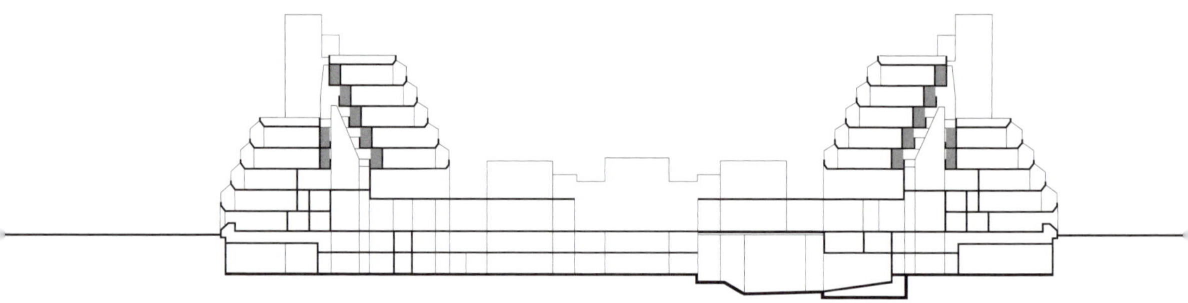

Floor plan 2nd upper floors, Cross-section, 1:1,000

A troubled history

The Brunswick was recognized as a high-profile architectural monument in 2000, listed Grade II and described in the Department of Culture, Media, and Sport's listing schedule as "a pioneering example of a megastructure in England: of a scheme which combines several functions of equal importance within a single framework. It is also the pioneering example of low-rise, high-density housing, a field in which Britain was extremely influential on this scale. [...] Brunswick developed the concept of the stepped section on a large scale and for a range of facilities, whose formality was pioneering."[2] But by that point the building was also very dilapidated following two decades of maintenance and changes in the council's housing allocation policy. It had also suffered greatly from negative press, residents' discontent, and a series of proposals since 1990 for its radical redevelopment in response to its perceived failures.

Since its completion in 1973 as a council housing development by the London Borough of Camden, above a ground-level shopping precinct in private ownership, the Brunswick has been experienced as a highly problematic living environment by many of its residents and by the council's housing managers, demanding a high level of maintenance and intervention to ensure the security of its inhabitants from intruders, including drug users and prostitutes.

At the same time, the Brunswick was favored by council tenants compared to neighboring blocks, because of the high standard of accommodation it offered in terms of the size and brightness of the flats. It also provided a large amount of sheltered public open space in its central precinct and first floor level terraces. Hodgkinson conceived these as "pleasure gardens" overlooking a "town room," with "professional chambers" opening onto the terraces.

However, these extensive upper-level spaces were eventually closed off from public use for security reasons, with the removal of the grand staircase drawing people up from the precinct and the installation of security doors to the open access points into the housing blocks from the street.

The shop units in the precinct were, for 30 years until the refurbishment of 2006, under-occupied and offered little in the way of local retail opportunity or public interaction, but in the last decade redevelopment as "a high street for Bloomsbury" has brought new

Brunswick, perspective through the atrium, Outline Planning Scheme 1963.

Resident on his terrace with the October issue of *Architectural Review* 1972 in hand.

life to the Brunswick's central public space—even though it may be relatively little-used by residents of the tiered housing above.

Hodgkinson described the project as being intended for "urbanites"—a gateway to the resources and pleasures of the central city, reflecting a particular positioning of Holborn as a residential area in close proximity to both the West End and the City of London, and to the major transport interchanges of King's Cross and St Pancras railway stations. In so doing, he made a distinction between the nature of the Brunswick development and other projects (such as his proposal for the Loughborough Estate), which were more family-focused. Camden Council's explicit intention when it took on the housing lease in 1965 was to use the scheme as a way of re-introducing family life into a neighborhood in which institutional usage was becoming increasingly prevalent, but by reducing the range of housing units in its cost-cutting exercise, it set inflexible constraints, minimizing household size. On the project's completion, some critics suggested that the building could never be expected to work successfully as a social housing estate, due to its innovative architectural design and aesthetic: "Council tenants, unlike the middle-income, middle-class inhabitants initially expected on the site, are unlikely to be respecters of the clean contemporary lines of the exterior."[3] The poet John Betjeman slammed the development in scathing and sarcastic terms in a piece suggestively entitled "The New Barbarism."[4]

In 1972, Theo Crosby, editor of the *Architectural Review*, referred to the new building as a "megastructure" for the first time, suggesting

that the form was inherently flawed as a model for successful urban development: "The megastructure, because it is self-contained, does not integrate with its surroundings. It is an alien growth, and for its own success it must eat up the surroundings as quickly as possible so as to impose its own order and system on every aspect of life there."[5] However, two female journalists who interviewed the first tenants reported more positive findings. Violet Johnstone wrote that they "find it provides a sense of identity"[6] and Ena Kendall noted that tenants appreciated the new environment, especially the open space it offered. Indeed, when the first crude, commercially driven proposals were made for redevelopment of the estate, they were strongly opposed by the residential as well as the expert community.

They ultimately led to the national heritage listing of the building for its own protection, as well as inspiring Hodgkinson's own tireless campaign to complete the work as originally conceived, which bore fruit in the regeneration project finally completed in 2006 by executive architects Levitt Bernstein.

A radical model: low-rise, high-density, mixed-use

In her report, Kendall also dismissed the term "urban megastructure" as a "lumpish description" for the new development,[7] and her comment underlines the importance of understanding the complex architectural history of the Brunswick in order to re-evaluate its significance as a model for mixed-used housing in the contemporary green city. As Hodgkinson was at pains to point out, one of its primary features was the fact that it returned 75 percent open space to the site compared to the original nineteenth-century terraced housing and backyards which stood on the site, along with what was intended to be a mix of housing types for people of different backgrounds, in close proximity to local shopping around a traffic-free square. The definition of the building as a "megastructure" was subsequently to become embedded in the architectural genealogy of the Brunswick as a result of Reyner Banham's eponymous book featuring the project,[8] but Hodgkinson hated the description due to its association with the ideas of authoritarian social control referenced by Crosby in his analysis.[9] By contrast, he embraced the critic Colin Rowe's more celebratory comparison of the Brunswick with the Palais Royale (1639) in Paris, and also cited as an antecedent the Adelphi in London, the grand speculative development of houses over vaulted warehouses near the Thames designed by the Adam brothers from 1768.

Indeed, in an architectural and planning climate dominated by the ruthless thinking and practice of Le Corbusier and the European school of functionalist Modernism, Hodgkinson's rich mix of influences and referents—English Gothic, Arts and Crafts, and the Festival of Britain, from Scandinavian Modernism to Futurism, and from Sartrian existentialism to Lewis Mumford's "precinctual" approach—was unusual. Hodgkinson's first ideas for the project were expressed in plans for brick-built, linear buildings organized internally around staircases, and externally around sheltered, bounded open spaces—an image of domestic tranquility as in a grand medieval house, monastery, or the universities of Oxford and Cambridge, quite different from the monumental, even futuristic presence of the A-frame structure that was eventually constructed. He subsequently developed an open-ended, linear configuration of buildings and sheltered spaces on the site, free of traffic, and elevated on a plinth to allow for underground servicing and car parking. It included a centrally placed circular recital hall (replaced by a covered shopping hall in 1963) and 54 shops on each side facing into the precinct, away from the traffic around the perimeter of the building.

The stepped section of the blocks was in place from an early stage, to provide midday sun into all the living rooms, east or west facing, and glass-enclosed "winter-gardens" for every flat. But the design for the monumental A-frame structure (developed with engineer Felix Samuely) which had emerged by 1965, with open terraces opening from the internal atrium level to overlook the shopping precinct below, was only a by-product of changes in building legislation that meant the structure had to be engineered and executed in reinforced concrete instead of brick. Hodgkinson objected to Banham's subsequent description of the Brunswick as a tribute to Sant'Elia, "the virtual inventor of the A-frame Terrassenhäuser section"[10] pointing to the less well-known Elberfeld hospital project of 1928 by Marcel Breuer and Walter Gropius, and Henri Sauvage's Rue Vavin apartment block in Paris of 1911–1912 as more significant influences. He emphasized his intention not to produce an oppressive, overbearing concrete megastructure detached from its urban surroundings, but to express an existential dimension to everyday life, allowing residents to look up towards the sky, above and away from the depressingly mundane street-level environment of post-war London.

Nevertheless, the scheme has also become notorious as a Brutalist building through its lifetime, its exposed concrete facades interpreted as representing the very opposite of green city values. Residents of the Brunswick have been clear during its lifetime that the material conditions of their lives have not been satisfactory, participating in a discourse of complaint focused on the local council and its failure to address the material inadequacies of the construction, manifested in leaks, stains, corrosion, and strange smells which have permeated the housing blocks over many years. But Hodgkinson later explained, "I myself reject Brutalism [...] because I felt it was inhuman and just a fashionable gimmick,"[11] insisting that he had never intended the materiality of the building as it was realized to be understood as an ideological statement. He embraced the opportunities offered by the refurbishment in 2006 to address some of the building's maintenance problems and cover its exposed facades as he had originally envisaged with a cream-colored finish evoking John Nash's grand stucco terraces at Regent's Park.

Framework for social change

When the redevelopment of the Brunswick Centre site in Holborn, central London, was first mooted in 1958, the proposals aroused a public outcry, and there was considerable dismay among locals at the prospect of what was described as a deeply-rooted population being displaced. But the decision to proceed was based on the principle of radical redevelopment in bomb-blasted London, established by Abercrombie and Forshaw's Statutory Development Plan of 1951, and housing on the site which had been condemned as substandard was demolished under subsequent legislation launching a major slum clearance program. By 1963, the Ministry of Transport had set out further recommendations to create traffic-free "environmental areas" in cities, surrounded by new highways for fast-moving traffic,[12] which built on clearance policies, and directly informed the design evolution of the Brunswick scheme as a "precinctual" approach to housing development.

Patrick Hodgkinson's mixed-use proposal needs to be understood as a radical counter-proposal to the original planning applications made for the site between 1958 and 1960 by developer Marchmont Properties and architects Covell and Matthews. Their scheme comprising a 40-story office block, three 20-story blocks of flats, and some long five-story blocks containing shops and hostel accommodation for the University of London was rejected by the London County Council, which was concerned about preserving the resi-

Brunswick pedestrian area, view of the shops from the south before the 2006 renovation

A new main shopping street for Bloomsbury: view of the pedestrian area after the renovation, with a new supermarket in the north

Living room with winter garden

dential character of the neighborhood. In 1959, Marchmont was advised to appoint Leslie Martin, who had recently left his position as chief architect at the LCC (where he had been responsible for the design of the high-rise Alton Estate in Roehampton, southwest London), because he could exert political leverage, and was also familiar with the Bloomsbury context. Hodgkinson was working in Martin's office on a number of low-rise, high-density housing schemes, including an alternative project for the LCC's Loughborough Estate in Brixton, and was opposed both to the slum clearance policies established by the County of London plan, and the Corbusian model of housing development embraced by the LCC.

Hodgkinson's vision for the Brunswick was of a coherent architectural framework which could bring public and private lifeworlds together through a network of spaces at different scales, connecting private dwellings to the street and the city across a series of thresholds. It would allow different households and communities to live alongside each other in relative privacy compared to the tight-knit traditional neighborhood street, and in many ways it establishes a model for inner-city redevelopment which does just that, notwithstanding the alterations to the architectural concept that have been realized over time to delineate and secure those boundaries more closely.

In 1992, the Architects' Journal commented that the way in which residents had "personalized" their external balconies had led to the Brunswick developing a rather exotic feel, comparable with Louis

Kahn's idea of "inhabited ruins."[13] Invisible, however, to the public eye have been the similar personalization of the common spaces inside the housing blocks—the atrium and access galleries at each level—and the transformation of individual flats that has occurred during the building's lifetime, reflecting the changing social mix and lifestyles of the residential community over three generations. A significant proportion of the 600-odd flats have gradually escaped into the private market and changed hands as a result of the "'right-to-buy" government policy initiative (for council tenants to buy their homes at a discount) introduced in the 1980s, while those that have remained in council ownership (including those units designated "sheltered" housing, with access to a warden service) have become a resource accessibly only to the most vulnerable and those declared homeless when tenancies become available. But, while the successful regeneration of the shopping precinct has created a new stage for public interaction and of course retail opportunity in this high-value area of central London, the experience of life inside the Brunswick has not really entered the public domain as the subject of discourse in its own right. As a place, perceived from within as a container of disparate people linked (or not) in space by many different threads, rather than observed from without as an external profile or aesthetic, monumental form, the Brunswick represents a multi-layered, multi-vocal social setting with its own internal dynamic. Now recognized as a landmark of national post-war cultural heritage, it has also during its lifetime offered residents a unique and generous spatial setting in which to sustain a private domestic life in close proximity to the opportunities offered by the central city as a theater of social exchange.

Notes

1 Hodgkinson, Peter. "Speculation with Humanity?" architect's objection to Tranmac's planning application, 10 July 1992.

2 Department for Culture Media and Sport (2000), Listing Schedule 798-1/95/10155: Brunswick Square (West side).

3 Murray, Peter. "Foundling Estate, Bloomsbury." In *Architectural Design,* 611, London: Academy Editions, October 1971.

4 Betjeman, John. "'The New Barbarism,' Nooks and Corners." In *Private Eye,* 13 August 1971 (CLSC np).

5 Crosby, Theo. "Brunswick Centre, Bloomsbury, London." In *Architectural Review,* 212, October: Vol. 152, No. 908.

6 Johnstone, Violet. "Another London 'Barbican', custom-built for Bloomsbury." In *Daily Telegraph*, 27 June 1972 (CLSC np).

7 Kendall, Ena. "Babylon Comes to Bloomsbury." In *Observer Magazine,* 33–34, 2 December 1973.

8 Banham, Reyner. *Megastructure: urban futures of the recent past.* London: Thames and Hudson, 1976, 185–189.

9 Crosby 1972, 212.

10 Banham 1976, 19.

11 Hodgkinson, Patrick. Letter to the author, 3 September 2000.

12 Buchanan, Colin. *Traffic in Towns.* London: Ministry of Transport, 1963.

13 Astragal. "Kasbahs in exotic Brunswick." In *Architects' Journal,* 49, 29 July 1992.

Bibliography

Astragal. "Kasbahs in exotic Brunswick." In *Architects' Journal,* 49, 29 July 1992.

Banham, Reyner. *Megastructure: urban futures of the recent past*. London: Thames and Hudson, 1976, 185–189.

Betjeman, John. "'The New Barbarism,' Nooks and Corners." In *Private Eye,* 13 August 1971, (CLSC np).

Buchanan, Colin. *Traffic in Towns.* London: Ministry of Transport, 1963.

Crosby, Theo. "Brunswick Centre, Bloomsbury, London." In *Architectural Review*, Vol. 152, No. 908, 211ff., October 1972.

Department for Culture Media and Sport, Listing Schedule 798-1/95/10155: Brunswick Square (West side), 2000.

Hodgkinson, Peter. "A Handful of Homes: British post-war housing." In *A3 Times,* No. 9, 19–21, Modern Urban Living, London: Polytechnic of North London, 1987.

Hodgkinson, Peter. "Speculation with Humanity?" architect's objection to Tranmac's planning application, 10 July 1992.

Hodgkinson, Peter. Letter to the author, 3 September 2000.

Johnstone, Violet. "Another London 'Barbican' custom-built for Bloomsbury." In *Daily Telegraph*, 27 June 1972 (CLSC np).

Kendall, Ena. "Babylon Comes to Bloomsbury." In *Observer Magazine,* 33–34, 2 December 1973.

Murray, Peter. "Foundling Estate, Bloomsbury." In *Architectural Design,* 605–612, October 1971, London: Academy Editions.

OFFICE
L.K.Bennett
vodafone

GLOBAL FOOD

Except cycles
LF57 YKG

BRUNSWICK

RENOIR
IN THE FOG
WHITE ELEPHANT
A LATE QUARTET
IN THE HOUSE
HANDEL'S CESARE
CINEMA
STRADA
OUR CHILDREN

theBRUNSWICK
Carluccio's

Carluccio's
ML09 BWH

Apartments 55
Built area ratio 64 %

Site area 4,400 m²
Built area 2,800 m²

Collective facilities, infrastructure: Events hall for 600 people, conference hall for 120 people, cinema, restaurant, snack bar, indoor pool, fitness center, sauna, shops, offices

Ivrea, Italy
Corso Botta 30

Architects
Iginio Cappai, Pietro Mainardis

Clients
Camillo Olivetti, CSpA

Planning and construction
1967–75

Site plan 1:10,000

La Serra, Ivrea

Iginio Cappai, Pietro Mainardis
1967–75

La Serra—Olivetti Social and Residential Services Center in Ivrea

Paolo Enrico Dalpiaz, Giulia Maria Infortuna

The building, formerly the Olivetti Social and Residential Services Center, then the Residential Unit East, and now the Hotel La Serra—in reference to the morainic hill that demarcates the Canavese territory to the east—is the result of the dynamics of the Olivetti company policy and of Adriano Olivetti's community ideals.[1] Together, these led to the recognition of Ivrea, known as the Industrial City of the 20th Century, as a World Heritage Site by the UNESCO in 2018.[2]

Hotel La Serra, bounded to the south by the Giusiana public gardens, to the north by Via Bertinatti, and to the east by Corso Botta, is part of a border space on the edge of the historic center, located on land that has been earmarked for expansion and urban renewal since the 1930s.[3]

La Serra is emblematic of Italian radical architecture, taking up the concept of connected cities from the utopias of the 1960s and 1970s; a city contained within a supporting infrastructure where highly functional housing cells and essential services are inserted, akin to Peter Cook's 1964 Plug-in City, in which technological innovation emphasizes the proposed city of the future, a science fiction city.[4]

"This is not a building [...] but an urban system: a district, a crossroad, a beehive, a medieval portico that gathers all the sounds and the [...] living, commercial, administrative, recreational paths. It does not therefore have a face, [...] but has foreshortenings, [...] views and

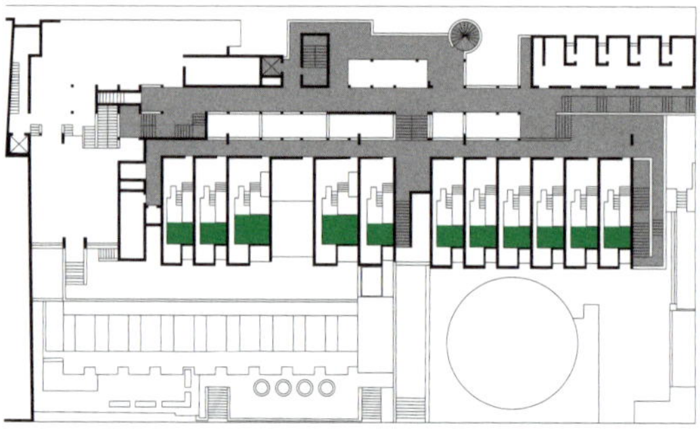

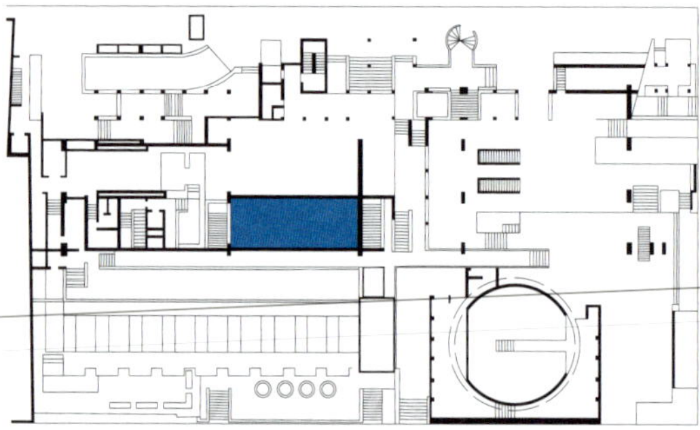

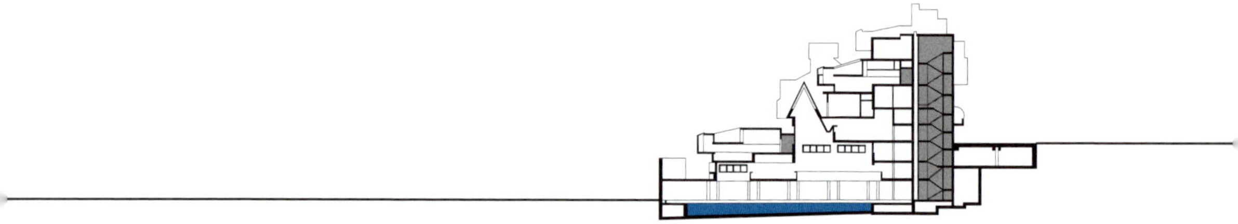

Floor plan 3rd and 6th upper floors, Cross-section, 1:1,000

predispositions to the landscape, to the body of the city,"[5] writes Paolo Volponi in 1976 about La Serra, a structure born by the will of the Olivetti company, designed to cross the natural boundary of the Dora Baltea River into Ivrea's historic center in order to realize Adriano Olivetti's idea (1901–1960) of a guest house providing the services necessary to meet the needs of the company and the city.[6]

Based upon these ideas, the project of the two Venetian architects Iginio Cappai (1932–1999) and Pietro Mainardis (1935–2007) develops 55 mini-apartments linked by a series of pathways—interposed with ramps, steps, and small bridges—to sports and cultural facilities open to both residents and the public. Indeed, the architects worked in such a way as to not categorize the various levels based on the type of use—private or communal—instead creating viewpoints related to the outside: a network of connections allowing users to benefit from the various services and live in the housing units as necessary.

A building complex, "that turns to the city (and everything that a city should feel is part of it), with a great many entrances, twelve in total, instead of a single main entrance. [...] The building's open spaces, hallways, and an escalator open it to all sides. But the entrances and connections always indicate something further. And this 'further' is a very special characteristic of the complex."[7]

Consisting of nine levels, the building originally featured an archaeological path through Roman remains found during excavation in the basement; a 600-seat *aula magna* equipped for cinema, assemblies, and concerts; a 25 by 10-meter swimming pool with sauna, gym, and a 150-vehicle parking lot; a domed hall for exhibitions and conferences on the ground floor with about 120 seats; and a restaurant, snack bar, and variously sized rooms for commercial use on the levels above.[8]

At the end, the housing units, located on a projecting element formed by four staggered terraced steps inserted into a structural grid, recall the shape of a typewriter and its keys. Made using four different modules, the apartments are designed to accommodate one to four people. The cells consist of a single, elongated open space organized on three staggered levels. The furniture is an integral part of the spatial design and everyday life: living room, study, bed, kitchenette, and bathroom.[9] A diagonally sliding opening system—a bay window made of porcelain sheeting based on aeronautical

Centro di servizi sociali e residentiali Olivetti, later: Hotel La Serra, photos 2018

South view with residential pods

technologies—in the study area allows one to look outside.[10] The whole building tends to resemble and work as a machine, with its technical perfection and maximum efficiency—for its time—meeting the minimum level of subsistence. The housing units are like cabins connected by naval bridges, the snack bar like a fuselage.[11]

View from Corso Botta with cantilevered building section over the forecourt: on the right, access to the apartments and shops; at the center, entrances to the cinema, auditorium and restaurant.

The failure of a utopian machine

The construction process was complicated from the very start: a building license was requested and obtained in 1968, but work was interrupted in 1969 when Roman ruins, part of a complex and extensive archaeological system, were discovered.[12] Construction was put on hold for about two years, starting again in 1970 but with a variant of the original project. There was never an official inauguration, as the complex started operation as the individual parts were completed: first the sports facilities with the gym, swimming pool, and sauna, then the residential units, the restaurant and bar, and finally the spaces for cultural and convention activities, such as the *aula magna* and the domed hall. In the original concept, the covered square beneath the cantilevered building section towards Corso Botta should have been a catalyst and an attractive element for the population of Ivrea due to its permeable conformation. However, the commercial spaces didn't start up until years later, and closed after a short time.[13]

The variation also modified the original project from a technological and functional point of view: the building was, in fact, designed using innovative technologies such as prefabrication. In the end, however, a mixed solution was chosen that included traditional building solutions. Prefabricated systems for residential units were integrated into reinforced concrete, with direct references to nautical construction systems such as hermetically sealed portholes, brass elements, and built-in concealed furniture.[14] "It must not risk becoming any

Snack bar near the fitness studio entrance on the first floor.

one person's. [...] It must instead remain public, a community building."[15] From a functional point of view, the second variant had far more serious repercussions. The management problems between the public and private spaces of the building led to the immediate conversion of the housing units—initially planned to temporarily accommodate technicians and scholars visiting the Olivetti company and the city—into a hotel, in order to guarantee better control of the interior spaces.[16]

This change led to a gradual and increasingly dominant exclusive and non-inclusive use of spaces, compromising the idea of the *promenade architecturale* and the public soul of the building, contributing to marginalization, progressive degradation, and a sense of abandonment.

Driver of development or vehicle of degradation?

"Graffiti, loose sheet metal, flaking concrete, rust, hallways and shops closed by metal gates, damaged and defect flooring, the typewriter is not running smoothly, and deterioration can be seen almost everywhere in the building."[17]

Despite being included in tours of Ivrea's Open-Air Museum of Modern Architecture (MaAM),[18] in recent years the building has undergone progressive architectural and social deterioration. The causes of the decline can be identified as a series of factors. The definitive shutdown of the four-star Hotel La Serra took place

Movie theater. In operation until 2014.

in 2001, bringing with it the increasingly progressive fragmentation of the building. In 2007, Pirelli RE, the owner of the property, began selling off sections to private individuals.[19]

Nevertheless, the desire to reclaim the collective social calling of the building, loved by architects, remained. In 2007, a small group of industrialists and professionals joined together to form a company named Effetto Serra S.p.a., purchasing the ground-floor atrium with shops and the *aula magna* for use as a cinema. The domed hall, previously donated by Pirelli RE to the municipality, was then also managed by the newly formed company. In the same year, the cinema hall—the covered square—became the heart of the new Cultural Center. A project by the architect Giorgio Ceradelli includes two pathways set into the floor that shape the spaces and guide visitors: a wooden boardwalk for the new food court and a steel walkway for the cultural space.

However, Effetto Serra's life span was short and troubled: in 2014, the high expense of renovations meant that the company was not able to cover the costs.[20] Due to the high investment costs, the poor profitability of the Cultural Center, and a ruinous public-private strategy, the cinema was closed in February 2014, the company went into bankruptcy, and the building has remained empty and unused ever since.

After this episode, the fate of the Unità Residenziale Est ex-Hotel La Serra has been one of progressive decline into abandonment and dilapidation. Fires and multiple acts of vandalism led to a decision by the residents to close the private section of via Bertinatti with gates.[21]

Starting in July 2017, public auctions were organized for the spaces of the former company, with inconclusive results, however. Meanwhile, the building is waiting, continuing into decline, with the exception of the swimming pool, which is still in active use, and the new sports center located in the former restaurant spaces. Academic and non-academic research on redevelopment scenarios continues, focused on defining a management model for the coordinated cultural management of the building, which is a complex system, a machine in continuous evolution. The synergy of its internal mechanisms and connections must be active and efficient in order for the structure to recover the economic and social role that it was never able to fully realize.[22]

"A plan to its preservation would promote Hotel La Serra as a unified building, a design object, a space for creativity and social activities, part of societal and architectural history and exceptional not only for the city of Ivrea."[23]

Notes

1 To learn more about the topic, see: Olivetti, Adriano. *Città dell'uomo*. Turin: Edizioni di Comunità, 2001; and Bonifazio, Patrizia, and Paola Scrivano. *Olivetti costruisce. Architettura moderna a Ivrea.* Milan: Skira, 2001.

2 "Ivrea è patrimonio mondiale Unesco, è il 54esimo sito italiano. Rinvio per le Colline del Prosecco," in: *La Stampa*, 01 Jul 2018.

www.lastampa.it/2018/07/01/societa/ivrea-patrimonio-mondiale-unesco-esimo-sito-italiano-bocciate-le-colline-del-prosecco-dLDFImS-Sz1DIb88hajJrbO/pagina.html (16 Jun 2018).

3 Olmo, Carlo. *Costruire la città dell'uomo. Adriano Olivetti e l'urbanistica.* Turin: Edizioni di Comunità, 2001.

4 Guisti, Maria A. "Ivrea: architettura parlante. Una macchina da scrivere nella città." In *Ananke,* No. 69, 64–70, May 2013, 65. Montanari, Guido. "Dall'utopia tecnologica al Decostruttivismo." In *Dellapiana*, Elena; and Montanari, Guido, *Una storia dell'architettura contemporanea,* Novara: UTET Università, 2015, 463–499.

5 Volponi, Paolo. "La macchina sociale. Un'architettura-ponte tra fabbrica e città." In *Architettura. Cronache e storia*, No. 249, 130–132, July 1976, 130. (Translation by the authors).

6 Rossano, Astarita. *Gli architetti di Olivetti. Una storia di committenza industriale.* Milan: Franco Angeli, 2000, 170.

7 Nannerini, Giuseppe. "Community and privacy. Un centro di servizi residenziali per Ivrea." In *Industria delle costruzioni*, 19–34, September/October 1973, 30.

8 De Simone, Ugo. "Residenziale Hotel 'La Serra' nel centro di Ivrea." In *Il Nuovo Cantiere,* No. 4, 18–26, April 1977.

9 Nannerini, Giuseppe. *Community and privacy* cit.

10 Pavan, Luigi. *Cappai e Mainardis. Laboratorio veneziano*. Rome: Testo & Immagine, 2004, 45.

11 Cappai, I., and P. Mainardis. "Centro di servizi sociali e residenziali Olivetti ad Ivrea." In *Architettura. Cronache e storia*, 134–186, No. 249, July 1976, 166.

12 Brecciaroli Taborelli, Luisa. "Ivrea. Scavo di una trincea nei giardini pubblici." In *Quaderni della Soprintendenza Archeologica del Piemonte,* No. 8, 221–223, 1988.

13 Zorzi, Renzo. "Olivetti: continuità e innovazione." In *Architettura. Cronache e storia,* Nr. 249, 132–133, July 1976, 132.

14 Caccia Gherardini, Susanna. "A stone's throw in the Neoclassical swamp of design. The Serra of Ivrea: guidelines for a restoration project." In *Restauro Archeologico*, No. 25, 62–77, 2016, 72.

15 Volponi, P. *La macchina sociale,* 131.

16 Tentori, Francesco, Cappai, Iginio e Mainardis, Pietro et al. "Ivrea. Centro di servizi Olivetti." In *Casabella*, No. 422, 41–57, February 1977.

17 Giusti, M. A. *Ivrea: architettura parlante* cit., 70. (Translation by the authors.)

18 Bonifazio, Patrizia, and Paola Scrivano. *Olivetti costruisce* cit., 175–179.

19 "Così Pirelli mette in vendita l'ultima 'macchina da scrivere'." In *la Sentinella del Canavese*, 01 Dec 2005. ricerca.gelocal.it/lasentinella/archivio/lasentinella/2005/12/01/IC3PO_IC301.html (accessed on 16May2019).

20 La Mattina, Liborio. "La Serra di Ivrea ad un passo dal fallimento." In *la Voce*, 10Jan2014. www.giornalelavoce.it/la-serra-di-ivrea-un-passo-dal-fallimento-32452 (last visit on 16 May 2019)

21 Bombonato, Simona. "Ivrea, stop ai vandali: la Serra blindata." In *la Sentinella del Canavese*, 28May2018. lasentinella.gelocal.it/ivrea/cronaca/2018/05/29/news/ivrea-stop-ai-vandali-la-serra-blindata-1.16891557 (accessed on 16 May 2019).

22 Coscia, Christina, Paolo Enrico Dalpiaz, Enrico Giacopelli, and Giulia Maria, Infortuna. "Il caso dell'Unità Residenziale Est - Ex-Hotel La Serra. Il Delphi Method a supporto di scenari di intervento per 'ri-Scrivere' la Città di Ivrea." In *Valori e Valutazioni. Teorie ed esperienze*, Vol. 22, 2019.

23 Giusti, Maria A., *Ivrea: architettura parlante* cit., 70. (Translation by the authors.)

Bibliography

Bonifazio, Partizia and Paolo Scrivano. *Olivetti costruisce. Architettura moderna a Ivrea.* Milan: Skira, 2001.

Bonifazio, Patrizia and Enrico Giacopelli. *Il paesaggio futuro. Letture e norme per il patrimonio dell'architettura moderna di Ivrea.* Turin: Umberto Allemandi & C., 2007.

Brecciaroli Taborelli, Luisa. "Ivrea. Scavo di una trincea nei giardini pubblici." In *Quaderni della Soprintendenza Archeologica del Piemonte,* No. 8, 1988, 221–223.

Caccia Gherardini, Susanna. "A stone's throw in the Neoclassical swamp of design. The Serra of Ivrea: guidelines for a restoration project." In *Restauro Archeologico*, No. 25, 2016, 62–77.

Cappai, Iginio and Pietro Mainardis. "Capsulated building for Olivetti employees in Ivrea is a beehive of many diverse activities." In *Architecture Plus*, No. 8, September 1973, 34–37.

Cappai, Iginio and Pietro Mainardis. "Centro di servizi sociali e residenziali Olivetti ad Ivrea." In *Architettura. Cronache e storia*, No. 249, July 1976, 134–186.

Coscia, Cristina, Paolo Enrico Dalpiaz, Enrico Giacopelli, and Giulia Maria Infortuna. "Il caso dell'Unità Residenziale Est—Ex-Hotel La Serra. Il Delphi Method a supporto di scenari di intervento per 'ri-Scrivere' la Città di Ivrea." In *Valori e Valutazioni. Teorie ed esperienze*, No. 22, 2019.

De Simone, Ugo. "Residenziale Hotel 'La Serra' nel centro di Ivrea." In *Il Nuovo Cantiere*, No. 4, April 1977, 18–26.

Feiersinger, Martin and Werner Feiersinger. *italomodern. architektur in oberitalien 1946–1976.* Vienna: Springer Verlag, 2012, 262–267.

Giusti, Maria A. "Ivrea: una macchina da scrivere nella città." In *Ananke*, No. 69, 2013, 64–70.

Huet, Bernard. "Centre de services sociaux er résidenties, Ivrea." In *L'Architecture d'Aujourd'hui*, No. 188, December 1976, 100–104.

Montanari, Guido. "Dall'utopia tecnologica al Decostruttivismo." In *Elena Dellapiana, Guido Montanari: Una storia dell'architettura contemporanea*, UTET University, 2015, 463–499.

Morris Dixon, John. "Utopian mechanism. Olivetti Social Services and Residential Centre, Ivrea, Italy." In *Progressive Architecture*, No. 8, April 1977, 74–81.

Nannerini, Giuseppe. "Community and privacy. Un centro di servizi residenziali per Ivrea." In *Industria delle costruzioni*, 1973, 19–34.

Olivetti, Adriano. *Città dell'uomo.* Turin: Edizioni di Comunità, 2001.

Olmo, Carlo. *Costruire la città dell'uomo. Adriano Olivetti e l'urbanistica.* Turin: Edizioni di Comunità, 2001.

Pacifici, Martina. "Esperimento Metabolista Italiano, 'La Serra' ad Ivrea." In *Lab 2.0 Magazine,* November 2014, 56–61.

Pavan, Luigi. *Cappai e Mainardis. Laboratorio veneziano*. Rome: Testo & Immagine, 2004.

Peverilli, Diego. "Möblierte Wohnungen der Olivetti in Ivrea." In *Werk*, No. 12, 1974, 1478–1482.

Rossano, Astarita. *Gli architetti di Olivetti. Una storia di committenza industrial.* Milan: Franco Angeli, 2000.

Segantini, Maria A. *Iginio Cappai e Pietro Mainardis. Architetti Contemporanei nel Veneto*. Viterbo: BetaGamma, 1999.

Tentori, Francesco, Iginio Cappai, and Pietro Mainardis et al. "Ivrea. Centro di servizi Olivetti." In *Casabella,* No. 422, February 1977, 41–57.

Volponi, Paolo. "La macchina sociale. Un'architettura-ponte tra fabbrica e città." In *Architettura. Cronache e storia*, No. 249, July 1976, 130–132.

Zorzi, Renzo. "Olivetti: continuità e innovazione." In *Architettura. Cronache e storia*, No. 249, July 1976, 132–133.

CS 362AS

HOTEL LA SERRA
CINEMA
ABC
AUDITORIUM LA SERRA
eclipse

1° TEMPO
2° TEMPO
ATTUALITÀ
INTERVALLO
VIETATO
FUMARE
ABC
È VIETATO

energie, cultura
solidarietà
metano
USCITA
SICUREZZA

The Return of Stepped Terrace Housing

Gerhard Steixner, Maria Welzig

Renouncing community

Until the mid-1970s, the curves of productivity growth and of wages were almost identical. From that point on, they became disconnected. Productivity increased while wages stagnated. Political development since the 1980s has seen a turning away from the community and the state, from Reagan's "trickle-down economics," Thatcher's "There's no such thing as society," Clinton's "It's the economy, stupid," to Schröder's and Fischer's: "Ich-AG," and Germany's Hartz 4.

The promotion of "Ich-AGs," quite literally "me-corporations," i.e. the self-employed, as a strategy to encourage consumption—every single person must now have everything. Consumption as a compensation for the isolation and the emptiness outside of making money and having a career. Economic and political interests are promoted by corresponding media images. One example is the perfectly executed 1990 cult series *Sex and the City*, in which four attractive, "hard-working," single young women featuring expensive hairstyles, dresses, and shoes are juxtaposed against the glittering backdrop of New York City.

As early as 1972, however, the Club of Rome's report had clearly pointed out "the limits to growth," a finding that was already clear 50 years ago. Architects and clients reacted to the developments mentioned above largely on a formal level. As far as housing was concerned, there was a return to a city of streets and facades. Stepped terrace housing, regarded in the 1960s as the ultimate solution to housing and urban development, a way of conserving land resources, of giving space to individual and community needs, and of efficiently creating a greener city, disappeared abruptly from urban planning and housing in the 1980s. Restoration and "critical reconstruction" became the motto of the moment. Mistrust of modernism's promises of salvation was great. In 1985, the City of Vienna put a striking end to this with the Hundertwasserhaus, the most internationally famous municipal building besides the Karl-Marx-Hof.

The stepped terrace typology, with its variety of accesses and apartment types, may also have disappeared because its planning required more effort than designing a standard floor. Greater effort is required, something only tolerated when paired with a commonsense belief that housing is not primarily an economic undertaking, but also an ecological and social one.

New experiments in the twenty-first century

It was only in the twenty-first century that people began to ask, "Why are we no longer building stepped terrace housing?" After all, stepped terrace housing has "almost only advantages. It blends into the landscape, the terraces are similar to the gardens of detached houses, and at ground floor level you don't stand in front of a vertical wall but in front of a greened slope. So why aren't we building them anymore? Because the gradient would overburden the building authorities? Because there are no standard floor layouts for developers?"[1]

Wienerberg residential building, Vienna 2005
Architects Wimmer und Partner
Swimming pool on the fourth panoramic deck, the Schöpfwerk housing estate and Alt-Erlaa residential park in the background.

Architects began rediscovering the potential of stepped terrace housing in the twenty-first century. Some have succeeded in convincing non-profit or private clients and political decision-makers of the advantages of the stepped terrace mode, although the scale has changed compared to the 1960s and 1970s. Large-scale complexes are still passé.

In 2004, on a joint red and green party initiative, the City of Vienna announced a competition for a stepped terrace apartment building with around 250 apartments. This was (seemingly) a signal to continue the successful stepped terrace housing projects of the 1970s. "With this project, we are responding to the wish of many Viennese to have their own terrace or garden."[2] In the same year, 2004, a study was published which again confirmed the highest level of satisfaction with and excellent social interaction in stepped terrace housing.[3] Surprisingly, however, the jury awarded the contract to a project with balconies and loggias, but no terraces.[4]

In Vienna, the stepped terrace housing typology has been taken up again since the turn of the millennium, by architects who grew up with the concept during their student days since the 1970s, and who pursue architecture as more than just a commercial endeavor. Helmut Wimmer,[5] Walter Stelzhammer, Artec Architekten—all firms that have realized numerous high-quality social housing projects, conceptually and innovatively, and have dared to tackle the challenging task of designing stepped terrace housing with different concepts and focal points.[6] The residents of all three of the buildings presented here

Wienerberg residential building, Vienna 2005
Architects: Wimmer and Partner
Stacked single-family homes, southwest elevation

Ödenburger Strasse residential complex, Vienna 2012
Architect: Walter Stelzhammer
The covered living street under the arcades on the north. The flat terracing creates generous open spaces for planting

enjoy using a swimming pool on the roof or a communal greenspace. This is an effective strategy for building community and reducing leisure travel.

The idea of stacked single-family homes with gardens was implemented in 2005 by the architectural firm Wimmer und Partner with the Wienerberg Stepped Terrace Apartments: a cooperative housing development with 141 maisonette apartments and a swimming pool on the fourth panoramic deck. Eight stories with four, stacked, double-story maisonettes: "Every resident has their own house, as it were, in a 'shelf system'—and has the possibility to individually design their immediate surroundings."[7] The casual elegance of the 170-meter-long, bent block, which rounds out Wienerberg City in the south, awakens memories of vacations in Mediterranean climes.

The architect Walter Stelzhammer was able to realize a social housing project on the outskirts of Vienna in 2012 as a stepped terrace building (plus row house complex). It is a five-story, almost 350-meter-long, curving block with terraces to the south, with balcony walkway access and various communal rooms on the northern side. The terraces, combined with loggias, are true outdoor spaces ranging from 25 to 40 square meters in size. The relatively flat terracing that results creates a large "overhang" on the north side. Similar to the Alexandra Road Estate (see p. 282 ff.), it evokes associations with the exterior of a stadium. Here, too, there is a south-facing swimming pool in the shared garden with a sauna and sundecks. Typologically, it has a profile similar to that of an extrusion press, comparable with

Le Corbusier's 1933 Durand stepped terrace project in Algeria (see p. 68 f.), using terrace as an element to shape the structure.

The Tokiostrasse apartments built in the Kagran West urban development area by Artec Architekten in 2009 is completely different. Here, the stacking of various residential forms defines the very concept of the stepped terrace building. In contrast to the previous complexes, the terraces are part of a composition of cubes and empty spaces. The dense urban structure accommodates 100 dwellings, an attractive community room, a playground for small children on the fourth floor, a swimming pool with a lawn for sunbathing on the roof, and space for temporary uses on the ground floor. Generous amounts of space and light are brought into the circulation areas of the double-winged street building by a 5-meter-wide hall with arcades and bridges that create private zones for parking bicycles and baby prams, illuminated from above. This "central-corridor-plus" prototype opens the east-facing maisonette apartments and west-facing multi-story apartments through generous two-story loggias, referencing the ATBAT residential structure by Candilis Woods in Casablanca from 1952 (see p. 72).

The number of stepped terrace buildings constructed since the turn of the millennium as social housing—a central focus of this book—is therefore still relatively small, while the desire of a broad swathe of the population for this type of housing is unmistakable. The typology is, however, projected and realized mostly in private and rather expensive projects, often also with a hybrid of uses, in Europe

Tokiostrasse—The Town Musicians of Bremen, Vienna 2009
Artec Architekten
Nature as part of the composition, east elevation

and Asia. The typology lends itself to the idea of a mix of uses, as seen in the most radical case in this book, the *Centro di Servizi Sociali e Residenziali Olivetti* in Ivrea.

In 2015, seven teams were invited to find new and innovative solutions in residential and urban development for a competition in Vienna's Aspern Seestadt urban expansion area.[8] Two of the teams, Atelier Kempe Thill from the Netherlands and Lacaton & Vassal Architectes from France, designed "green mountain housing." The realized project was by Helen & Hard of Norway, who had proposed a structure stepped on the narrow sides and thus with a relatively low proportion of terraces. It is one of the rare projects with mixed uses, combining student dormitories, privately financed apartments, office and commercial spaces, adult education center, restaurants, and commercial premises on the ground floor.

What Barke Ingels and Jakob Lange (BIG) succeeded in realizing in 2008 in Copenhagen with the Mountain Dwelling project, a combination of multi-story garages and a terraced, compact low-rise building, has so far remained on paper for the Dutch firm NL Architects. They proposed the typology of stepped terrace housing for a public cultural building, the Guian Urban Planning Museum in China or the ArtA art center in Arnhem. With their programmatic design for a stepped terrace apartment building in Amsterdam with 50 owner-occupied units, they realized a six-story extrusion profile in 2017. The central corridor on the ground floor provides access to the south-facing apartments and maisonettes on the northern side, while the

MTN The Mountain,
Copenhagen 2008
Bjarke Ingels Group
Swept under the carpet:
A compact, low-rise building,
staggered over eleven floors
to create the roof of a
multi-story car park

first floor has southern sun exposure. The apartments on the four floors above are accessed via balcony walkways. This is a classic typology that provides all apartments with a spacious terrace.

Brandlhuber + Emde, Burlon und Muck Petzet Architekten designed and built a similar typology with their stepped terrace structure for Berlin-Wedding in 2018. It has an open-plan, hybrid profile, the circulation of which is reminiscent of Adolf Loos's 1923 stepped terrace housing for workers. In both cases, the individual units are accessed from the outside via terraces about 6 meters deep. It is up to the residents to define the relationship between public and private. The building has pedestrian access via two cascade staircases flanking the terraces, leading all the way to the roof. Two elevators are also accessible from the covered public forecourt, making about 20 units on the upper floors (offices, studios, living, and working) barrier-free and directly accessible. The robust structure is open to different uses and has a high potential for appropriation. The experimental building uses resources and space efficiently and is progressively detailed and strives to do less.[9]

De Klenke or Terras op Zuid,
Amsterdam 2017
NL Architects
Elevation rather than a facade

Onwards!

It is time for a renewed attempt at making architecture and urban development more democratic and more ecological. These outstanding examples of social housing, designed and built since the 1920s, show that innovation and high quality are indeed compatible with building for great numbers of people. An analysis awakens awareness for what is really possible.

The great prosperity often claimed today is contrasted by a somewhat different reality. Rental costs in Vienna, for example, have risen by 48 percent since 2008,[10] while the average annual income of salaried employees has stagnated since 1998 after adjustment for inflation, and wages of blue-collar workers have even fallen by 13 percent.[11] The current discussion about affordability brings to mind a time when the mayor of Red Vienna, Karl Seitz, described the situation in 1924 as follows: "Then came the building period of bleak tenement buildings, where every last patch of land was made usable. That was a time in which the Viennese were struggling under capitalism, with anyone in a rental apartment dreading the terrible payment deadline." A return to the *Gründerzeit* era, with smart solutions? Apartments are affordable when their occupants once again earn decent wages for their work. At the same time, it is becoming increasingly necessary to decouple the housing question from market forces, as well as to communalize land.[12] Housing is a human right, not a commodity.

Lobe Block Stepped Terrace Housing, Berlin 2018
Brandlhuber + Emde, Burlon and Muck Petzet Architects
Over time, the residents will turn the cold structure into a verdant hill.

We build worse housing today than we actually could. And it's not a question of money. It's as if there were a latent political view that people should not be too well off, latent fears that individual freedoms—which are strongly linked to the housing situation—make people less controllable.

"Tighten your belt," they say. Yes! In consumption, energy, transport, and resource use as a whole. In housing, however, investment is what is needed. There must be a reform program for housing subsidies, with clear guidelines as to which measures should be stimulated, and these must reflect the ecological requirements of a Green City and the needs and wishes of those who live in it, since it is they who provide the funding for it through paying rent and taxes. The relationship between the city and nature must be rethought; otherwise the inhabitants will remain mere extras in an architectural scene.

With the individually designable private exterior spaces of stepped terrace housing, the punchline when looking at their rational construction methods, is the echo of Hundertwasser's famous symbolic demand from his "Mouldiness Manifesto against Rationalism in Architecture": "The apartment-house tenant must have the freedom to lean out of his window and as far as his arms can reach transform the exterior of his dwelling space. And he must be allowed to take a long-brush and as far as his arms can reach paint everything pink, so that from far away, from the street, everyone can see: there lives a manwho distinguishes himself from his neighbours, the pent-up livestock!"[13]

Bessemerstrasse residential complex, Vienna 2014
Architect Gerhard Steixner
The terrace as extended living space, make it your own, easy living.

"Luxury for All" exhibition, TU Wien 2017

So why don't we build stepped terrace housing anymore? After all, in light of climate change, they are more relevant than ever. One of the reasons for the lapse since the 1980s is probably education. After all, Europe's architecture schools have also adapted to the general political climate, withholding a wonderful understanding from over two generations of students: Luxury for all is possible!

From 2009 to 2019, as head of the Research Department for Building Construction and Design 2 at the TU Wien,[14] the editor has been able to question well over a thousand students on social housing in the Green City. Prototypical stepped terrace housing structures were developed at large events with over 500 participants and in several design studios. A set of rules formed the basis for the design, with two fundamental parameters for all groups: At least 20 percent of living space must be planned as open terraces and loggias, and at least six percent as gardens. In addition, based on the prototypical building sites, urban planning specifications such as orientation, access, number of stories, and building height had to be taken into account. Relevant building parameters for the user, such as the ratio of residential to non-residential use, minimum number of dwellings per access core, a minimum room height of 2.7 meters, and others, were also to be observed. The rules were strict, aimed at achieving both high living quality and economic efficiency.

The students used the stringent parameters to create imaginative interpretations, with no house quite like another. More than 300 projects with a total of over 20,000 residential units were designed

in the large-scale experiment. This is a rich inventory of prototypes, ranging from stepped terrace hill houses to super-hybrids. As part of the exhibition "*Luxus für alle. Prototypen für die grüne Stadt*" (Luxury for All. Prototypes for a Green City) in January 2017 at the TU Wien,[15] the project models were assembled like building blocks to create an 80-square-meter mock-up city with a variety of different spatial milieus: the Green City took shape.

Notes

1 The Viennese architect Sabine Pollak in her article: "Warum gibt es keine Terrassenhäuser mehr?" Architecture blog of *Der Standard*, 19 April 2017, https://www.derstandard.at/story/2000056052743/warum-gibt-es-keine-terrassenhaeuser-mehr

2 https://www.wien.gv.at/presse/2007/09/21/terrassenhaus-buchengasse-wohnen-mit-licht-und-sonne

3 Wiener Wohnstudien: "Wohnzufriedenheit, Mobilitäts- und Freizeitverhalten." Stadtentwicklung Wien, MA 18 – Stadtentwicklung und Stadtplanung (ed.), Vienna 2004. The examples studies included Alt-Erlaa and the Inzersdorfer Strasse stepped terrace apartment complex.

4 Buchengasse "stepped terrace estate", architect Rüdiger Lainer.

5 Helmut Wimmer worked on the Wohnen Morgen project in Vienna in the 1970s, see p. 344–356.

6 The Viennese architecture firm PPAG refers to the "Glückian" stepped terrace prototype in its 2013 Europan competition project in Vienna-Simmering. In contrast to Glück's model, however, the focus of the highly dense residential building is not on plantable terraces, "luxurious" ancillary facilities, or communal greenspace, but rather on internal circulation.

7 From the explanatory text on the Wienerberg residential building by the architects Wimmer und Partner (WUP): http://www.wimmerundpartner.com/index.php?seite=projekte&projekt=wienerberg&id=1&lang=de

8 Initiated and carried out by the Architekturzentrum Wien in cooperation with Wien 3420 aspern Development AG as part of the Vienna Biennale 2015: Ideas for Change.

9 In France, too, young architecture firms are trying to reactivate the stepped terrace concept for social housing ("The Return of 'Sauvage Terraces'"), even if attempts have so far remained unbuilt. New interest in the stepped terrace models of the 1970s in housing and urban planning is demonstrated by the model of the Jeanne Hachette Center in Ivry (see p. 79) by the architects Aoibheann Ní Mhearáin and Mary Laheen for the 2018 Venice Architecture Biennale. The Vietnamese architectural firm H&P is testing the stepped terrace structure as a possibility for combining urban architecture and agriculture.

10 Cf. *Wiener Zeitung* from 28 June 2019 https://www.wienerzeitung.at/nachrichten/politik/wien/2024508-48-Prozent-teurere-Miete-seit-2008.html

11 2018 General Income Report of the Austrian Court of Audit.

12 A scandalous example of the privatization of social housing in Austria is the sale of 60,000 non-profit apartments (Buwog apartments) from the government to a private investor in 2004.

13 Friedensreich Hundertwasser: "Verschimmelungsmanifest gegen den Rationalismus in der Architektur," 1958. English translation from http://www.hundertwasser.at/english/texts/philo_verschimmelungsmanifest.php (accessed on 18 July 2020).

14 Seidel, Michael, and Gerhard Steixner (eds.). *Society now! Architektur. Projekte und Positionen 2009–2019.* Gerhard Steixner/TU Wien, Research Department for Building Construction and Design 2, Zurich: Park Books, 2020.

15 "Terrassenhäuser als Idee für Wien: 'Danke Harry Glück'", in: *Die Presse online*, 30 January 2017, https://www.diepresse.com/5162025/terrassen-hauser-als-idee-fur-wien-danke-harry-gluck; "80 m² großes Modell zeigt 'Luxus für Alle'", in: *Tageszeitung Heute*, 31 January 2017; Zoidl, Franziska: "Terrassenwohnungen: Studierende entwickeln 'Luxus für alle'", in: *Der Standard*, 2 February 2017; "Studierende entwickeln 'Luxus für alle'", in: *Die Presse*, 4 February 2017; "TU fordert mehr Natur im Wohnbau," in: *Der Standard*, 4 February 2017.

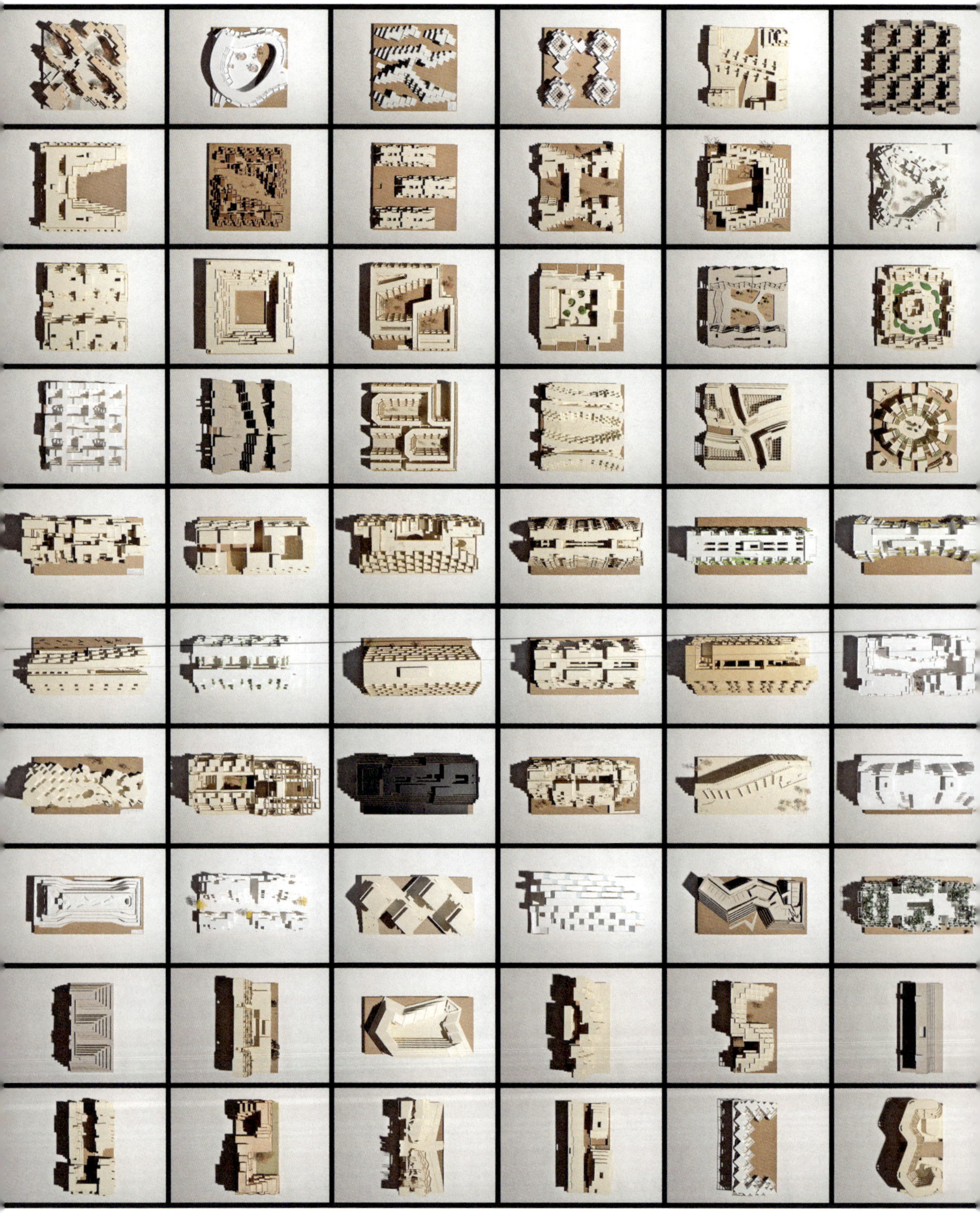

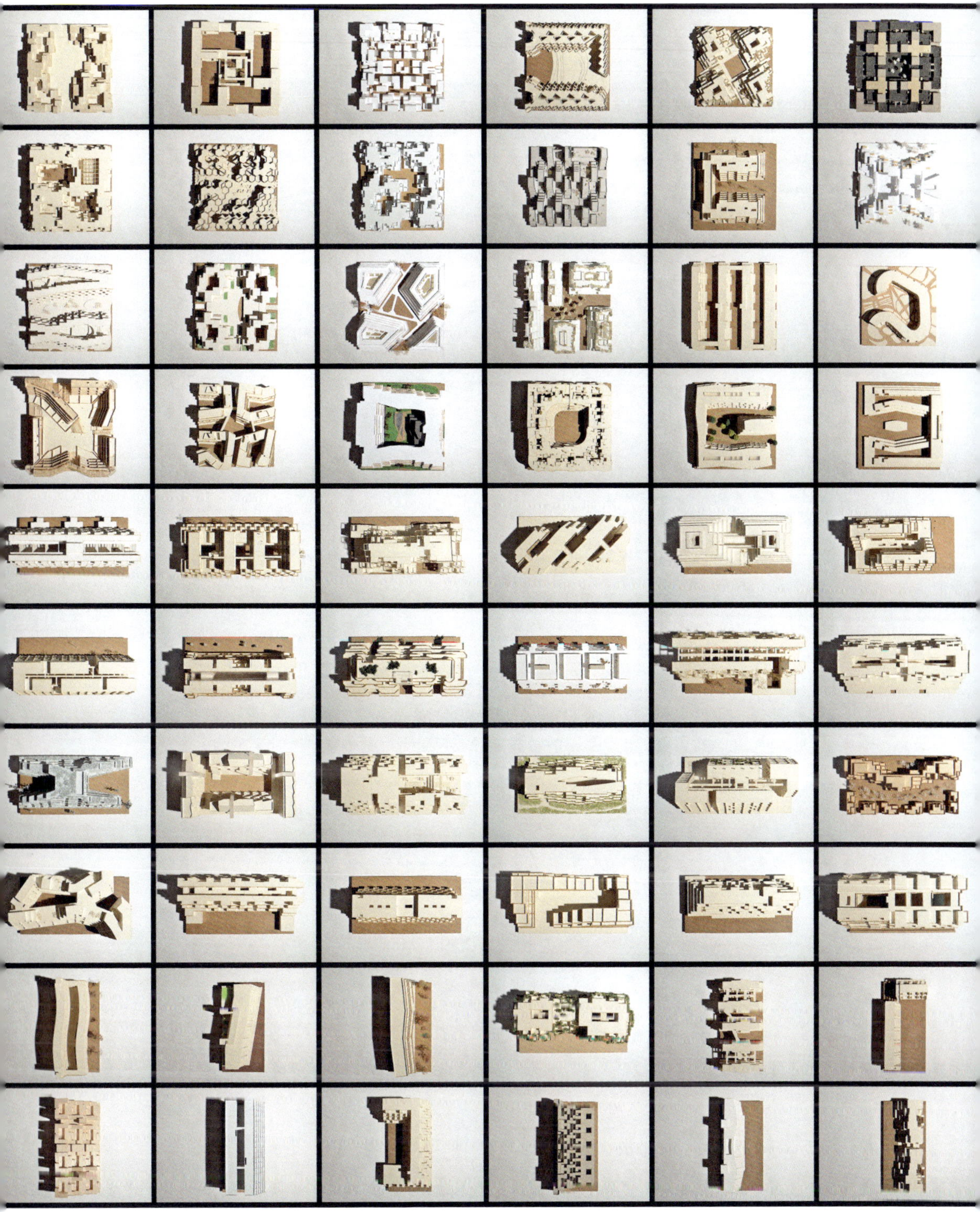

Author Biographies

Karen Beckmann Dr. Eng. Architect

studied architecture in Hanover, Germany and Rouen, France. In 2014 she earned a doctorate with her dissertation titled *Urbanität durch Dichte? Geschichte und Gegenwart der Großwohnkomplexe der 1970er Jahre* (Urbanity through Density? Historic and Present Situation of Large Housing Complexes of the 1970s). In 2015 and 2018 she held a lectureship at the Institute for History and Theory of Architecture, Faculty of Architecture and Landscape, at Leibniz University Hanover. Her research focuses on the interface of theory and practice on topics of architectural reception and production, with an emphasis on complex urban development structures. Beckmann lives and works as an architect, author, and researcher in Hanover.

Paolo Enrico Dalpiaz M.A.

after completing his undergraduate scientific studies, Paolo Enrico Dalpiaz attended the Torino Polytechnic. In 2018, he earned a *magna cum laude* master's degree in Architecture for the Restoration and Enhancement of Heritage with a thesis titled *Unità Residenziale Est—Ex Hotel La Serra. The Delphi Method to support intervention scenarios to reinvigorate Ivrea City*. Currently a student at the Postgraduate School of Beni Architettonici e del Paesaggio, Dalpiaz works as a freelancer in an architectural design studio.

Silke Fischer DI

studied architecture at the Bauhaus University Weimar and at the Southern California Institute of Architecture (SCI-Arc) in Los Angeles, USA. She has taken part in numerous competitions and completed residential, educational, and industrial buildings in various architectural offices. Since 2015, Fischer has been active in teaching and research at the Structural Engineering, Construction, and Design Department at the TU Wien. She lives and works as an architect in Vienna.

Natalie Heger Dr. Eng.

worked as a set and costume designer before studying architecture in Berlin and Barcelona. In her doctoral thesis, she explored the history of planning and ideation of the Olympic Village in Munich. For more than ten years she taught and performed research in the Department of Architecture, Urban and Landscape Planning at the University of Kassel and was co-founder of the interdisciplinary working group *u Lab, Studio für Stadt und Raumprozesse* in Berlin. Since 2018 Heger has worked in the research laboratory for post-war modernism at the Frankfurt University of Applied Sciences.

Giulia Maria Infortuna M.A.

after completing her undergraduate scientific studies, Giulia Maria Infortuna attended the Torino Polytechnic. In 2018, she earned a *magna cum laude* master's degree in Architecture for the Restoration and Enhancement of Heritage with a thesis titled *Unità Residenziale Est—Ex Hotel La Serra. The Delphi Method to support intervention scenarios to reinvigorate Ivrea city*. Currently a student at the Postgraduate School of Beni Architettonici e del Paesaggio, Infortuna works as a freelancer in an architectural design studio.

Nataša Koselj Ph.D.

is a Ljubljana-based architect with a Ph.D. in post-war modernism. She has studied and worked in Slovenia (University of Ljubljana), Finland, the UK (Oxford Brookes University), and France (Cité de l'architecture et du patrimoine). She currently serves as chair of Docomomo Slovenia and established the course "Twentieth Century Slovenian Architecture" at the Ljubljana Faculty of Architecture. Koselj has published extensively since 1995, and in 2014 was awarded the Plečnik Medal.

San-Hwan Lu DI Dr. techn.

studied architecture at the TU Wien and has worked in both Vienna and Asia. Until 2010 he collaborated on projects with Richard Rogers and Kisho Kurokawa, and he worked with Hans Hollein until 2014. Currently, Lu teaches and performs research at the TU Wien, with a focus on building regulations and the cultural context of building.

Clare Melhuish Ph.D.

is Director and Principal Research Fellow in the UCL Urban Laboratory. Her research focuses on the processes and impacts of large-scale urban developments in the U.K. and abroad, and conceptualizations of urban heritage within transformative processes of change in multicultural cities. Melhuish has a disciplinary background extending across architectural history and criticism, anthropology, and human geography, drawing on ethnographic and visual research methods and analysis of architecture and the built environment as social and cultural setting. Her particular areas of interest and expertise include the Modern Movement and contemporary architecture, postcolonial urban aesthetics and heritage, and urban regeneration policy and practice, with specific area specializations in architecture and planning of the U.K., France, the Gulf, and the Caribbean.

Gerhard Steixner Univ.-Prof. i. R., Mag. arch.

studied architecture at the Academy of Fine Arts Vienna, Master Class of Roland Rainer. In 1983 he established his architecture office, based in Vienna, with a focus on eco-solar building, prefabrication, and prototypes. From 2009 to 2019, Steixner was university professor for building construction and head of the Building Construction and Design 2 research department at the TU Wien. His research on European and non-European modernism between 1958 and 1978 focused on housing construction.

Mark Swenarton Ph.D.

is an architectural historian, critic, and educator. In 1981 he established the U.K.'s first master's degree in architectural history with Adrian Forty and in 1989 co-founded *Architecture Today*, which he edited until 2005. Subsequently, he was head of the architecture school at Oxford Brookes University and inaugural James Stirling Chair in Architecture at Liverpool University, where he is now professor emeritus. He has written numerous books, including *Homes Fit for Heroes, Architecture and the Welfare State*, and, most recently, *Cook's Camden*.

Maria Welzig Mag. Dr.

studied art history at the University of Vienna, completing her doctoral thesis on the architect Josef Frank. She has served as head of research projects for the Austrian Science Fund on architecture in Austria since 1968 and on the Vienna Hofburg since 1918. Visiting professor at the University of Applied Arts Vienna, photography class 2008/09. Welzig has worked as a curator and published several books, including *Josef Frank – das architektonische Werk, Die Architektur und ich, Kulturquartiere in ehemaligen Residenzen* and *Die Wiener Hofburg seit 1918*. She has worked at the Architekturzentrum Wien since 2019.

Index of Names

List of Illustrations

The Potential of the Green City

Page 14: https://de.wikipedia.org/wiki/Elektrolokomotive#/media/Datei:First_electric_locomotive,_built_in_1879_by_Werner_von_Siemens.jpg. Copyright-free.

Page 24: https://commons.wikimedia.org/wiki/Category:Flammarion_Woodcut?uselang=de#/media/File:Из_Фламмариона.jpg. Copyright-free.

Page 25: https://upload.wikimedia.org/wikipedia/commons/4/40/Rousseau_Ermenonville.jpg, User: Docteur Ralph. Copyright-free.

Page 26: https://de.wikipedia.org/wiki/Datei:Karlsruher_Stadtansicht.jpg. Copyright-free.

Page 28: Den svenska staden https://commons.wikimedia.org/wiki/File:Miletos_stadsplan_400.jpg

Page 29: David Rumsey Historical Map Collection, http://www.davidrumsey.com/maps4124.html

Page 30: Photo: Sasha Stone, from *Berlin in Bildern*, ed. by Adolf Behne, Verlag Dr. Hans Epstein, Vienna and Leipzig, 1929.

Page 31: from *Die Wohnung für das Existenzminimum*, ed. by Städtischen Hochbauamt Frankfurt am Main and the Internationalen Kongressen für Neues Bauen, Frankfurt am Main, 1930

Page 32: Le Familistère de Guise collection, anonymous photo, 1890.

Page 33: https://de.wikipedia.org/wiki/Arbeiterkolonie_Westend#/media/Datei:Arbeiterkolonie_Westend,_Krupp,_Essen.jpg. Copyright-free.

Page 34: https://upload.wikimedia.org/wikipedia/commons/3/3d/Garden_City_Concept_by_Howard.jpg, Copyright-free.

Page 35: © Gerhard Steixner

Page 36: © Christos Vittoratos 2013, CC BY-SA 3

Page 37: © Gerhard Steixner

Page 38: Sigfried Giedion, *Befreites Wohnen*, Orell Füssli Verlag, Zürich and Leipzig 1929, book cover.

Page 39: © F.L.C. / image rights, Vienna 2020

Page 40: © Georg Fayer 1927, ÖNB, Bildarchiv Austria, Inv. No. Pb 580.555-F 44 Copyright-free.

Page 41, left: © Bezirksmuseum Ottakring, photo Gerlach

Page 41, right: © Stadt Wien Bäder

Page 42: © Thomas Ledl, 2016, CC BY-SA 4

Page 49: https://de.wikipedia.org/wiki/Utopia_(Roman)#/media/Datei:Isola_di_Utopia_Moro.jpg. Copyright-free.

Pages 52-53: Archiv Büro Glück

Page 56: © Raphael Azevedo Franca, Copyright-free.

Page 57: © Firaxis Games, Sid Meier, computer game Civilization

The *Invention* of Stepped Terrace Housing

Page 64: © Gerhard Steixner

Pages 66, 67 left: © Fonds Henri Sauvage. SIAF/Cité de l'architecture et du patrimoine/Archives d'architecture du XXe siècle

Page 67 right: © Richard Anderson

Page 68: © F.L.C./ image rights, Vienna 2020

Page 69: © Architektursammlung der Albertina Inv. No. ALA401

Page 71: © NASA / William Anders

Page 72: © Fonds Candilis. SIAF/Cité de l'architecture et du patrimoine/Archives d'architecture du XXe siècle

Page 73 left: from Hoffmann, Ot / Christoph Repenthin: *Neue urbane Wohnformen*, Bertelsmann Verlag, Gühtersloh and Berlin 1965, p. 186

Page 73 right: https://neverwasmag.com/lower-manhattan-expressway

Page 74: © Archiv Safdie Architects

Page 75: © Marlies Breuss

Page 76: © Gerhard Steixner

Page 77: © Wolfgang Theiss

Page 78: © Gerhard Steixner

Page 79: © Paul Maurer

Page 80: © Gerhard Steixner

Page 85: © John Boughton (Municipal Dreams) 2013, https://municipaldreams.wordpress.com

La Grande Motte

Page 90: from Prelorenzo, Claude / Antoine Picon, *L'aventure du balnéaire. La Grande Motte de Jean Balladur*, p. 66, fig. 24

Pages 92–94: © Maria Welzig

Page 95: Merian 1971

Pages 96–97: © Maria Welzig

Pages 100–101: © Maria Welzig

Milestones in European Stepped Terrace Housing

Olympic Village, Munich

Pages 118-119, 122-123: © Nikolaus Koliusis

Pages 126–127, 130–134, 136–137: © Gerhard Steixner

Pages 128, 129, 135: © San-Hwan Lu

Alt-Erlaa Residential Park, Vienna

Page 144: from *Architektur.aktuell*, Vol. 3 (1969), No. 14/15

Page 145: http://www.dasrotewien.at/Page/liesing

Page 146: from Reininger, Hans: Wien. In: Glück, Harry / Freisitzer, Kurt: *Sozialer Wohnbau. Entstehung. Zustand. Alternativen.* Molden Verlag, Vienna 1979

Pages 147, 149: from *Architektur.aktuell*, Vol. 10 (1976), No. 56

Pages 158–169: © Gerhard Steixner

St. Peter Housing Estate, Graz

Page 176: © Gerhard Steixner

Pages 177–179: © Walter Kuschel

Pages 184–193: © Gerhard Steixner

Koseze Housing Estate, Ljubljana

Page 198: from *Kako so Nastajala Moja Naselja*, Pust, Viktor, Univerza v Ljubljani Fakulteta za arhitekturo, 2012, pp. 44, 49

Page 200: Still from *Apprenticeship of the Inventor Polz* by Jane Kavčič, 1982.

Pages 201, 202: from *Kako so Nastajala Moja Naselja*, Pust, Viktor, Univerza v Ljubljani Fakulteta za arhitekturo, 2012, pp. 46, 49

Page 203: © Janez Kališnik, Stane Bernik Archiv

Pages 206–217: © Gerhard Steixner

Heinz-Nittel-Hof, Vienna

Page 222: © Archiv Büro Glück

Page 223: © Felbermayer Fenster GmbH, 1210 Vienna, 2019

Page 225 left: from Marchart, Peter: Wohnbau in Wien, Compress, Vienna 1984, p. 58

Page 225 right: © Gerhard Steixner

Pages 232–243: © Gerhard Steixner

Hadikgasse Residential Complex, Vienna

Pages 252 left, 253–256: © Gerhard Steixner

Page 252 right: © Archiv Büro Glück

Pages 258–269: © Gerhard Steixner

Alexandra Road Estate, London

Pages 274–275: © Image courtesy of Martin Charles, RIBA collection

Page 278: © tumblr_pudbwjDNJl 1snysgoo5_1280

Page 279: © The Modern House_04_ 20160216-DSC_2702-WEB

Pages 282–291: © Gerhard Steixner

Autobahnüberbauung Schlangenbader Strasse, Berlin

Page 298: © Landesdenkmalamt Berlin, Wolfgang Bittner

Page 299: from www.pettydesign.com/2012/03/11/life-above-the-autobahn/

Page 300: © David Kasparek, 2015, flickr CC BY 2.0

Page 301: © Nils Richter

Pages 306–317: © Maria Welzig

Inzersdorfer Strasse Residential Complex, Vienna

Pages 326–327: © Archiv Glück

Pages 331–343: © Gerhard Steixner

Wohnen Morgen, Wien

Pages 348, 350, 351: from Marchart, Peter: Wohnbau in Wien, Compress, Vienna 1984, pp. 164, 165

Page 349: © Maria Welzig

Pages 358–365: © Gerhard Steixner

Brunswick Centre, London

Page 372: British Architectural Library, RIBA, London

Page 373, 376, 377: © Clare Melhuish

Pages 382–388, 392–395: © Gerhard Steixner

Pages 389–391: © Laurenz Steixner

La Serra, Ivrea

Pages 400–403: © Giulia Maria Infortuna

Pages 410–411, 416: © Archiv HB2, TU Wien

Pages 412–413: © Giulia Maria Infortuna

Pages 414, 417–419: © Gerhard Steixner

Pages 415, 420–421: © Filippo Poli

The Return of Stepped Terrace Housing

Pages 425, 426:
© Gerhard Steixner

Page 427 left:
© Gerhard Steixner

Page 427 right:
© Laurenz Steixner

Page 428: © Richard Manahl

Page 429: © Gerhard Steixner

Page 430: © Marcel van der Burg

Page 431: © David von Becker

Pages 432, 433: © Gerhard Steixner

Pages 436–437: © Hertha Hurnaus

Pages 438–439:
© Archiv HB2, TU Wien

Pages 440–441: © Gerhard Steixner

Pages 442–443: © *Tageszeitung Heute*, Helmut Graf

Imprint

Editors
Gerhard Steixner
Maria Welzig

Text Editors
Maria Welzig
Gerhard Steixner

Our thanks to
Vera Kumer from the Department of Building Construction and Design 2 at the TU Wien and Nikolaos Kombotis for his many years of collaboration and support for this project.

With contributions by
Karen Beckmann
Paolo Enrico Dalpiaz
Silke Fischer
Harry Glück
Natalie Heger
Giulia Maria Infortuna
Nataša Koselj
San-Hwan Lu
Clare Melhuish
Gerhard Steixner
Mark Swenarton
Maria Welzig

Acquisitions Editor
David Marold,
Birkhäuser Verlag

Content and Production Editor
Angelika Gaal,
Birkhäuser Verlag

Translation
from German into English
Anna Roos

Copy Editing
Word Up!

Layout
Büro Ferkl

Plans
Laurenz Steixner
Markus Rupprecht

Lithography
Pixelstorm

Printing
Holzhausen, die Buchmarke
der Gerin Druck GmbH

ISBN 978-3-0356-1884-6

e-ISBN (PDF)
978-3-0356-1887-7

German Print-ISBN
978-3-0356-1880-8

Library of Congress Control Number
2019955726

Bibliographic information published by the German National Library
The German National Library lists this publication in the Deutsche Nationalbibliografie; detailed bibliographic data are available on the Internet at http://dnb.dnb.de

P.O. Box 44, 4009 Basel, Switzerland
Part of Walter de Gruyter GmbH, Berlin/Boston

9 8 7 6 5 4 3 2 1

www.birkhauser.com

Printed with the kind support of

Beatrix Becker-Glück

Bundesministerium
Kunst, Kultur,
öffentlicher Dienst und Sport

City of Vienna Housing Research Programme (MA 50)